D1068306

ANTHROPOLOGY OFF THE SHELF

In memory of Gay Becker and Octavia Butler,
original members of this project
They stay close through their words

About the cover art

Observer by Roslyn Zinn

The "observer" in the painting is outside of the painting, looking at Roz as she kneels before the fireplace, favorite paintings on the wall in front of her (Picasso, her friend Elly Rubin). A self-portrait, really, and I like to think the "observer" is myself, watching her, perhaps as a humanist anthropologist observes the world, from afar, but with affectionate concern.

Howard Zinn

Anthropology off the Shelf:
Anthropologists on Writing

EDITED BY

ALISSE WATERSTON AND
MARIA D. VESPERI

A John Wiley & Sons, Ltd., Publication

GN
307.7
.A59
2009

This edition first published 2009
© 2009 Blackwell Publishing Ltd except for Chapter 12 © 2009 Irma McClaurin

Blackwell Publishing was acquired by John Wiley & Sons in February 2007. Blackwell's publishing program has been merged with Wiley's global Scientific, Technical, and Medical business to form Wiley-Blackwell.

Registered Office
John Wiley & Sons Ltd, The Atrium, Southern Gate, Chichester, West Sussex, PO19 8SQ, United Kingdom

Editorial Offices
350 Main Street, Malden, MA 02148-5020, USA
9600 Garsington Road, Oxford, OX4 2DQ, UK
The Atrium, Southern Gate, Chichester, West Sussex, PO19 8SQ, UK

For details of our global editorial offices, for customer services, and for information about how to apply for permission to reuse the copyright material in this book please see our website at www.wiley.com/wiley-blackwell.

The right of Alisse Waterston and Maria D. Vesperi to be identified as the authors of the editorial material in this work has been asserted in accordance with the UK Copyright, Designs and Patents Act 1988.

All rights reserved. No part of this publication may be reproduced, stored in a retrieval system, or transmitted, in any form or by any means, electronic, mechanical, photocopying, recording or otherwise, except as permitted by the UK Copyright, Designs and Patents Act 1988, without the prior permission of the publisher.

Wiley also publishes its books in a variety of electronic formats. Some content that appears in print may not be available in electronic books.

Designations used by companies to distinguish their products are often claimed as trademarks. All brand names and product names used in this book are trade names, service marks, trademarks or registered trademarks of their respective owners. The publisher is not associated with any product or vendor mentioned in this book. This publication is designed to provide accurate and authoritative information in regard to the subject matter covered. It is sold on the understanding that the publisher is not engaged in rendering professional services. If professional advice or other expert assistance is required, the services of a competent professional should be sought.

Library of Congress Cataloging-in-Publication Data
Anthropology off the shelf : anthropologists on writing / edited by Alisse Waterston and Maria D. Vesperi.
    p. cm.
  Includes bibliographical references and index.
  ISBN 978-1-4051-8920-0 (hardcover : alk. paper) 1. Ethnology–Authorship.
2. Literature and anthropology. 3. Anthropologists–Attitudes. I. Waterston, Alisse, 1951– II. Vesperi, Maria D.

  GN307.7.A59 2009
  306–dc22

2008051199

A catalogue record for this book is available from the British Library.

Set in 10 on 12.5 pt Sabon by SNP Best-set Typesetter Ltd., Hong Kong
Printed and bound in Malaysia by Vivar Printing Sdn Bhd

1 2009

Contents

Acknowledgments   vii

Notes on Contributors   ix

Foreword   xiii
Cheryl Mwaria

1   Introduction: The Writer in the Anthropologist   1
    Maria D. Vesperi and Alisse Waterston

Part I   Conceptions   13

2   Speaking Truth to Power with Books   15
    Howard Zinn

3   Remember When Writing Was Fun? Why Academics
    Should Go On a Low Syllable, Active Voice Diet   21
    Karen Brodkin

4   The Bard   35
    Carolyn Nordstrom

5   Saggin' and Braggin'   46
    Lee D. Baker

6   Stories for Readers: A Few Observations from
    Outside the Academy   60
    Andrew Barnes

Part II   Creations   63

7   Writing Poverty, Drawing Readers: Stories in *Love,*
    Sorrow and Rage   65
    Alisse Waterston

University Libraries
Carnegie Mellon University
Pittsburgh, PA 15213-3890

 8 Write-ous Indignation: Black Girls, Dilemmas of Cultural
    Domination and the Struggle to Speak the Skin We Are In   79
    Signithia Fordham

 9 Writing Truth to Power: Racism as Statecraft   93
    Arthur K. Spears

10 Remembering Octavia   101
    Sharon Ball

11 Believing in Anthropology as Literature   106
    Ruth Behar

Part III Receptions   117

12 Walking in Zora's Shoes or "Seek[ing] Out de Inside
    Meanin' of Words": The Intersections of Anthropology,
    Ethnography, Identity, and Writing   119
    Irma McClaurin

13 Off the Shelf and into Oblivion?   134
    Catherine Kingfisher

14 "Don't Use Your Data as a Pillow"   146
    S. Eben Kirksey

15 The Trope of the Pith Helmet: America's Anthropology,
    Anthropology's America   160
    Micaela di Leonardo

16 The Book that Wrote Me   172
    Roger Sanjek

17 Fighting Words   182
    Paul Farmer

18 Taking Chances   191
    Maria D. Vesperi

    Index   203

Acknowledgments

The four extraordinary panels that led to the creation of this volume were presented at the Annual Meeting of the American Anthropological Association in 1999, 2000, 2003 and 2005. We would like to thank the Association of Black Anthropologists and the Society for the Anthropology of North America for their enthusiastic sponsorship of the first three: Anthropology off the Shelf at the Turn of the Millennium (Chicago), Anthropology off the Shelf in the Year 2000 (San Francisco) and Anthropology off the Shelf for the 21st Century (Chicago). The fourth panel, Anthropology off the Shelf: Speaking Truth to Power with Books (Washington), was sponsored by the Executive Program Committee of the American Anthropological Association. We are grateful to AAA Meetings Director Lucille Horn for her assistance in planning the logistics of these four large sessions.

A series of panels held over the course of six years presents a particular challenge to assembling the presentations as a book. We would like to extend particular thanks to our original panelists for joining the conversation and staying with us to explore the possibilities of working as both an anthropologist and a writer: Lee D. Baker, Sharon Ball, Andrew Barnes, Ruth Behar, Karen Brodkin, Micaela di Leonardo, Paul Farmer, Catherine Kingfisher, S. Eben Kirksey, Irma McClaurin, Cheryl Mwaria, Roger Sanjek, Arthur Spears and Howard Zinn. We would also like to thank Carolyn Nordstrom for accepting our invitation to contribute, and Tim Sieber for his insightful review of the manuscript at its early stages. Elly Rubin worked tirelessly to make our cover art possible. Finally, in a competitive marketplace of ideas, we would like to thank Rosalie Robertson of Wiley-Blackwell for believing in our session-to-book project and bringing it to fruition. Deirdre Ilkson and Julia Kirk of Wiley-Blackwell have provided invaluable assistance along the way.

Maria D. Vesperi would like to express her deep gratitude to Alisse Waterston for the long-term collaboration that led to this book. The idea for a series of panels about writing sprang up between us a decade ago

viii *Acknowledgments*

and we have delighted in nurturing it together ever since. I would also like
to thank all of the contributors to *Anthropology off the Shelf* for their
sustained attention to the development of this volume. I am grateful to
Lee D. Baker and S. Eben Kirksey for their helpful comments on drafts of
my own chapter, "Taking Chances."

I owe much to Vincent Crapanzano and Jane Kramer, who believed early
in my ability to write, and to Andrew Barnes, who gave me the chance to
write professionally and who has served as my mentor in journalism for
more than two decades. My late father, Arthur E. Vesperi, was always my
first reader and best critic, a role that passed to my daughter, Corinna
Calagione, whose sharp eye and sense of structure I can always trust. I draw
sustenance from the steady exchange of thoughts and observations with
my smart sister, Molly Barnes. And none of my current work would be
possible without the love, intellectual companionship and support of Jay
Sokolovsky, my husband and partner in comedy.

Alisse Waterston gives special thanks to her dear friend and colleague
Maria D. Vesperi who is wise, kind, smart and a pleasure to work with.
Our collaboration on *Anthropology off the Shelf* is one of several I have
enjoyed with Maria over many years, and I look forward to future projects
with her. I am deeply grateful to our amazing contributors who heard our
request to "write about writing" and took off with it, taking us to places
where knowledge, creativity and communication have come together in very
special ways.

My gratitude extends to my family and friends for their encouragement
of my own writing efforts, especially my mother Louise M. Waterston,
my children Leah Horowitz and Matthew Zuckerman, and Adrienne
Waterston, Barbara Rylko-Bauer, and Herlene Lawton. I want to express
loving appreciation to Howard Horowitz, my husband, my best critic and
editor, my mainstay.

Notes on Contributors

Lee D. Baker is Dean of Academic Affairs, Trinity College of Arts and Sciences, Duke University. He is currently completing a book entitled *Anthropology and the Racial Politics of Culture*, examining the role anthropology played in various "culture wars" that were waged throughout the twentieth century.

Sharon Ball is currently Executive Director of the Broome County Arts Council in Binghamton, New York. She is the former Senior Cultural Editor at NPR News in Washington, D.C. In the village of Whitney Point where she lives, she is an active member of the Community Planning Committee and the Main Street Development Committee and is working to transform the small, 100-year-old church that she bought last year into a cultural center.

Andrew Barnes is the retired editor and CEO of the *St. Petersburg Times*. He chaired the Pulitzer Prize Board and the Newspaper Association of America. He currently chairs the Florida chapter of the Nature Conservancy, and continues to be a trustee of the Poynter Institute for Media Studies.

Ruth Behar is an anthropologist, writer, and documentary filmmaker. In her latest book, *An Island Called Home: Returning to Jewish Cuba*, she recounts her journey back to Cuba and the Jewish communities she discovers there. Behar's other books include *Translated Woman: Crossing the Border with Esperanza's Story* and *The Vulnerable Observer: Anthropology that Breaks Your Heart*. She has also published essays, poetry, and short fiction. Behar is Professor of Anthropology at the University of Michigan and the recipient of fellowships from the MacArthur Foundation and the John Simon Guggenheim Memorial Foundation.

Karen Brodkin writes about race, gender and activism. She is author of *Making Democracy Matter: Identity and Activism in Los Angeles*, and *How Jews Became White Folks and What That Says about Race in America*. Her forthcoming book is *Power Politics: Environmental Activism in South Los Angeles*. She is Professor Emerita in Anthropology and Women's Studies at UCLA.

Micaela di Leonardo is Professor of Anthropology and Performance Studies at Northwestern University. Her co-edited *New Landscapes of Inequality: Neoliberalism and the Erosion of American Democracy* appeared with SAR Press in 2008. She is currently finishing *The View from Cavallaro's*, a historical ethnography of political economy and public culture in New Haven, Connecticut, for University of California Press. She also has an ongoing project on black radio, progressive politics, and the American public sphere.

Paul Farmer is Presley Professor of Medical Anthropology in the Department of Social Medicine at Harvard Medical School, Associate Chief of the Division of Social Medicine and Health Inequalities at the Brigham and Women's Hospital, and a co-founder of Partners In Health (PIH), a non-profit organization that provides free health care and undertakes research and advocacy on behalf of the destitute sick. His current focus is on the public-sector scale-up of PIH's model of care in rural Haiti, Rwanda, Malawi, and Lesotho.

Signithia Fordham, who teaches in the Anthropology Department at the University of Rochester, takes lived experience as central to her critical analysis. The author of *Blacked Out: Dilemmas of Race, Identity and Success at Capital High*, she is currently writing a fictionalized ethnography, tentatively titled *Downed by Friendly Fire*, based on her observations and interviews regarding aggression between and among socially defined Black and White girls in a suburban high school. Interrogating the gendered performance of racial scripts, she explicates how subordination and the desire to belong compel young Black women to learn to breathe with "no air."

Catherine Kingfisher is Professor of Anthropology at the University of Lethbridge, Alberta, Canada. Her current book project, *Traveling Politics, Traveling Policies: The "New Zealand Experiment" at Home and Abroad*, has two simultaneous foci: first, the travel of neoliberal cultural formations of gender, personhood, poverty and work from Aotearoa/New Zealand to Alberta (facilitated by the visit of a former NZ finance minister); and second, the differing experiences of Native and non-Native poor single mothers in Canada, and Pakeha (white/European), Maori, and Pacific Island poor single mothers in Aotearoa/New Zealand in the context of welfare state restructuring.

S. Eben Kirksey earned a Ph.D. from the History of Consciousness Program, University of California at Santa Cruz, in early 2008. His writing has appeared in major newspapers and he has served as a source for journalists in print and broadcast media. Currently he is completing a book about the idea of freedom (*merdeka*) in West Papua that combines multiple genres and narrative forms: indigenous parable, figural realism, the "view from nowhere," ethnographic vignettes, oral history, and memoir. A postdoctoral fellowship in the National Science Foundation's Science and Society program (2008–10) will allow him to conduct an ethnographic study of tropical biology.

Irma McClaurin is Associate Vice President for System Academic Administration and Executive Director of the first Urban Research and Outreach/Engagement Center (UROC) at the University of Minnesota. Two children's books have been published by Marshall Cavendish. She is working on two new children's books, and a longer-term project on Zora Neale Hurston that examines Zora's contributions as a scholar/writer, and her continuing omission from the canon of innovative ethnographic practices. She conducts writing workshops and continues to write poetry and essays. As Executive Director of UROC, her goal is to use public and engaged anthropology to develop programs and infrastructure.

Cheryl B. Mwaria is Professor of Anthropology at Hofstra University and Executive Director of the Africa Network, a consortium of liberal arts colleges. Currently she is working on two research projects – a cross-cultural comparison of the ethical debates surrounding the use of pre-implantation genetic diagnosis and a longitudinal ethnographic study of efforts to eliminate disparities in interconceptional care received by women who have given birth prematurely. The latter study is being undertaken in conjunction with the Drexel University College of Medicine and the University of North Carolina at Chapel Hill.

Carolyn Nordstrom is Professor of Anthropology at the University of Notre Dame. Having struggled for years to fit the world's vast roiling multiplex realities into an academic epistemological universe too small to accommodate them, she is writing a book challenging the academy to update its theoretical foundations for the twenty-first century. She conducts fieldwork in war zones worldwide and was recently awarded John D. and Catherine T. MacArthur and John Simon Guggenheim Fellowships. Her books include: *Global Outlaws*, *Shadows of War*, and *A Different Kind of War Story*, plus several edited volumes.

Roger Sanjek is Professor of Anthropology at Queens College, City University of New York, where he has taught since 1972. In addition to his Gray

Panther experience, he has done fieldwork in Brazil, Ghana, and Queens, New York City. His next project will be a collection of essays on ethnography – past, present, and public.

Arthur K. Spears is Professor of Anthropology and Linguistics at the City University of New York Graduate Center. At City College, he is Professor and Chair in the Anthropology Department and Director of the Black Studies Program. He is President (2007–9) of the Society for Pidgin and Creole Linguistics, the largest international body devoted to promoting the study of contact languages. Professor Spears's current book projects deal with Haitian Creole; African American English and Caribbean creole languages; and introductory linguistics, focusing on increasing diversity within the discipline.

Maria D. Vesperi is Professor of Anthropology at New College of Florida and a trustee of the Poynter Institute, a school for journalists. She is currently completing a book on the relationship between ethnographic narrative and narrative journalism. By examining where ethnographers and journalists struggle with similar writing challenges and where their experiences diverge, she hopes to foster discussion that will help anthropologists work more effectively with the media and lend new depth to journalists' understanding of the ethnographic process. She is also working on a long-term project, a 150-year social history of a utopian community turned company town.

Alisse Waterston is Professor, Department of Anthropology, at the John Jay College of Criminal Justice, City University of New York. She edited *An Anthropology of War: Views from the Frontline* with Berghahn Books in 2008 and is working on two projects: *Out of the Shadows of History and Memory: Writing My Father's Life* is an intimate ethnography of her father's experiences (as a Jewish child in Jedwabne, Poland, a young man in Havana, and an old man in San Juan, Puerto Rico); *Narrating Poland* is an ethnography of Polish-Christian immigrants from northeastern Poland, now living in New York. Her goal is to write family tales that reveal larger histories.

Howard Zinn is Professor Emeritus of Political Science at Boston University. He is currently involved in adapting his book *A People's History of the United States* for a television series. It will be called *The People Speak*, and there will be four one-hour programs, with each hour concentrating on a different issue: class, race, women, war. Well-known actors will read the words of historical figures such as Frederick Douglass, Mark Twain, Emma Goldman, Helen Keller – people who have kept alive the spirit of dissent and rebellion in this country.

Foreword

Cheryl Mwaria

I cannot remember how many people have asked, upon learning that I am an anthropologist, "What is it that you do? Dig up bones? Study people in far-off places, like Africa? Study ancient civilizations?" Writing and teaching are seldom mentioned. Instead, there tends to be a romantic notion attached to anthropology combined with a sense of surprise that a full-grown adult could or would spend her time in such an inconsequential way. This, even from people who have taken an anthropology class and declared it their "favorite subject." The most succinct comment I've heard came from an 81-year-old African American woman, the grandmother of a good friend, who declared, "I know what you do, you mind other people's business!" This I confess is true, but to what end do we do it? What is it that we anthropologists, as perpetual students, learn from those willing, generous and patient enough to teach us? What then is the significance of writing anthropology in such a way that not only we, as anthropologists, but also others from disparate parts of our societies can learn from what we write?

Anthropology is a broad discipline. We pride ourselves on being "holistic," studying all aspects of the human condition, from our biological evolution and make-up which gave us the capacity for culture, to the varied lives we live through cultural lenses. It is an eclectic discipline, but not one that is without order. Species-wide we are social animals, primates that depend upon the formation of social groups and alliances that change over time to meet our biological and emotional needs. Politics come naturally to us. Anthropology helps us see who we are and why we are who we are. It does so by training its practitioners to observe, to listen, to participate and to question. In essence, we look for patterns and details in human behavior. We begin with a basic principle: that every human being is socialized to specific ways of seeing the world and responding to it, behaviorally, through culture. Culture is, as Dorothy Lee so eloquently said, "a symbolic system which transforms the physical reality, what is *there*, into experienced reality" (1959: 1).

Whether or not we consider Ibn Battuta, or Herkouf, an Egyptian explorer of the Fourth Dynasty who described the Pygmies living in the great forest to the west of the Mountains of the Moon as tiny people who sang and danced to their god (Turnbull 1961: 15) to be among the earliest anthropologists, each had the essential gifts of any good anthropologist: an eye for intimate details that make the "exotic other" sympathetic, an ear for the language of good storytelling, and a basic curiosity and intellect for discerning that which is significant, but significant to whom? The discipline began in an ominous way in the service of the state. The rise of colonial empires, particularly in Africa and Asia, was accompanied by the birth of the classic ethnography, written often by those in the employ of the state to be used to better control local populations. Moreover, those who got to tell the story did so more often than not from their own ethnocentric perspectives, thereby reinforcing hierarchies, particularly of race and gender. By the twentieth century the insights of anthropologists had entered the public discourse in earnest and they contested prevailing notions about human cultures, race and evolution. Franz Boas, the "father" of American anthropology, led the challenge to overthrow widespread assumptions held by scientists and the public alike about race and cultural hierarchies by giving his first public speech on the subject in 1894 (Baker 1998: 104). While Boas trained almost all of the leading American anthropologists of the first half of the twentieth century, and they in turn took on some of the most important topics in anthropology, it was two of his female students who caught the public eye for their literary skills – Margaret Mead and Zora Neale Hurston. They were followed by many others – Colin Turnbull, Elizabeth Marshall Thomas, Victor Turner, Edmund Leach, Mary Douglas, Claude Lévi-Strauss and Clifford Geertz to name but a few – who showed an interest in literary theory and practice. Free of the shackles of academic convention, these writers embraced more creative literary forms to tell their stories, as do the contributors to this volume. The latter half of the twentieth century saw anthropological writing change once again with the powerful introduction of emotion in ethnographic description and in the voice of the anthropologist her- or himself. Renato Rosaldo's *Culture and Truth* made a powerful argument for moving away from the authoritative voice of the classic norms in ethnographic description in order to include "myriad modes of composition . . . moral indignation, satire, critique and others" (1993: 60). A range of such voices are present in this anthology.

So where do we find ourselves as anthropologists at this stage of the twenty-first century? Our ranks have swollen to include colleagues from many of the cultures we have studied. Their voices have provided new insights and fresh critical perspectives. We have also learned to take the criticisms of our informants as we would those of our colleagues, as can be seen in several of these essays. There is, however, a discomfort here, a conundrum of sorts. Our informants can be "insightful, sociologically correct, axe-grinding, self-interested or mistaken," as Rosaldo warned (1993: 50). We humans are, after all, creatures of agency and conscience. Whose interests do we serve? Anthropologists, having honed the tool of cultural relativity to combat ethnocentrism in ethnographic discourse, often find themselves in a curious and unenviable position. Far too often we have fallen into what may be called a relativistic fallacy – a misguided idea that it is impossible to make moral judgments about the beliefs and behaviors of members of other cultures. All cultures are not equal any more than are all ideas. This is a compelling truth at a time when myriad moral dilemmas face us in our research, whether we are focused on the biotechnological revolution and its implications for the very nature and direction of our biological makeup, the consequences of massive immigration, the rise of fundamentalist movements, the use of limited resources, gender, class and ethnic inequalities, or the use of force or violence to obtain objectives. Anthropologists, particularly those who see themselves as practicing advocacy anthropology, increasingly face the complexities and challenges of these dilemmas, as several of these essays show.

Our post-9/11 world is increasingly Orwellian – democratically elected governments are overturned in the name of democracy; dissent is suppressed in the name of freedom of speech; the right to privacy is restricted in the name of protecting our liberties; even the celebration of diversity has often erupted in racial and religious hatreds. As Kenan Malik argues, "The quest for equality has increasingly been abandoned in favour of the claim to a diverse society. Campaigning for equality means challenging accepted practices, being willing to march against the grain, to believe in the possibility of social transformation. Conversely, celebrating differences between peoples allows us to accept society as it is – it says little more than 'We live in a diverse world, enjoy it'" (2002).

Where are we to go from here? How can anthropology and anthropologists meet these challenges? First and foremost, we must continue to engage in the struggle to bring clarity to just what the issues and interests are in any area of contention we are describing and to do so with anthropological insights into human behavior. We must also use the tools intrinsic to our discipline – by observing, listening, questioning and participating in the everyday lives of humans with a critical eye. As this volume demonstrates, good writing that engages a wide audience is a priceless asset to this enterprise.

References

Baker, Lee D. 1998. *From Savage to Negro: Anthropology and the Construction of Race, 1896–1954*. Berkeley: University of California Press.
Lee, Dorothy. 1959. *Freedom and Culture*. New York: Prentice Hall.
Malik, Kenan. 2002. Against multiculturalism. *New Humanist* 117 (2). www.kenanmalik.com/essays/against_mc.html. Accessed April 29, 2008.
Rosaldo, Renato. 1993. *Culture and Truth*. Boston: Beacon Press.
Turnbull, Colin. 1961. *The Forest People*. New York: Simon and Schuster.

1

Introduction: The Writer in the Anthropologist

Maria D. Vesperi and Alisse Waterston

Off the shelf and into the hands of well-informed general readers. That's the *where*.

The *who* are increasing ranks of anthropologist-writers, folks whose words could burn right through the covers of the prestigious journals where they might consign them if their eyes weren't fixed on that *where*: the bookstore window, the policy library, the bedside table.

The *what* are texts these anthropologists-writers produce, mostly ethnographies but also history, critical analysis and works of creative non-fiction.

The *why* is the weight of this work, too imminent to contain, too heavy to be borne by those who would publish simply not to perish. These are stories that must be told, sometimes at the risk of personal rejection or professional failure. "We have taken upon our shoulders an enormous responsibility that is beyond any allegiance we might owe to the academy or any desire for tenure," writes Irma McClaurin in her contribution to this volume. "We hold in our words, real people's lives."

The *when* is right now, before the policy is made, the hope crushed, the genocide completed.

It's not that anthropologist-writers believe their work can change the world, although some admit freely to outsized assumptions about the potential impact of a book or article. It's just that they won't give up on the job of sharing anthropological knowledge in straightforward, powerful ways.

"I think it is enough to be able to document carefully and clearly what is happening," suggests Paul Farmer. "That is my idea of speaking truth to power with books."

Encouragement in that direction comes from Andrew Barnes, a journalism leader and Pulitzer Committee veteran. "Too much of our public discussion is superficial," he observes. "We need more ideas grounded in fieldwork and rigorous thought. It's worth your effort to take anthropology to the broadest possible audience."

Increasing numbers of anthropologists agree. But for many who would take it public, the *how* is the rub.

Ruth Behar opens her contribution to *Anthropology off the Shelf* with comments from an editor who sought to remove "cultural anthropology" from the blurb touting her newest book, *An Island Called Home* (2007). The editor explained that "since we're marketing the book as a trade book, we need to reach the general reader, and any reference to an academic discipline is a turn-off. They say it's toxic. They've done studies."

"They" say a lot of things but Behar resisted, as any discipline-based writer might. After all, many scholarly books are reviewed in the mainstream press, featured in bookstores, selected for prizes that signal to readers: "Pick this one! A must read!" Well-crafted books about language, ideology, history, politics, war, race, poverty, health, gender – and so much more – routinely find their way onto "must read" lists and win non-fiction awards, in part because their orienting premises and narrative structures are accessible to diverse audiences. Few anthropology books meet this criterion and even fewer enjoy such notice, even when they treat the same topics.

At the core of *Anthropology off the Shelf* is a critical analysis of whether the models anthropologists use for framing, illustrating and contextualizing information and ideas facilitate or hinder engagement with the well-informed general reader of non-fiction. The project began as a way to approach this problem by tracing specific books from their intellectual origins to publication and beyond. In a series of four panels presented between 1999 and 2005 at the American Anthropological Association annual meetings, some 20 writers and editors offered straight talk about the desire to reach intended readers and how this goal became wedded to the writing process – for better and for worse. They revisited difficult, sometimes painful choices about conceptualization, crafting and marketing. They discussed, in retrospect, which strategies were effective and which ones fell flat. They revealed specific decisions about theoretical framing, unit of analysis, contextualization and narrative structure in representing ethnographic material. Bravely, they probed further to expose the rich but rarely tapped lode where commitment, inspiration and motivation are pressed hard by racism, sexism, real and imagined critics, ethical quandaries and ingrained writing habits, productive or otherwise.

Sometimes the result is a diamond.

From the start, "Anthropology off the Shelf" sessions drew large audiences brimming with questions. People were hungry for frank conversation about the passions that prompt a researcher to enter the public conversation through scholarly literature, and where acting on such passions might lead. Talk remained sharply focused on the process of writing: what anthropologists really do in their everyday writing lives and how they get folks to read what they write.

Our decision to follow in the tradition of the "writers on writing" genre promoted engagement across a broad range of research topics and anthropological allegiances. Despite the purported intellectual and praxis divide in anthropology, the opportunity to talk about writing itself revealed more overlap, more fluidity than the much-discussed boundaries between such camps seem to suggest. Participants could agree to disagree as they shared fresh insights about how theory, epistemology, methodology, ethics, politics and potential applications shape the structure and texture of a book.

It's no secret that conference-to-book projects can lack collective spark. Sometimes readers are left to wonder what unites a collection of essays beyond that ephemeral moment when their authors shared a skirted table under hotel ballroom lights. Surely, there was excitement in the room. The audience was engaged. So much seemed possible. Too bad it didn't survive the telling.

In the case of *Anthropology off the Shelf*, however, the four panels generated dialogue and reflection that continued to develop and mature. All but one of the contributors to this volume participated in the original four panels. And as they persisted in grappling with the issues – and equally important, persisted in living their lives as writers – many were moved to radically revise their essays. Some are altogether new. As a result, the collection reveals important new patterns in the ongoing, often frustrating, rarely celebrated process of taking books or articles from their initial conception to their fruition, and beyond to their reception by targeted readers.

Anthropologist-writers reveal a clear pattern when they discuss the power of imagining the audience for a particular work. In many cases, the Oz-like images of teachers who drove graduate school writing in certain directions gave way first to equally constraining fantasies of scowling colleagues at peer-reviewed journals. "Every time I sit down to write, I knock a host of academic critics off my shoulder who tell me I *can't, shouldn't, wouldn't* write what I believe in; that I *must* follow their guidelines for 'truth,' academic style," reports Carolyn Nordstrom.

"When I think of my own progression as a writer," reflects Ruth Behar, "I believe I have gone from trying to write for my teachers to trying now, in the most recent phase of my work, to write for my mother so I could write for the world."

There is general agreement that dialogue with institutional phantoms must be abandoned before an anthropologist-writer can hope to be understood beyond the academy. "The key, of course, is to present things in such a way that they can be heard and taken in," notes Catherine Kingfisher, "a goal anthropologists also pursue in the classroom when teaching about topics such as racism, colonialism and gender inequality."

"The norms and conventions of citation determine so much of how you tell your story, and these conventions become ingrained, to the point where the writer often thinks everyone can read that dialect," Andrew Barnes observes. "A lot of us can't, and won't."

Dialect is a polite word for jargon and the tortuous sentence structures required to support its weight. It's a bumpy read. Would-be social scientists become inured to the ill effects of this writing style through a slow but effective inoculation process that begins in college. They might protest at first, but by graduate school most are fully accommodated to this dense code and more or less eager to reproduce it. Colleagues and students for whom the going remains hard are left to stammer along as best they can. Some drift away from academia for this reason; they aren't motivated to sustain the code-switching required to hold forth in academic high jargon.

In contrast, general readers out grazing for knowledge are free to taste, reject, leave the "lardballs," as Karen Brodkin aptly names them, half-chewed. Through conversation or bad reviews, they warn others off their feed as well. Like any shoppers, folks who invest in books gauge the quality of the medium before they spoon up the message. If it's lardy, they leave it on the shelf. If it's tougher to open than a shrink-wrapped compact disc, well advised, they move on.

The title of Marie Cardinal's *The Words to Say It* is a haunting mantra, a compelling summary of the longing associated with novelists but experienced by anthropologist-writers as well. *Anthropology off the Shelf* reveals the persistent question behind this desire: the words to say *what* to *whom*? Who can be counted among the readership by those who would aim beyond the captive audience of tenure and promotion committees? How wide is the potential audience for an anthropologist's work?

"I think that progressive anthropologists *can* reach large popular audiences, as I hope to do with my New Haven book, with skillfully written, accessible, historical ethnographic narratives that eschew biting the public cultural hand that feeds them," writes Micaela di Leonardo, reflecting on a work-in-progress.

Lee Baker structures his historical writing to help students "think differently and critically," beyond the familiar dualities. "I always write for my undergraduate students, and I often have a specific class in mind when I begin to tackle a research project," he explains.

Karen Brodkin writes for "two different but connected audiences," undergraduate students and "a community of kindred political intellectuals, both activist and academic." Over the years her audiences have changed, but each has been clearly envisioned. *Caring by the Hour* (1988), for example, "used as jargon-free a style as I knew how." The book remains in circulation two decades later, Brodkin is pleased to note, and "my greatest joy has been the fact that, so I've been told, at least two unions engaged in hospital organizing in the South and on the East Coast have used it as an organizing manual and in organizer training."

Some frame particular writing projects by imagining direct, point-counterpoint engagement with readers. In her work for the editorial and op-ed pages of the *St. Petersburg Times*, Maria Vesperi learned that the efficacy of opinion writing springs from accurate, balanced data collection and clear delivery to closely targeted readers. Some editorials have a "readership of one" – the governor, say – while others, the ones that are toughest to write, speak to broad but vividly imagined communities.

Signithia Fordham employs the term "counternarrative" to describe her engagement with the public through popular media. "The determination to claim a space in American public discourse for a viewpoint that comes from my position as Black and female is an integral part of my quest for justice," she explains. "In an effort to practice writing as a form of social activism, I submit op-ed pieces for publication by well-known newspapers and magazines."

Similarly, "I wanted to *talk back to* those mothers of my daughter's classmates who believe it when the tabloid press, some popular politicians and social scientists depict *other* women as undeserving and disreputable," recalls Alisse Waterston in describing her imagined audience for *Love, Sorrow and Rage*. And, at the same time, "I wrote *in dialogue with* an imaginary interlocutor, my colleagues in anthropology, especially those with a critical, political-economy perspective and those interested in urban poverty issues in North America, including the US."

Academic writing comes with disciplinary qualifiers: there is anthropological literature, historical literature, area scholarship. Prompting that general reader to reach for one's book obliges the writer to move beyond academic caveats, to aim for "something we call literature," as Ruth Behar puts it. Behar titles her essay "Believing in Anthropology as Literature," and belief – faith in one's skills – is required if a book is to fly off the shelf and into a canvas tote on the shoulder of that well-informed general reader.

Among the contributors to this book are scholars who peruse Clifford and Marcus's *Writing Culture* (1986) as a guide to form, in the same way they might pick up an edition of Strunk, White and Angell's *The Elements of Style*. They are not deterred from Clifford Geertz's call to craft in *Works and Lives* by his ironic caution that tradition trusts "plain texts" as credible ethnographic work, discounting attention to writing as odd, "suggestive even of sharp practice" (1988: 2). They aren't hampered by canons or schools or even disciplines, because the readers they seek don't respond well to the narrative conventions required.

Moving beyond the foundational qualifier "anthropology" is a difficult step, however, and not one the contributors to this volume seem eager to make. Instead, they demonstrate eagerness to work seriously with form in ways that enlarge anthropology's potential to provide accessible, in-depth information and analysis about things that are amiss in the world.

As a result, however, they must take risks with their writing, pushing the safety zone of disciplinary protocol in ways that are rarely welcomed by colleagues. There is perhaps no greater example than the career of Zora Neale Hurston, who shines posthumously as an enduring beacon for those who would risk mislabeling and misunderstanding to position themselves between the reflexive tasks of a scholarly life and progressive engagement with the world.

Discussing the privilege and inspiration of "Walking in Zora's Shoes," Irma McClaurin foregrounds how Hurston "linked ethnographic observations and anthropological analysis with literature" in powerful and compelling ways. McClaurin explains why it is "important to write in ways that move our communication beyond the scholarly constraints that have shaped most academic writing, and truly get at what Zora called 'de inside meanin' of words.'"

The late Octavia Butler created fictional worlds that reached deep for the inside meaning of real ones. Her work inspired anthropologists and also journalists such as Sharon Ball, the former cultural desk editor at National Public Radio. Ball confided to Butler herself a special dream that "I, too, always intended to write. At that point, [Octavia] looked up and said, not unkindly, 'Well, you'd better get to it!' and she smiled right at me."

Butler understood the need, the *sine qua non*, for a writer to grasp that elusive *how*. "There was that voice, soft and strong, telling funny stories and offering straightforward advice about the key elements of a writing life: Research; Realism; Description; Details; Family stories; Serendipity; Persistence; Go on Learning; Walk the Ground You Want To Write About; Write Your Passion," Ball remembers gratefully. "As you see, I took notes."

"More and more, I dare to think I can call myself a writer, plain and simple," ventures Ruth Behar. "But I can't forget that I took up the pen for the same reason all anthropologists do: because we care passionately about the worlds that others inhabit and not just about our own small worlds." Of course, she notes, many fiction writers share the same concerns. Yet, "Our imaginations are in service to real communities we know first-hand and to real journeys we've taken across land and sea. And this isn't a bad thing at all, so long as we know how to spin a tale about all that we've witnessed."

In the essays found here and in less formal conversations about writing, memories of those who would undermine the writer's confidence and ability to "spin a tale" float vividly to the surface. Remarking on his early experiences, Arthur Spears shared this: "Throughout my schooling I was accused of plagiarizing papers because 'no reasonable person' (black teacher or white professor) could possibly believe that I had written them, this though I was an honor student throughout."

Let no good writing go unpunished.

Signithia Fordham begins her chapter this way: "She writes like a (Black) girl." Fordham revisits the sentence, turning it this way and that, revealing at each stage how her efforts to write in her own voice were "blacked out": "Nowhere was this blackout more apparent than in how my schoolmates and I were required to write. Narration, the academic benchmark used to judge the adequacy of our presumed or compulsory transformation, was highly stylized and formulaic. Writing in our native voices – regardless of the circumstances or our level of sophistication – was either erased or repeatedly edited by our teachers and other school officials to fit a preexisting template."

"Research," Maria Vesperi concluded in her middle-school years, "meant a trip to the public library and diligent paraphrasing from the dog-eared offerings on hand in the Juvenile Section." A dry affair, mechanical, less compelling than the daydreams that competed for her attention, and usually won.

From childhood through graduate school and well beyond, contributors to this volume have struggled to pry free of preexisting templates and the numbing conventions they impose. Each anthropologist-writer identifies tension between the creative impulse to tell a story and the formal constraints of the anthropological canon. "You're not good enough, never will be," whisper Carolyn Nordstrom's imagined critics. "Even kindly friends and unctuous journal editors trying to help me by explaining 'how it is done' and why my style 'just won't work' join the others on my shoulder."

Writing teachers such as Peter Elbow (1998a, 1998b) and Chip Scanlan (2005) cite the babble of imagined critics as a source of paralyzing writer's block. In his workshops with writers, Scanlan urges them to ignore such voices – at least for the moment – or risk failing to find their own.

Anthropologists confront ongoing ethical and epistemological challenges in their efforts to represent others, and contributors to *Anthropology off the Shelf* are no exception. This collection demonstrates that some must reach even further, first confronting how racism and/or sexism complicate efforts to represent *themselves* as individuals, as social observers and as writers. Signithia Fordham, for instance, points to "the rapacious hegemony of the pen" that leads African American schoolchildren to "fear our own writing, and to fear that what we wrote would further distort our lived reality."

"Whether it is baggy pants inspired by prison garb or a simple white t-shirt that belies any gang affiliation, the pattern is the same," observes Lee Baker. "When black people appropriate it as their own, the meaning changes and the object, or sound, or food, or clothing takes on a new meaning. Sometimes it's negative, but often it is positive; most always it is shot through with ambivalence and anxiety."

Popular response to *How Jews Became White Folks* (1999) taught Karen Brodkin a lot about self-positioning. While she dubs the book "my biggest success at reaching a readership that goes far beyond the usual suspects," she was also prompted to think further about where the anthropologist in the writer should aim to be: "I think that what is missing in this book is a better sense of what do you do once you recognize you have race privilege? I'm not sure that there is, even now, a political community that is asking that question. I think we should be asking it very seriously."

Evidence of a book's reception can be painfully thin, particularly for its creator. "I think it is important not to fool ourselves about what it is that our books do," Paul Farmer states pragmatically. ". . . generally, if we're lucky, our books are read by 5-, 10-, 15,000 people or maybe a few more – but the sales don't lie." Farmer suggests that anthropologist-writers might come closer to their goals by pairing writing with activism and dispensing with the conceit that their books have clout. "Do we really need to claim that we are altering the impact of noxious social forces with our writing? I think it is better to simply acknowledge we don't, and then have our own reasons for doing what it is that we do."

"In the face of being outflanked by big power, activists taught me the importance of incremental and partial victories," observes Eben Kirksey.

Looking back on a long career as reader and writer, scholar and activist, Howard Zinn remains convinced of the book's ability to speak truth to power. "I am persuaded about the importance of books simply by my own experience," he states.

At the same time, Zinn acknowledges that it can be hard to comprehend fully what books *do*. "One reason is that it is very rare to find a direct line between the writing of a book and the changing of a policy," he explains. "But I think you can find indirect lines, and you can find eras in which writings appeared and people's consciousness was raised and policies were changed, sometimes after decades had passed. The long trajectory between writing and changing consciousness, between writing and activism and then affecting public policy, can be tortuous and complicated. But this does not mean we should desist from writing."

Catherine Kingfisher doesn't plan to desist, but she wants to know more about who pays attention to her research findings – and why. She offers this advice to other anthropologist-writers: "Systematically tracing the processes associated with the production and travel of knowledge would allow us to determine whether our ventures off the shelf are leaps into oblivion or jumps to places that may someday prove beneficial."

As a historian of anthropology, Lee Baker shares Zinn's long view. "I am perfectly aware that studying the history of anthropology makes an insignificant contribution to the marginal field of history of science," he offers candidly. "I do not have the immediate, life-saving impact of someone like Paul Farmer. Yet, I still believe my efforts are important for better understanding how racism works by trying to document how even the most progressive social scientists and most thoughtful political activists usually fail to shake loose the noose of racism that constricts and tightens the harder one fights."

In "Racism as Statecraft," Arthur Spears describes his effort to meet students' need for an anthology that "laid out the principal issues connected with racial categorization and racism and that clearly articulated these issues with those relevant to gender, ethnicity, class, and sexuality." The initial reception by his publisher was, well, chilly. While *Race and Ideology: Language, Symbolism, and Popular Culture* earned positive reviews from readers, Spears continues to wonder about how publishers treat authors whose work "speaks ugly truths to a many-tentacled power."

"I did have great hopes of contributing to important scholarly conversations about gender, race, and class shifts in American history, politics, and culture," writes Micaela di Leonardo, reflecting on the reception of *Exotics at Home*. "I have had modest success here. . . . I do not, however, expect to reach a large popular audience with the book, because of its scholarly tone, because of its intransigent anti-postmodern stance, because of its radicalism in a conservative era – but most importantly, because the book offers a serious critique of precisely the public culture in which popular reviews would appear."

Eben Kirksey, the youngest contributor to this volume, entered college in the mid-1990s. He describes the climate for a new generation of anthropologists when he writes: "In creating an anthropology that is ready to travel off the shelf we should be prepared to face multi-directional demands for accountability – from informants who "talk back," from libel laws, and from a reading public who desire particular narrative forms. Being deceptive, presenting flimsy knowledge claims, will clearly not aid the political struggles of people who seek us as allies. Learning to follow the epistemological standards that operate in different domains, and mediating among these systems of knowing, can produce knowledge claims that stick."

Claims that stick, words that matter – these are the elusive prizes that drive anthropologist-writers to place their critiques, analyses, and social criticisms in the public domain. "To succumb to the belief in our own ineffectiveness is to play into the hands of the worst of distorted political arguments and to provide fodder for furthering our own marginalization," Alisse Waterston asserts.

The Gray Panthers' refusal to succumb to social injustice without a fight drew Roger Sanjek to them when he was barely out of graduate school. He participated in the activist group for years, only later deciding that their story "could be the subject of a book" that he could write. Or could he? "I was a participant, not an observer, and I had taken no fieldnotes," he recalls.

Sanjek refers to *Gray Panthers* (2009) as "the book that wrote me." He points out that it "has little to do with research proposals, standard fieldwork, or academic career hurdles. Still, it is the work of a social anthropologist who has attempted to employ an ethnographic sensibility and adhere to canons of validity he advocates." Equally important, as Sanjek explains, it is the work of someone who has lived the story and who is willing to embrace the moral responsibility of positioning himself as storyteller.

Anthropologists write stories across the broad range of the human condition: things that go wrong, things that go right, those that need fixing and those that call for celebration right now. Anthropologists place their stories in the public record, in print, knowing that they can be used to affirm or indict – if not today, perhaps tomorrow. Stories have unanticipated endings; some become weapons in the hands of those who tell or those who hear.

Despite these uncertainties, where there is passion about something that needs to be said, the writer in the anthropologist survives.

That's the hope.

"The fact that the war orphan's story has seen the light of day means the fight is worth it," writes Carolyn Nordstrom. Whether anyone reads it, now or later, is something that anthropologist-writers are willing to take on faith. There are role models. Although she did not live to see it, Zora Neale Hurston's writing has endured that "long trajectory between writing and changing consciousness" described by Howard Zinn.

Its trajectory off the shelf may be long, but time disappears when a book is in readers' hands. "Now, when I feel that itch to talk to Octavia," writes Sharon Ball, "I read something she wrote and I remember the promise she made as we ended each of our conversations: 'I'll be talking to ya.' And in the way that mattered most to her, she still does."

That's the victory.

References

Elbow, Peter. 1998a [1973]. *Writing Without Teachers*. Oxford: Oxford University Press.

Elbow, Peter. 1998b [1981]. *Writing with Power: Techniques for Mastering the Writing Process*. New York: Oxford University Press.

Geertz, Clifford. 1988. *Works and Lives: The Anthropologist as Author*. Stanford, CA: Stanford University Press.

Scanlan, Chip. 2008. The Best Writing Tip of All Time: Sit. www.poynter.org/column.asp?id=52&aid=140738. Accessed September 15, 2008.

I
Conceptions

CONTRIBUTORS

2

Speaking Truth to Power with Books[1]

Howard Zinn

I will start by introducing the most crucial issue of all with regard to writing, and that is, what in the world does it do? What effect does it have? Does it help change the world? After all, the first decision a writer has to make is like the first decision a teacher has to make: why am I doing this? In what way is it going to help people, or am I doing it just to advance myself professionally or just to get a book published?

We want to know what books do and get at least a partial answer to the question – partial because I do not think we know exactly what books do or what writing does. One reason is that it is very rare to find a direct line between the writing of a book and the changing of a policy. But I think you can find indirect lines, and you can find eras in which writings appeared and people's consciousness was raised and policies were changed, sometimes after decades had passed. The long trajectory between writing and changing consciousness, between writing and activism and then affecting public policy, can be tortuous and complicated. But this does not mean we should desist from writing.

I am persuaded about the importance of books simply by my own experience. Sometimes people ask me, "What made you what you are?" I laugh and pretend I don't know what they mean. But I think they are trying to say something nice about me. They are trying to say, "What made you a socially conscious person, an activist?"

And I think: was it my background? Was it my growing up? And I think of all the people who grew up in roughly the same environment I did, and who did not end up thinking the same way or doing the same things. And the closest I can come to an explanation is: I read certain books. Really. I think you know that when you are 15, 16, and 17, you read certain books

[1] A transcription of remarks presented in "Anthropology off the Shelf: Speaking Truth to Power with Books," December 2005.

which have a very powerful effect on you. My parents did not have a single book in the house, but when I was 14 years old, I discovered books. I found a book on the street. And then my parents knew that I was interested in books even though they didn't have any. And so they sent away to a newspaper – it was the *New York Post* – which was offering a set of Dickens, volume by volume, if you sent away a coupon with ten cents for each volume. Well, my parents thought, "Oh yes, he likes books." They had never heard of Dickens. But that is what they did. And so I started reading Dickens. It had a powerful effect on my thinking, and still does.

I imagine others have had the same experience. There are books that seriously affected you. Now how to make a connection between how they affected you, and what you then did, and then the connection between what you then did, and what other people did, and then what connection between what everybody did and then what happened in the world. Well, that's complicated. But if you do not start that trajectory, even if you don't know where it is going to end, it will go nowhere. You have to begin.

I know this. There are people who have said to me, "This book changed my life." The first time I heard that, it surprised me. I had been invited to speak at the University of Hawaii and afterwards I was sitting in the cafeteria. There was a student sitting across the table from me, and I saw the book she was reading, *The Color Purple* by Alice Walker. I didn't want to say, "Oh, Alice Walker was a student of mine," because I would never say *that*. So I just said to her, "What do you think of that book?" She answered, "This book changed my life." That startled me. But I have heard that many, many times since. "This book changed my life." So, yes, I think books can do that. And if a book changes somebody's life by changing somebody's consciousness, it is going to have an effect on the world, in one way or the other, sooner or later, in ways that you probably cannot trace.

Books operate in many ways to change people's consciousness. We know that scientists always number things, and since everyone wants to be scientific, they also number things. I remember when I was going to school, I would hear the statement, "These are the four causes of the French Revolution." I realized that if you number the things you say it is very impressive even though it is totally meaningless. Let us just say there are a number of ways in which books can change consciousness. First, they can introduce an idea that the reader never thought of before. This has happened to many of us. We read Herman Melville, *Billy Budd*, and we are confronted with a situation where everybody obeys the law, everybody dutifully follows the rules. The chaplain follows what he thinks is the word of God and everyone else follows the word of some authority, and Billy Budd, an innocent guy, is put to death. You have to think at that point, "Maybe there is a difference between law and justice." Maybe the rule of law needs to be examined, and maybe authority is not to be revered, or innocent people will die.

We grow up being taught that we should obey the rules, obey our parents, the teacher, right up to the President. But at some point in our lives, especially if we read widely, we stop and say, "Why should we do this? Why should we go along with this and why don't we think for ourselves?" It is an insight that you can get from a book even if it is only hinted at. It may just be implied in a story, yet it has that powerful effect.

Here is another idea that may occur to people, perhaps after reading a book, especially if they are reading unorthodox history. It may strike you that we do not all have the same interests. This is not an easy thing to come by because we are all confronted with language that presumes a common interest for everyone in the nation. We are told that some policy is in the "national interest," that something must be done for "national security," or "national defense." The pretense is that the interests of "the nation" encompass us all. If I had read Kurt Vonnegut's *Cat's Cradle* at an early age I might have questioned this because Vonnegut invents the term "granfalloon" to describe "a proud and meaningless association of human beings" and he places nations among such unnatural abstractions. But it was a different book that, when I was a young man, first led me to consider that we are not one great family in this country, that the idea of ourselves as a nation cleverly conceals the struggle of clashing interests for fear we might then enter that struggle knowing clearly who our friends are and who are our enemies.

It is always a little embarrassing to realize that you lived many years before a certain important realization came to you. You want people to think that what you know now, you knew at birth. Teachers will present something with great authority, but it may be something they just learned last week. So I will confess that it was only at a certain point in my life that I read Charles Beard's *An Economic Interpretation of the Constitution*, and it was a revelation. We grow up in a country where everyone reveres the Founding Fathers and the Constitution (or at least I thought so, not knowing until an even later time in my life that black scholars had deep reservations). The Constitution is a holy document, and so you cannot say anything against the Constitution, you cannot say anything against the Founding Fathers. You look at all the volumes of books that come out about Adams and Jefferson and Madison, volumes upon volumes upon volumes upon volumes; almost always they are admiring.

Charles Beard, however, dissected and analyzed the 55 men who gathered in Philadelphia to write the Constitution. He tells you who they were, how much land they owned, how many slaves they owned, how many bonds they held, what class they belonged to. These were rich, white men and they framed a Constitution that would serve their interests. "Professor Beard, you mean the government may serve interests which are not *my* interests?" That is a dangerous idea. Does it mean that Marx was right? Well, there is an important insight: society is divided into classes, and governments generally follow the dictates of the people with the most wealth and the most power. This is a matter of life and death. If you do not know that the government may very well represent interests different from yours, you will listen very dutifully to what the government tells you, and obey what it tells you to do, and you may end up dead.

So yes, there are insights that come from books. Here's another, this one out of Charles Dickens. The first time I read Dickens's *Hard Times* I was just a kid and only understood it on a superficial level. Later I read it again, and was struck by the character of the schoolmaster Gradgrind who advises a young teacher, "Remember, just give them facts, nothing but facts." I pondered this advice about "facts, nothing but facts," and came to the insight that there are no such things as pure facts unadorned by judgment. That is, as soon as facts are presented, as soon as facts are put out in the world (you put them out in the world or somebody else puts them out to you), they represent a judgment. The judgment is that these particular facts are important for somebody to know and there are other facts we are not going to tell you about, which are not important for you to know. I remember Senior Bush, George H. W. Bush, talking about education because he knows a lot about education and he knows that kids must learn facts. You see this represented in multiple-choice tests, and true/false tests, and test scores and so on: facts and facts and facts. But once you understand that certain facts are held out in full view and others are not, and that the selection is not innocent, that is a leap of social consciousness.

There are entire sets of data which people just had no idea about, and which, when they were revealed in a book, shocked readers into an important awareness. I am thinking of Rachel Carson's *The Sea around Us* from 1951. People simply did not think about what is happening to the air and the water and the environment. It just never occurred to them, and she calmly told all of us what was going on. She didn't have to make judgments, she didn't have to editorialize. She just had to say what was happening. Today, we know about what is going on. We know, for example, what is going on in the Sudan. You do not have to editorialize about it. Sometimes just telling people about something that they do not know about is an important thing to do, because that alone may move them to a greater consciousness and even into action.

I will say something about Christopher Columbus. When my book, *A People's History of the United States* came out, I began to get mail from around the country. I found that most of the mail dealt with the first chapter of the book, which of course made me very suspicious! I refused to accept or believe that people only read the first chapter. Instead, I came to the conclusion that all the mail about the first chapter was because it was upsetting to those brought up in the United States who learned about Columbus the hero, Columbus the great discoverer, Columbus the pious Bible reader. To read about Columbus as a murderer, a torturer, a kidnapper, a mutilator of native people, a hypocrite, a greedy man looking for gold, willing to kill people and mutilate people – it was shocking.

At one point, I received a letter from a teacher in California, saying, "You know, you got me in trouble. A student brought your book home, her mother read the first chapter or maybe the first five pages of the first chapter, and said, 'I'm going to talk to the school committee. I think your teacher is a communist!'" That's a case where just to learn the facts about Columbus may lead to a revolution in one's thinking. When you learn about information that has been withheld from you, it may lead you to wonder what else has been withheld. There is a wonderful teacher in Oregon named Bill Bigelow who made it a kind of crusade to go around the country, taking time off from his own teaching, to talk to other teachers. He told them about Columbus so they could then teach in a different way. One of his own middle school students, a girl named Rebecca, wrote in her little paper: "Well if I've been lied to about Columbus, about what else have I been lied to?" Just giving people certain information about one situation may lead them to look for what else has been concealed from them.

There is still another way in which books can have a powerful effect. Very often, people believe they know something when they really do not. White people in the United States have always "known" in some distant and antiseptic way that black people have been kept down. But there is a difference between knowing in that superficial sense – "Oh yes, there's racial discrimination," "Oh yes, there's segregation" – and reading Malcolm X's *Autobiography* or Richard Wright's *Black Boy* or James Baldwin's *The Fire Next Time*, or the poems of Countee Cullen, and feeling, truly feeling, at least beginning to feel what it means to grow up black in this country.

The same goes for the phenomenon of war. Everyone knows, and it is repeated endlessly: "War is hell," now let's move on. But there are books that will not let you move on. It is possible to read that there are 100 million landmines buried in the earth all over the world, and think: "That's terrible," and move on. But if you read Gino Strada's book, *Green Parrots: A*

War Surgeon's Diary, and you begin to feel what it is like to amputate the legs of a child who has just been hit by a landmine, or has picked up a cluster bomb in a field, you cannot just move on.

I was a bombardier in the Air Force in World War II, and I dropped bombs on cities, towns, people. And yet I did not know what bombing did to human beings. I dropped bombs from 30,000 feet high and I saw no human beings, heard no screaming, saw no blood, did not see children dismembered by the bombs. I was guilty of the murder of innocents but did not understand what I had done. Shortly after the war was over, I read John Hersey's book, *Hiroshima,* where he visits Hiroshima and talks to the survivors and brings them before your eyes: people without arms or legs, or blinded, with skin that you cannot bear to look at. Reading John Hersey's book, I finally understood: this is what we do when we drop bombs on people.

So there is knowing and there is knowing and there is knowing. The most powerful anti-war book I ever read, that brought me close to understanding war, was Dalton Trumbo's novel, *Johnny Got His Gun.* It is told in the first person by a soldier on a hospital bed, a person who has no legs, no arms, who is blind, deaf, mute, just a torso with a beating heart and a thinking brain, reflecting on his life and on war. I would have my students read it because it did more to get to the reality of war than any five lectures of mine.

There is still another way that books and writing have an effect, and that is through the literature of absurdity, in the tradition of Jonathan Swift and Franz Kafka and Mark Twain. For our time, I think of Kurt Vonnegut's books, such as *Cat's Cradle* and *Slaughterhouse-Five.* I am thinking, too, of Joseph Heller's *Catch-22.* Heller creates a scene with Yossarian, the World War II bombardier, in a brothel in an Italian town, talking to an old Italian man who says, "You know, Italy will win because she is so weak. The United States in the long run will lose because she is so strong." This is an absurd idea. But it makes you think.

A final word. There is something important that writing can do, aside from all the other things. This was put into words by Kurt Vonnegut, who was often asked, "Why do you write?" Vonnegut would reply, "I write so you would know there are people who feel the way you do about the world, that you are not alone." That is an enormously important thing to accomplish, to have people feel that they are not alone. And it does something for you too, the writer.

3

Remember When Writing Was Fun? Why Academics Should Go On a Low Syllable, Active Voice Diet

Karen Brodkin

Not all that long ago I was sitting in a roomful of kindred academics. We were the new editorial board for a prestigious academic journal. What were we talking about? Actually, we weren't talking. The editors had asked how we could make the journal more interesting. Dead silence from 20 heavy hitters seldom at a loss for a polysyllable. Finally, one brave soul said, "I never read this journal; it's too dull." Many nods. Then another, "I avoid journal articles like the plague; they put me to sleep." More nods. A diplomat changed the subject and we all breathed a multi-syllabic sigh of relief. Full disclosure: I was person 2.

I really do fall asleep reading journal articles, and a fair amount of other academic writing as well. I'm not getting senile; it's been going on since I was an undergrad. All scholarly writing, actually any writing, has to frame the story it tells – and has to *tell* a story. Fiction writers talk about how to tell a story, and journalists talk about how to spin a story. There is a lot of overlap in framing, telling and spinning. They all get readers' interest by telling them what larger lesson a story teaches, what bigger issue it helps one see in a new, better way. But somehow, proper academic framing has slipped and slid from linking our stories to larger stories and findings by kindred scholars. We seem to do less debating and building knowledge collaboratively, and more genuflection-by-citation, usually to dead old white guys. As in: "This paper presents a Foucauldian analysis of governmentality." The only purpose a sentence like this serves is to put the writer into an intellectual kinship chart that links her/him to illustrious intellectual ancestors. In order to read this kind of journal article, I often feel as if I have to first swallow a turgid chanting of intellectual loyalties and ancestry. It feels like swallowing a lardball of jargon. Sometimes the rest of the article doesn't get any better, and I quit.

This rant was fun to write. It's what I was thinking about when I made up the title for this chapter. I've written a fair number of lardball productions myself, so I don't think ill of those whose work I have abandoned. Still, the lardball/no story problem seems to have a broad distribution these days, including in anthropology and women's studies, the two disciplines I know best. Was turgid and obscure always better? Is there something unprofessional about telling a story or explaining something? I don't think so. That doesn't mean boring is a recent invention in the academy; there is more than one way to put a reader to sleep.

After I got through ragging on a situation we've all experienced, I began to think seriously about why so many of us write this way at least some of the time, and in these times in particular. What I learned from the exercise, and what I will try to show here, is that an antidote to the current form of boring, the academic equivalent of a Big Mac – too many syllables and not enough content – is participation in intellectual communities, for me political ones, from which academic research and writing come.

A Retrospective Credo

So what's my alternative? Being asked to explain why I write what I do and how I do it has been a very helpful exercise. All my research has been about trying to figure out what it takes to create a more democratic and socially just society in today's world. That task has two intellectual parts. The first is speaking truth to power – finding information and telling stories that challenge conventional wisdom and then interpreting those data in ways that give readers an alternative wisdom. This part is about critique and Gramscian ideological struggle. The second part is offering a vision of what a better world could look like by analyzing people's efforts to change their social circumstances for the better. These are both long-term projects. I try not to write critique without also offering a vision of alternatives.

But I don't enjoy writing any of this as grand and abstract theory. I much prefer to tell a good story and maybe create a little new theory in the process. As I have written more, I have become more conscious about what I do in the way of story making. Here it is: I write about things that are familiar to and taken for granted by my audience, and I defamiliarize them.

I do this by telling stories that destabilize common sense and replace it with a new understanding, which serves as the political or conceptual lesson, or punch line. I write academic stories that have a plot, narrative tension and characters. I make myself a character in the story, usually the person in search of illumination. At my best, I'm light on the citations and genuflections, but clear that I'm one of a community of people who have been trying to figure out how to answer the particular question. At my worst, I've written lardballs as dense, obscure and boring as any I've ever read. Sometimes I have been aware of what I was writing about at the outset; other times I had to figure it out by writing many lardballs and non-stories.

I also have become more self-conscious that I write for two different but connected audiences. The first is an audience of "the unconverted," people who are unfamiliar with academic and political jargon and perhaps also with progressive or left perspectives. Any academic's best chance of reaching this audience is in undergraduate classrooms, and that is whom I write for. I count on my second audience, a community of kindred political intellectuals, both activist and academic, to use my work in their undergraduate classes, and they do. I try to offer this community the kind of article and book that can speak equally clearly to undergraduate students and non-academic activists. The "unconverted" is my audience because I was one when I was an undergraduate, and I can testify to the power of clear and unpretentious stories to change one's life.

I am a walking advertisement for the power of social movements to make people want new answers to old questions and to make new questions important. I was a student in the sixties, when the left had reason to be optimistic, when socialist revolutions in Cuba and China were young, and when the Civil Rights Movement was making great strides at ending legal segregation. Between 1962 and 1967, my thinking went from apolitical, slightly artsy, suburban middle-class to anti-racist, socialist, and very pro-proletarian, Marxist, and feminist, in roughly that order.

The best "before" picture I can offer of myself comes from 1962. Kathleen Gough was the catalyst that started all the dominoes falling. She was my undergraduate mentor. During the Cuban missile crisis, Kathleen gave a speech at a public forum at Brandeis University praising the Cuban revolution. Fear ran high across the nation about nuclear war erupting between the US and the Soviet Union. Herbert Marcuse, also a speaker, but less forthright, praised Kathleen for her courage in speaking truth to power. After her talk I congratulated her on her courage, but also said, "But you don't believe all that crap you said about Cuba do you?"

"What have you read, Karen?" Kathleen asked.

"*Time* magazine," says I.

"There are several books I could lend you." she replied.

I did not take her up on the offer.

Brandeis University's administration persecuted Kathleen Gough for her speech, and I joined the many students and a few faculty who fought for her rights. Fast forward a few weeks. I was in Kathleen's office when an anthropology grad student came by to return a book. "Thanks for the book on China."

"You mean Red China?!" I asked.

"Yes," said Kathleen; "why are you so surprised?"

"Because *Time* magazine says no one can get into Red China."

"There are lots of books by people who went to China."

"Can I borrow that book?"

I read Felix Green's *China*, and then Edgar Snow and then some more. I didn't like what I read; it contradicted everything I knew for sure. I had already participated in demonstrations at Woolworth's supporting integration of lunch counters. I knew that segregation was wrong, but thought it was an anachronistic blot on a pretty good and democratic society. That everyone around me (in the North) thought so too, and that so did *Time* magazine, confirmed my general view. But communism is good? Too much. Still, there was lots of specific, first-hand information and testimony in all those books about China. I came to the conclusion that I'd been systematically lied to about all sorts of things, and got very angry. It was the beginning of turning all my thinking around: all was not as it should be and not like "they" said it was.

I lived in opportunity-rich times. I found the National Association for the Advancement of Colored People and the Congress of Racial Equality in Boston and worked on civil rights and tenant organizing. For budding activists, there were two important things to do in the summer of 1964. One was to participate in the Student Nonviolent Coordinating Committee's Freedom Summer in Mississippi; the other was to travel to Cuba to see the revolution and to challenge the US travel ban. Civil Rights workers Schwerner, Chaney and Goodman had just been murdered in Mississippi and I was afraid to go there. Instead I seized the opportunity to go to Cuba for two months, when the revolution was an extraordinarily exciting mass movement that people in the streets claimed as their own. In all these contexts I met lots of radicals of all stripes and began to think like one myself. When I transferred from graduate school at Harvard to the graduate program in anthropology at the University of Michigan in 1966, its anthropology department was a hotbed of anti-Vietnam War activity. I became very active in anti-war politics on campus, and with other graduate students organized sessions against the war and imperialism at the American

Anthropological Association meetings. When Students for a Democratic Society had its first women's liberation workshops in Ann Arbor, I realized feminism was what I'd been waiting for all along and joined a consciousness-raising group. I discovered that I was now a Marxist feminist. These were heady times. I changed my mind and so did lots of others; many things in the society changed for the better. People thinking differently and working together made a difference on a big scale. A better world was indeed possible.

Writing as Part of a Community

As a graduate student at Michigan, I was part of a political cohort and community that rested quite solidly inside anthropology. Our faculty's activism modeled engaged scholarship and gave an immediacy and significance to intellectual work, to teaching and to writing. Like other graduate students in my cohort, I dreamed of studying the social revolutions that were then taking place. I wrote a quasi-ethnographic article about my Cuba trip, comparing Cuban state farms and small producer agricultural coops, extolling both but coming down strongly on the side of the latter, as I recall. It probably had a readership of two, me and the editor of the *Papers of the Michigan Academy of Science, Arts and Letters.* By this time though, with two children and a burgeoning feminist movement in the United States, I began to think about research closer to home. I've stayed in my own backyard ever since.

My first contact with the feminist movement at Michigan changed my life. Now my life was part of the Revolutionary program. In my consciousness-raising group, and among the women grad students in anthropology, we talked a lot about how to get rid of sexism, patriarchy and male chauvinism in society. Many of us began to engage with what anthropology could tell us about sexism and equality. It took me a while before I understood how anthropology could be relevant to this project. Feminist poet and writer Robin Morgan was way ahead of me. When she was putting together contributions for *Sisterhood is Powerful* (1970), the first and probably most widely read anthology of early women's liberation, she went looking for someone to write an anthropological perspective. "So what's an anthropological perspective?" I asked Robin.

"You know, Margaret Mead, Engels."

I wrote "Social Bases of Sexual Equality," which became the germ of my dissertation, and published the article "Engels Revisited" in both Rosaldo and Lamphere's *Woman, Culture and Society* (WCS), and Rapp's *Toward an Anthropology of Women* (TAW) in 1974 and 1975 respectively.

All this was exciting, but it also tended to marginalize budding feminists in anthropology. With the exception of Norma Diamond (who contributed to *TAW*), the faculty simply did not get feminism, certainly not the way they got and often took the lead on things pertaining to imperialism and Marxism in anthropology. But given their politics and the politics of the times, they did not get in the way of our efforts to create feminist anthropology either.

My experience with writing a feminist dissertation and trying to use anthropology to think about feminism led me to think that cohort-based communities are where new intellectual and political projects are born. The editors of both the first feminist anthropology collections were anthropology grad students when they got bit by the feminist bug; so were most of the contributors. We were part of feminism's third wave. WCS came out of the Harvard–Stanford cohort, and was more cultural and psychological. *TAW* drew on the Michigan cohort, and was more political economy, cultural evolutionary and Marxist. But these two books created a feminist anthropology with a clear question: Why are women subordinated in so many societies? We wanted to figure out what caused sexism and what a society without it would look like. Was it a cultural universal or were there egalitarian societies and matriarchies? My contribution was a comparative analysis of the kinds of social organizations that supported gender equality in several pre-colonial African societies, including the ways in which class mapped onto gender systems.

Reasonable feminists disagreed on whether or not gender-egalitarian societies ever existed, often reading the same evidence differently. But what we all shared was a firm conviction that conventional anthropological wisdom, that women *must* be socially subordinate to men because that is the way all societies are organized, was totally bogus. I think it's fair to say that a major success of the early feminist anthropology project was that we shredded that idea – helped mightily by the real changes the feminist movement made in our own society. We never answered our big question, but feminist anthropology did help the wider feminist movement radically destabilize conventional assumptions about "natural" gender relations – at least for a few decades.

Why didn't we answer our big question? I think because it became obvious that the paradigm from which we worked did not fit the world as it was going. We all used some version of a comparative method that rested on comparing supposedly discrete, autonomous, and timeless cultures and societies. As a good Marxist I acknowledged history and imperialism messing this situation up. But my approach was to look instead for a time-less time before the West spread its brand of sexism around the world. I held to the belief that there was a time when, as Eric Wolf put it, cultures were like billiard balls; they collided, but the eight ball always remained the eight ball.

When I wrote *Sisters and Wives* (1978), half my intent was to critique sexist ideas in anthropology, to expose all the ways they were wrong. I had a wonderful time savaging the thoughts of most of anthropology's greybeards. The other half was to rethink social structures of gender from a Marxist and feminist perspective, to figure out what the social requisites of gender equality might be. My dissertation research convinced me that the concepts of matriarchy and patriarchy were too vague and their specifics too rooted in contemporary Euro-American culture to be helpful.

This book sat at the border of my involvement with two overlapping political communities – efforts in the seventies to develop Marxist anthropological theories of pre-capitalist modes of production; and efforts by feminists to develop Marxist feminism as a way to link feminist activism to the political Left, and criticize the sexism that prevailed on the male-dominated Left. I argued that kinship was a way of organizing a society's relationships to the means of production, and was the heart and soul of political economy in non-class societies. Prior to feminist interventions, Marxists and anthropologists conceptualized women solely as reproducers in stereotypic ways. *Sisters and Wives* helped to develop a more complex Marxist and feminist theoretical framework for approaching kinship. It argued that the relationships of "sister" and "wife" in the patrilineal societies I examined were gender-specific relations to the means of production, so that the same woman could be empowered in her relations as a sister, even if she were subordinate to her husband's kin in her relations as a wife. The wider theoretical point was that relations to the means of production are necessarily gender-specific (though hardly uniform), that gender is an integral dimension of political economy: women are producers and owners as well as reproducers.

By the late seventies, the early feminist anthropology project and my Marxist intervention in it were past their sell-by date. But the gender struggle with and within the Left was in full flood. Conventional wisdom on the male Left was that women were invested in the household and didn't make great workplace activists. It just wasn't worth trying to organize women workers.

The next project among my cohort of left feminists, both activist and academic, was to answer smug male Marxists and unionists, and to show them that women were workplace leaders and activists, no doubt better than their male counterparts. Every woman activist knew this was true and that conventional male wisdom was wrong. In the mid-seventies, Dorothy Remy and I organized a conference of feminists in our cohort on women and work. We brought together anthropologists, sociologists, economists and historians to talk about Big Ideas for feminist political research. With the exception of Louise Lamphere, who was already doing ethnographic work with women garment workers, and Evelyn Nakano Glenn, who was doing similar work in sociology, the rest of us were wannabes. We were all interested in the ways that women fought back against sexism and exploitation. Our edited collection, *My Troubles are Going to have Trouble with Me* (1984), brought together case studies of what women were up against in the workplace and the everyday ways they resisted. The only problem was that none of us could really show what women's intentional and collective activism looked like.

A post-doc at Carol Stack's Family Policy Research Center at Duke University let me try to find out. There was a union drive going on at Duke Medical Center and the workers were overwhelmingly women. I participated in it and, with workers' permission, conducted research on: Did women organize? Were they leaders? What did these things look like when women did them? *Caring by the Hour* (1988) was the result. Its key answer to these questions was to develop the concept of centerwomen. These are women who hold together the networks that make up the informal social structure of women's workplaces. They are leaders in part because they embody and articulate the core understandings of work and social relations that govern women's work culture. *Caring by the Hour* documented the large amount of unrecognized and unremunerated skill, knowledge and responsibility that went into the daily performance of so-called unskilled labor. And it detailed the informal structures of mentoring, recognition and affirmation of the skills of that work that underlay the informal work culture and social networks of women workers. This remains a challenge to unions' prevailing acceptance of management's definition of hourly work as unskilled. I showed how women's work culture included a familistic idiom of resistance. That is, women, especially centerwomen, learned organizing skills as part of family life, and women used family-derived values about adulthood, work and respect to assert and legitimate their positive evaluation of their own skill and worth in opposition to the hospital's denigration of them. Women's activism had its own informal structure and cultural values embedded in workplace networks. Women learned those roles and many of the values that animated workplace networks in families. The informal structures and values by which non-professional hospital workers organized their daily work lives became the organizational platform for unionization and social change. Union leadership and organizational strength rested with the informal activities of centerwomen, especially of African American women's work-based networks. Women's informal networks and family-derived work culture were the informal structure and culture of the union movement. When union spokespersons and organizers worked within that frame the movement flourished; when they strayed, it withered.

Although I focused on women's activism, it had to be understood in a wider social context. Two linked national structural shifts were key: the massive growth and industrialization of health care in the 1950s and '60s, and the rise of the Civil Rights Movement. The former led to a worsening of conditions for many hourly workers, while the latter lent force and legitimacy to demands for social justice. Because African American workers took the lead in unionizing, the union struggle combined racial and class consciousness in a movement that sustained itself for more than a decade. These were the widest levels of structural conditions supporting politicization of African American women's social networks within and beyond the hospital. A more proximal set of structures segregated women's jobs by race, and the race of the job in turn structured its working conditions as well as the availability of alternatives and mobility. These directly shaped the informal networks and oppositional work consciousnesses that were at the core of the union movement, making some jobs and departments hotbeds of activism and others not.

I wrote *Caring by the Hour* for activists and unionists, feminists and not. I used as jargon-free a style as I knew how. I also framed it by making me an animating character in the book; my research quest, a feminist wanting to challenge the prevailing sexism, was the theoretical frame of the book. I used my mistakes to highlight the differences between middle-class and mainstream notions of leadership and the actual forms that grassroots leadership takes. I also showed how workers' race and gender shaped the kind of work they did, their treatment, and how management saw the skill required for their jobs.

The time was right to take on this question, but this was a book with a foot in several small markets: labor history, budding anthropology and sociology of work, US anthropology, labor studies. *Caring by the Hour* did not make me rich or famous, and its politics did almost prevent me from getting hired at UCLA. But it has stayed in print and been used for two decades now. I managed to get a one-page piece about Duke Hospital women workers into *Ms.* magazine. However, my greatest joy has been the fact that, so I've been told, at least two unions engaged in hospital organizing in the South and on the East Coast have used it as an organizing manual and in organizer training.

By the late eighties, the solid, comfortable day-to-day intellectual, political, cohort-based communities that I experienced inside anthropology at Michigan in the sixties, and among a multi-disciplinary group of feminist activists around women and work in the seventies and early eighties, seemed to have dissipated. It may be that cohorts have a finite life, that we age out, and newer cohorts of younger scholars take over the job of developing new projects for new times. In any event, by the late eighties I often felt like an academic ugly duckling, working in a borderland of several disciplines – Marxist and feminist scholarship, sociology, ethnic studies, social movement theory, critical race theory, US labor and women's history, with no homeplace.

I don't think I've aged out, and I don't think my experience is especially unusual, but I do think that my relationship to intellectual political communities has changed. The intellectual communities in which I now participate are more imagined communities that include several generations of progressive cohorts across disciplines than day-to-day networks of collaborators whose questions I share. Looking back, my early involvement with the feminist movement prepared me for this kind of community. My involvement with early feminist anthropology made me something of an oddball within anthropology. My jobs have come through Women's Studies more than anthropology. Doing field research in the US in the seventies and eighties didn't help either. One consequence is that I've participated in a variety of intellectual and political conversations, but do not feel like a specialist in any one of them. Another is that my work often combines disciplines in unorthodox ways, mixing history and ethnography, memoir, narrative analysis and occasional miscellaneous muckraking.

And still a third is that I have written my share of lardballs as I try to frame my work for imagined audiences. Cynthia Strathmann and I worked with union organizers to figure out why union-busting campaigns worked, what organizing strategies countered them and why. We ultimately wrote "The Struggle for Hearts and Minds: Organization, Ideology, and Emotion" and published it in *Labor Studies Journal* (2004), but not before I tried mightily and unsuccessfully to give it a framing for an anthropological journal. At one point, I shared a draft with a research and writing seminar of graduate students for critique. They dutifully read it, and met me with dead silence. Finally, one brave soul said, "You always tell us our writing needs to have plot and characters; this has no plot and no characters." She was right; it was a beautiful exemplar of a lardball. We couldn't imagine a clear community inside anthropology as its audience. Framing it for a labor studies journal was a no-brainer. Maybe part of the lardball framing problem comes from a disjuncture between our disciplinary heritages, which disciplinary journals need to represent, and emerging intellectual communities that cross disciplines.

How Jews Became White Folks and What That Says about Race in America (1999), began as – and remained – a book for an imagined community. It represented a shift in my writing in several ways. First of all, from the beginning, it was a book intended for undergraduate classes and non-academic audiences. Second, it was a topic that did not deal with activism or what a better world might look like. I didn't even start out to write about Jews, but rather to write an interpretive synthesis of the large, multi-disciplinary and often arcane literature that explored the ways race, class, gender and national identity were mutually constructed in US culture. That would have been a fine project when I began to write in 1992 or '93. By the time I got down to writing seriously, that need was filled because lots of people had explained it really well. That was fortunate, because it turned out that I don't like writing about abstract ideas at all. But as part of the narrative, I thought I still needed a chapter that put the structures of gender in the foreground to show how race and class shaped different versions of womanhood and manhood in US history. That chapter is loaded with jargon, and is as boring to read as it was to write. It is a little lardball-like.

When I rethought what kind of book I could write about race for an undergraduate audience, I realized that I had scooped myself by having put the book's first (and best) chapter, "How Jews Became White Folks" in Gregory and Sanjek's collection, *Race* (1994). So the question became: where to go from there?

For several years in the early nineties I was part of a writers' group led by the poet Eloise Klein Healey. I was trying to learn how to write creative non-fiction. I had written a short memoir about growing up in New York's suburbs, and now I began to look at it as a way into writing about Jews' shift from being stigmatized to being given the social privileges of the WASPly white. I rewrote and expanded it so that it made my family the archetypal Eastern European, non-observant and unaffiliated Jewish characters whose story the book would tell. As the book's Introduction, it told the story of the three generations of Jewish women in my household as I grew up in the 1950s. Each came of age under a different set of racial structures; each historical set of constraints and opportunities influenced the ways our different generations shaped our Jewish womanhoods and our class privileges and aspirations. This set up the narrative tension and framed the book: what were the structures that shaped us?

The first three chapters analyzed them – first the federal policies and institutional practices that removed barriers of racial discrimination against Jews and other Eastern and Southern European immigrants in the wake of World War II, thereby "whitening" them. Then I examined the forces that made Jews less than white for most of the preceding century, and how working-classness has been constructed racially in American history, and how gender figures in the story. The last two chapters looked at how Jewish women responded to their historically different racial assignments – in my grandmother's turn-of-the-century Jewish New York, and in the late forties and fifties in which I grew up.

This book has legs. It's gone through five printings and keeps selling well almost a decade after its publication. I've lost count of the number of class-room anthologies and number of editions that have reprinted parts of the book. It even has a non-academic readership. It's my biggest success at reaching a readership that goes far beyond the usual suspects. That's the good news – and the bad news. I discovered fairly quickly, when I gave talks to Jewish groups and read reviews from Jewish scholars, that Jews either loved the book or hated it, and neither group was shy about telling me why. Some Jews resonate with the book's argument that Jews today occupy a status of racial privilege. For others I believe that argument is deeply threatening. Overall, it has been a healthy kind of controversy in that it has opened up intellectual spaces for Jews to engage constructively with issues of race, affirmative action, and the ways that Jewish organiza-tions use the Holocaust to enlist their support for right-wing Israeli politics.

But here's the thing: I didn't write this book as part of a political/intel-lectual community. Academic community yes, and it is part of many schol-arly weddings – mainly critical race theory and critical studies of whiteness. But I think that what is missing in this book is a better sense of what do you do once you recognize you have race privilege? I'm not sure that there is, even now, a political community that is asking that question. I think we should be asking it very seriously.

After the publication of *Jews*, I returned to thinking about activism, with activists and with imagined communities. What I'm interested in is vision: what does a better world look like today? For those of us who are socialists of one or another stripe, what would a better, post-socialist world socialism look like? *Making Democracy Matter: Identity and Activism in Los Angeles* (2007) is also designed for the classrooms of progressive faculty, and for activists themselves. It is based on long conversations with sixteen activists and I tell the story largely in their own words. I'm the framing character here too, the old leftie who notices that, to paraphrase Steinbeck, the young, they're not like us. But the tools for figuring out what the young are like come from the younger feminist scholars of color who developed theories and insights that come from living in social and cultural borderlands. The question I pose is: what visions and practices of democracy are the upcoming cohort of labor and immigrant rights workers developing for our times? I argue that what makes a social movement a *movement* is the vision of something better and the sense that we can make it happen. I try to show how that contagious energy comes from the personal transformations of a cohort of activists to the new political and cultural identities they create, and from the resonance of those identities with a mass constituency. This is still another book that doesn't rest comfortably in one of academe's boxes, although it looks as if it might be happiest in labor studies, ethnic, and women's studies. Too soon to know what its audience might look like or what work this book might do.

What I've learned from this exercise is that in writing as in research, the questions we ask are as important as the answers. Asking, "What work does this piece of writing do?" directs us to approach our scholarship as a form of building social relationships with audiences and interlocutors. Sometimes writing destabilizes our audience's common sense and suggests alternatives. Sometimes we help existing communities form new kinds of self-consciousness; and occasionally we help nurture new forms of community building. And at the very least, if we all thought about scholarly writing as a kind of relationship building, maybe we would spare the world a few academic lardballs.

References

Brodkin, Karen. 1968. Agrarian Reform in Cuba. *Papers of the Michigan Academy of Science, Arts and Letters*, 53.

Brodkin, Karen. 1970. Social Bases for Sexual Equality: A Comparative View. In *Sisterhood is Powerful: An Anthology of Writings from the Women's Liberation Movement*. Robin Morgan, ed., pp. 455–69. New York: Vintage.

Brodkin, Karen. 1974. Engels Revisited. In *Women, Culture, and Society*. Michelle Rosaldo and Louise Lamphere, eds., pp. 207–22. Stanford, CA: Stanford University Press.

Brodkin, Karen. 1975. Engels Revisited: Women, the Organization of Production, and Private Property. In *Toward an Anthropology of Women*. Rayna Reiter, ed., pp. 211–34. New York: Monthly Review Press.

Brodkin, Karen. 1982. *Sisters and Wives: The Past and Future of Sexual Equality*. Champaign: University of Illinois Press.

Brodkin, Karen. 1988. *Caring by the Hour: Women, Work and Organizing at Duke Medical Center*. Champaign,: University of Illinois Press.

Brodkin, Karen. 1994. How Did Jews Become White Folks? In *Race*. Steven Gregory and Roger Sanjek, eds., pp. 78–102. New Brunswick, NJ: Rutgers University Press.

Brodkin, Karen. 1999. *How Jews Became White Folks and What That Says about Race in America*. New Brunswick, NJ: Rutgers University Press.

Brodkin, Karen. 2007. *Making Democracy Matter: Identity and Activism in Los Angeles*. New Brunswick, NJ: Rutgers University Press.

Brodkin, Karen and Dorothy Remy, eds. 1984. *My Troubles are Going to Have Trouble with Me: Everyday Trials and Triumphs of Women Workers*. New Brunswick, NJ: Rutgers University Press.

Brodkin, Karen and Cynthia Strathmann. 2004. The Struggle for Hearts and Minds: Organization, Ideology, and Emotion. *Labor Studies Journal* 29, 3: 1–25.

4

The Bard

Carolyn Nordstrom

The war orphans have gotten me through academia.

Every time I sit down to write, I knock a host of academic critics off my shoulder who tell me I *can't*, *shouldn't*, *wouldn't* write what I believe in; that I *must* follow their guidelines for "truth," academic style, and that (by the way) I'm not good enough, never will be. The delegation contains everyone from my former graduate school advisors to the anonymous reviewer who said I might as well quit anthropology altogether and chuck my writing (and why not myself, by the way) off the Golden Gate Bridge as my work was hopelessly terrible. Even kindly friends and unctuous journal editors trying to help me by explaining "how it is done" and why my style "just won't work" join the others on my shoulder. Some are particularly hard to knock off: one of the worst whispers, "You think you can put *that* out there . . . they'll think you're stupid."

And then I remember why I'm writing.

I remember sitting on dusty broken street curbs amid the cacophonous swirl of life and war with kids who gently and patiently explain what it means to be human, to have dignity, to survive on a very unequal playing field. Kids whose theories of life are as vibrant as any scholar's I've met. Children who have been exposed to the worst violence humans have invented and yet continue to care.

They help push the academic judges and juries off me:

"We're the story. We are why you travel, why you write."

And they bring in their own reinforcements, sitting not on my shoulder, as the judges do, but alongside me – sprawled ephemerally in my mind's eye in the tropical sun, twirling bits of grass in their fingers, clapping one another on the back in affectionate camaraderie, offering a cool drink when things get hot. Reinforcements like the starving Mozambican village woman who punched out a murderous soldier humiliating her with such force that the troops left, fearing she was sparking a revolt. Like the Sri Lankan teenage girl killed by troops and left crucified on a barbwire fence as a "warning." Like the tough African traders who carried the last of their food across enemy lines to help feed those under attack. People whom I suspect will be found by future researchers to be more courageous about the truths of theory and practice than those of us writing today.

One of the spirits who continues to shine brightly in my life was my close friend Anita. She is particularly adept at staring down the judges of epistemology. I met her the first day I arrived in Africa, and we struck up an immediate friendship. She showed me how to work the informal markets, hitchhike across Zimbabwe, cook sadza (corn meal porridge), and graciously visit everyone from local elites to impoverished street musicians. To this day, I have not met anyone who had more of the anthropologist's gift, or more love of Africa. We got caught by sheer bureaucratic oversight in Mogadishu when political violence erupted nation-wide and all foreigners were expelled. Except us. She told me then, as we scrounged for food, that she had been raped in a similar circumstance in another country by a man she was working with during a military curfew. It was the only time she had unprotected sex. One month later she found out she had AIDS. Anita decided that before she died she wanted to study anthropology, specialize in Africa, and write a thesis, then a book, on identity, sexuality, the warmth of relationships and the post-modern dynamics of power. I encouraged her. But I had forgotten about the judges. About the fact that while some are fictitious creations of nightmares, some are real. When she applied, they moved from my shoulder to tell her she just wasn't good enough. Didn't invoke the liturgy, ah, theory, in the right sequences; didn't honor the ancestors, our grand theoreticians, in the right way, by date and title. Application: Denied. With Humiliation. Maybe in dying she was just too alive for theory. She died some years ago – thinking she was too stupid for anthropology. Maybe Anita suffered not one but two rapes. She reminds me who my audience is.

What role makes it easiest for me to translate these roiling realities into word? The bard. The person who translates the unfettered wilds of raw experience and human interaction into philosophical story. The lens of reflexivity. The conduit through whom the story of one reaches many, and philosophies are crafted across time and space.

The role of the bard is reassuring: the bard lives in the world, among friends, within experience. The war orphans knock the judges off my shoulder and fellow anthropologists whose light burns bright help forge an anthropology free of harsh critics and hidebound rules. They are too big to sit on my shoulders, but they have shaped my writing in exciting ways.

They, too, struggle with the demons of academia, searching for innovative solutions to our discipline. Their words have freed my writing. There are too many to cite by name, thank goodness. But examples come easily. I remember panicking while writing one of my first articles after defending my dissertation, and calling JoAnn Martin. As I poured out my anguish at my terror of writing trash, I heard her start to laugh. "OK, Carolyn, I'm looking at my watch. You can whine away for 15 more seconds, and then I want you to sit down and get that fucker done." I recall Bruce Kapferer saying to me a few years back, "Good God, woman, let loose; shake up the Academy, write something New." I feel warmed by the gentle kindness of colleagues such as Victoria Sanford who know the value of support and the words "I love our work." I hold them dear when fellow anthropologists, ostensibly peaceful, attack with verbal savagery. On days when the war orphans need some assistance, I am inspired by Paul Farmer's honesty and heart: "It's ok for scholarship, for anthropology, for us, for me, to care." These are good antidotes to those late-night existential quandaries – the ones I describe as sitting on the dusty crumbling curb of our fieldsite at three in the morning ripping out our guts and inspecting them with a cheap plastic flashlight we bought in the street market for a buck: "What am I offering to life?" And the invitations that make it possible to go on: dinner with Tony Robbins' family, Burma with Monique Skidmore, sitting in the middle of the parking lot at midnight at the American Anthropological Association meetings with Rob Borofsky, all of them saying, "Hey, we can do it."

Do I see myself as some voice, some savior of the war-afflicted? Of the violated and the orphaned? No. This strikes me as offensive. It certainly strikes the war-afflicted as offensive. I have learned a more palatable view from the in-field philosophers: we all, as humans, have a responsibility to creatively offer something to the world. Not more than one person can. Just our bit.

Creativity is not an individual act. In my opinion, it takes meaning only when it adds to the sum of our humanity. The traders offering their last bit of food to those being bombed on the front are forging a better world in the midst of violence, and one that is easily as important (perhaps more) as the one academics create with their publications and policies. The peasant who lives Foucault in resistance to abusive violence may well be more innovative than a scholar critiquing his work for a grade or a promotion.

What's my bit? I tell my students to research and write about what sets their hearts aflame; what they care about enough to jump out of bed after a few hours' sleep to study; what their intellects truly love because it takes them to worlds deeper and more meaningful than they thought possible. Not about any notion of *should*.

These passions are a curious and intangible blend of history, creativity, imagination, guts, self-identity, and serendipity. In my case: I inadvertently witnessed a massacre of peaceful political demonstrators when I was an undergraduate. As a graduate student, I got caught in an eruption of severe political violence. In my small and sleepy Midwest hometown, one of my best childhood friends was beaten to death with a brick. I found out another of my closest childhood friends was gang-raped during the time I was researching rape camps overseas. The stories continue, but somewhere along here I realized a simple fact: war doesn't make sense. Violating those who can't protect themselves and fight back is unconscionable. There is no glory in bodies exploding into bits. Too many of my friends have died unnecessarily. This is what gets me up on cold rainy days to follow a story. When the judges sitting on my shoulder are particularly brutal (*"You'll be flipping hamburgers at McDonald's for a living if you try to publish this crap"*), I dedicate my writing to those I have known who have died. Or those battling on the frontlines for survival who have entrusted me to tell their stories. They are particularly adept at challenging the hegemony and onerous rules of academic gatekeepers.

i'd like
to write
like
this . . .

sometimes.

and once in a while burst into laughter at the joy of it all
or scream with pain

howling like a wounded animal
at the night
sky

the wild heartbeat of words across the page
caressing theory like
a
sizzling lover

but . . .
i don't

well, at least not in
   public.

you should
see
my field notebooks.

i show them to my students who are having existential
crises
and every time
they
just
sit
there
and hold them

and then
   smile.

'i can do this'
they say,
and they mean
not
   just
anthropology

but life.

I tried publishing an article in an anthropology journal recently, an article that broke the rules of convention. Nothing as raw as what is written above. A tamer but equally earnest version. "Sorry," they wrote back. "Not sufficiently ethnographic: put in more data. Quote Bourdieu and explore Agamben. Make your argument more clearly." I wrote back to thank them for their reviews; and noted that Bourdieu and Agamben wouldn't be able to publish in this journal given their writing styles.

When I write at my university, the walls fade away into open savannah, and the sounds of students in the hallways give way to the raucous murmurings of open markets and backyard gatherings. My colleagues know this, and make cheerful noise when they come in my door to alert me to the fact that I'm in the USA, in my office, in a day filled with appointments cut into 15-minute slots. They are used to the fact that if they approach silently, I look at them blankly for a moment, wondering what they are doing in Africa, or Sri Lanka; and worse, what I am doing in an office. Going to the place I am writing about in my head is an old trick of mine. It's a feeling akin to allowing yourself to be in a movie you are watching. I can feel the sun on my face, the intangible ripples of war's violence shaping the day, the emotions of the people I'm talking to. And that's what I write.

But for me, it's far better to actually write on the road. I'm most comfortable juggling my laptop on a rickety table in the field, the sounds of life swirling about me. Death is a lot closer in the field, but somehow that makes my writing more honest. The looks in the eyes of the people I'm talking to, writing about, remind me not to sanitize death, write out the pain, abstract the raw in bloodless theory.

There, on the frontlines of life, I can see what theory is meant to be – and here I speak of theory in the most encompassing sense: of the epistemologies that define our intellectual efforts in this era . . . meta-thought both intended and unwitting; the "definitives" of the Academy, capital A, poetry and power entwined. And simultaneously, in the field I see what the people I speak with intend it to be:

Alive. Vibrant. Passionate. Creative. Daring.
Ontology infused with searing insightful thought.
Epistemology that howls after a military attack. While deconstructing it.

People in the midst of living and dying understand this kind of theory. They encourage it. Many from the frontlines of wars I have met across Africa and Asia have said to me that western religious iconography is full of blood (pointing out Jesus on the cross), and its academic work bloodless. To them, this is about as useful as a body without blood: it is missing its lifeforce.

It is fascinating to me that when I take the jargon out of academic theory and explain it to people who may never have seen the inside of a classroom, they can engage with me on a level as deep as any of my university colleagues. I've discussed Foucault's ideas about power with farmers in Sri Lanka ("Foucault basically has it right, but needs to factor in humans' ability to react to power on at least five simultaneous planes: a non-thoughtful submission to oppressive power, the thoughtful spark of creative resistance to this, the tools of history, the potential of the [creative] unknown, and the grounding of individual as social will"). African peasant women have patiently explained to me that western epistemologies of knowledge lack an understanding of the fact that perception is never a mere linear process; that even asking the question of whether sense, perception or raw knowing precedes knowledge misses the point ("Knowledge can be embedded in raw perception, knowing is sense, and in battles the survivors have learned perception-is-action-is-knowing-is-perception").

They couldn't care less about the academic judges sitting on my shoulder telling me how I must engage with the idea of power and perception if I am to be published. For them, the war orphans are better critics.

If we can manage to keep them alive.

It isn't enough to say I write for the war orphans. That keeps my sanity. But it doesn't explain why I write. Why I go to warzones and get malaria and shot at and truly educated.

There are several reasons. One of them is *not* that I get an adrenaline rush by violence, or that I'm addicted to the heightened senses – living a life more intense than life – that come in the midst of war. People in warzones *never* ask that question of me. Hearing talk about the adrenaline rush of violence reminds me that we have a lot yet to learn about war. About human dignity. About research and the nature of being human. No one asks people if they study tuberculosis because of the neurochemical high they get, or assumes people investigate financial derivatives or the Japanese sense of self-identity for the rush.

Nor do I research violence because I decided to. It decided me. I was a student studying medical anthropology when I got caught in the epicenter of the 1983 rioting in Sri Lanka in which thousands of people were killed and one-sixth of the country's infrastructure destroyed in seven days. I gave up what I was working on in order to study violence. I had seen something I couldn't explain; and every explanation in print that I saw was inadequate. It feels physical, that Why? Why do some people hack vital lifeforces up into dead bits? Why do others risk their lives protecting someone they don't know? Why can I so seldom find answers in print that match the reality of violence lived? Why care?

As I get older, and traveling in warzones and along extra-legal global pathways gets harder on my bones, I wonder why I still do it. The academy gracefully pardons its veterans (the tenured) from ongoing bouts of grueling fieldwork; it embraces equally those who go to the frontlines and those who go to soft beaches for fieldwork. And I have come to accept that there is something deeper that drives people to do what they do. Something that is perhaps the intellectual equivalent of the sex drive: a curiosity that drives the evolution of thought-lived. The kind of knowledge that makes us possible.

I remember reading about the man who illuminated turbulence theory. I can't remember his actual job, but in my memory, he is something like a postal clerk. Certainly not a well-paid scientist in a laboratory. There was no career-related obligation for him to care. Nor am I sure he actually had the brown La-Z-Boy recliner chair that I picture. But he did come home from work each day and pull his home-made turbulence machine out from behind his living-room chair and throw himself into discovering the force explaining not only a foundation of water's movement, but chaos theory. Why, I always wonder, would a man come home from work, tired and hungry, and instead of going for a beer with his mates, try to discover a fundamental force of our universe? Why do any of us leave the comforts of home to place ourselves on the brink of chaos? Whatever force it is – turbulence or otherwise – it feels tangible, and rather inescapable. As if along with eye color and kidney function, each of us is born with some burning question. The sum total equals humanity.

In addition to this, in warzones I discovered how big life really is. As an acquaintance once summed up: "It's not that we go to warzones for the rush; it's that we find out there is so much life."

On the frontlines, every single person matters.

The good and the bad are conjoined in the dance of life and death, and neither is edited out, either in the daily telling or in the bard's accounting.

In academia, we have "marginal topics" – the ones that usually aren't in plenary sessions at the annual meetings; the ones that if you focus on, you have to look hard for a job, and worry more than usual about tenure. The ones that start to define your identity rather than your research site. When I came up for tenure, I had publications on just about every aspect of warzone ethnography conceivable. I learned my work on the economics of war was "masculine," and therefore fundamentally weighty. So too with politics – but that was a bit more dodgy: whose politics? Publications on frontline actors – from soldiers through civilians to rogues – were seen as "gutsy," and therefore respected. The quotes, however, from these actors were "art": cool, but a bit insubstantial. And this bled over to define not merely my anthropology, but me. My work on children and war concretized this view, but lent it heart. Amid all this I had half a dozen articles on rape. Those, I was told, my committee took out of the packets that were being sent to my tenure reviewers. The committee felt they were acting in the best of faith: worried that the guardians of anthropology, the powers-that-be – those unnamed good people across the breadth of our universities – would be prejudiced against me if they associated me with work on rape.

And so in the annals of economics there are few articles on the economics of rape; and those on the politics of rape are far more often found in gender studies than in government science. Job openings follow along these same lines. Promotion is segregated.

Many tell me I am not alone when I escape to the field to find reality. To breathe in the vitality of life-lived. To feel free to cry at the stories we hear, and dance the joys of theory that begins to pulse with blood.

To revel in the fact that everyone matters.

Everything we cover in our research – from lies to love, from professors to war orphans –is part of a vast interrelated story of the human condition. To take out the economics, the children, the rapes, the evening meals, the nightmares spreading across the countryside, the creative solutions that walk hand in hand with the terrors, the politics, the smiles . . . renders it all false. It bleeds out the color and paints humanity in black and white. It hurts.

As I write this, I realize that in going to our disciplines' inter/national meetings for more than two decades, I have heard not scores, but hundreds of heart-rending presentations on topics from HIV/AIDS to torture, from poverty to child abuse. Twice, I recall having heard people become emotional or cry while giving these papers.

Coming back from the field to our "day jobs" – to the academy – is often like going into another kind of warzone. This is a nearly universal feeling in my experience. Virtually everyone I know has some kind of existential crisis. I call it the "cereal aisle meltdown." For me, it happens on the first trip to the western supermarket. I am stopped cold in front of the cereal section. And the crash begins, the clash of competing worlds: "One hundred kinds of sugar-flour when just yesterday I was talking to kids scrounging for a meal; a world where shoppers can name more brands of cereal than human rights laws." And I mull: Reason that this is so? Unknown. Reason: none, literally. Conclusion: (the world is) unreasonable. And so it goes.

Everyone has ways of dealing with it. My students returning from overseas often break into tears in my class and office. Friends rage against the system. Some by writing what they know to be true, others by drowning their feelings in drugs and alcohol. And others still by leaving. The rules of what we can write and not-write, indeed of what we can see and not-see, chafe like straightjackets. Or worse. I think of my friend whose husband died from stepping on a landmine: she is expected to write him out of her thesis; or, if she writes him in, to write out emoting. She loves Renato Rosaldo, who refused to do either when his wife died in the field. Or my colleagues and students who live with the intangible but powerful traces of tragedies witnessed, and are expected to adhere to a strict academic apartheid: write words, not traces. These people often love the work on subjectivities by Veena Das, Arthur Kleinman, Mamphela Ramphele, and Pamela Reynolds. Personally, I find works like Bao Ninh's *The Sorrow of War* – that craft the larger truths of life lived through the creative interplay of non/fiction – powerful theoretically as well as poetically. As effective in the classroom as the more classical academic books. This seemed to me an excellent way to render into word the vibrant turbulence of research lived. Until I found out the academic presses I work with are not able to publish creative non/fiction under the title of anthropology.

Within all these considerations, I am continually astounded that we actually accept that a division *can* exist between theoretical and applied, between academic and activist, between Bao Ninh and ethnography; and that we – who write on the abuses of value hierarchies – allow them to be applied to these arbitrary divisions: this is cool, this isn't. As if theory isn't an interactive process that shapes what it comes into contact with – as if it isn't activism. As if active work could ever be disentangled from epistemology.

Those first days back, the landscapes of my academic life look like barren wastelands; theory seems eviscerated, caring unacceptable.

And then we settle in. One eye always on the horizon.

And over coffee and the internet, most of the anthropologists I know, and certainly the ones I love best, promise that we will work to craft a new anthropology, forge a new kind of epistemology. Kinder, gentler: writing in the vibrancy of life and taking out the terrors of tenure competition and the brutality that can be found in the publishing world. The fact that with so much good will among so many good people the "gatekeeping rules" change so slowly gives pause: what, actually, is being served?

On days when I'm having an existential thunderstorm, with the winds of questions kicking up eddies in my mind, I wonder, "If I were going to make a discipline that had the ability to see the larger realities defining our worlds, both internal and external, *and* I wanted to make sure it had as little impact on the political world and its power systems as possible, what would I create?" And the answer for me is always the same: the academy as we know it today. A tenure system that makes people fearful and cowed. A publishing system with rules of jargon and distribution that ensure only a handful of fellow specialists will ever read the discipline's works. And a personal system where competition rather than camaraderie is supported.

A system where not everyone matters.

And on those times when I'm struck by lightning in the storms of my mind, I have to laugh: we research and publish on people's resistance to oppressive hierarchies around the world, while so often accepting the ones defining our own academic lives.

Who, I find myself asking again, will the future historians looking back on our era define as courageous? As world-creating?

I dedicated my last
book
to the war
orphan

like
so many friends
I have fought hard
to
maintain
my own writing style
the voice I like
best

the fact
that the war orphan's story
has seen the light
of day
means the fight
is
worth
it

things change

5

Saggin' and Braggin'

Lee D. Baker

Don't get caught with your pants down in Delcambre, Louisiana; it will cost you $500.00 or six months in jail. Carol Broussard, the mayor of this bayou township with fewer than 2,000 people, signed into law an ordinance passed by his town council on June 11, 2007. The ordinance criminalizes those ubiquitous baggy pants worn by young men, and some women, that are at once a fashion statement of urban cool, a sign of youthful rebellion, and a clever way for heavily branded boxer briefs to compete with denim jeans over the visible real estate on the bodies of members of the coveted 16–24 demographic, many of whom seem to relish paying top dollar to become walking billboards for designers of their favorite gear.

The new law states that "it shall be unlawful for any person in any public place or in view of the public to be found in a state of nudity, or partial nudity, or in dress not becoming to his or her sex, or in any indecent exposure of his or her person or undergarments, or be guilty of any indecent or lewd behavior" (Associated Press 2007a). Within a month the town of Mansfield, Louisiana passed a similar law and other towns are planning to follow suit (Associated Press 2007b).

Although Louisiana has public decency laws on the books, the stiff fine and "drawz clause" were added in an effort to both discipline and punish the mostly black and brown youth who sport this unique style, a style that has been putatively associated with gang violence, disrespect of authority, and in my opinion, a general sense that it is possible but not probable to make it in America – so why try? These men, who for the most part are undereducated and underemployed people of color, know that it's a long shot to achieve the American Dream by simply working hard and playing by the rules. In some respects, this is a much more productive response to the long shot of achieving the American Dream, because others resort to abusing methamphetamines, alcohol, or food, which leads to rampant addiction in many white communities and to type II diabetes in Native American communities.

Wearing baggy pants, or saggin' as it has become known, is a fashion statement that has emerged by articulating a consistent pattern of creative adaptation that involves inverting and transmuting the monikers and symbols of racism, disrespect, and humiliation into symbols of power, pride, and respect. Yet such symbols are always already steeped in contradictions and complicated; unintended consequences immediately become read and interpreted within a racial politics of culture and a cultural politics of race. It is widely believed that saggin' as a style was adopted from prison culture, where belts are prohibited and ill-fitting prison garb the norm (Christian 2007: 16). Judge Greg Mathis, who hosts his own eponymous courtroom television show, has become a self-proclaimed fashion critic, or at least a critic of this fashion. He told readers of *Jet Magazine* that "you have this in[t]erchange of what is cool and hip in the 'hood and what is cool and hip in prison. You have a rotating door" (Christian 2007: 18).

In the wake of particularly draconian dress codes in schools and prisons, young men have been routinely told what and what not to wear. Frankly, there are few options because a wide palette of colors – as well as a wide range of National Basketball Association and National Football League mascots – are associated with gang membership and subsequently banned from schools, recreation centers, and other public spaces. An interesting trend has emerged among urban and rural youth, which I think must be understood as explicit, sardonic cynicism. They have begun to sport simple, all white t-shirts, thus transforming the unassuming tee into the latest must-have gear. As if on cue, the white t-shirt became the target of policing and censorship. Although not yet as inimical to the customs and mores of middle America as sagging jeans, the long white t-shirt is now increasingly associated with gang violence and pathological behavior, and sanctioned under strict dress codes. If a t-shirt is violet and emblazoned with Tommy Hilfiger or Sean John it's fine. If a young adult wants to don gang-neutral garb and ad-free gear, however, he might not be able to go to school, get into a night club, or dine at a restaurant (Ayad 2006: B1). Wittingly or not, a large swath of the fashion-savvy hip-hop/wired generation have begun to tog out with the most innocuous and least offensive piece of clothing one could imagine. By doing so, they have collectively forced the so-called powers-that-be to demonstrate that the real subject of policing is not the clothes but the bodies of black and brown boys. The white t-shirt is, by definition, unmarked; but on these bodies it is assigned a mark of urban degeneracy that cannot be worn in many venues because it putatively promotes violence. Whether it is baggy pants inspired by prison garb or a simple white t-shirt that belies any gang affiliation, the pattern is the same. When black people appropriate it as their own, the meaning changes and the object, or sound, or food, or clothing takes on a new meaning. Sometimes it's negative, but often it is positive; most always it is shot through with ambivalence and anxiety.

Inverting, Converting, and Subverting

In the case of hip-hop, jazz – and, one could argue, food, religion, fashion and sport – the inversions and interpretations are appropriated and consumed around the world as authentic urban America. This is often just a euphemism for poor and black, but it sells and becomes integrated into the global mainstream. This pattern of inversion and reappropriation is nothing new. Zora Neale Hurston, in her unevenly balanced but emphatic "Characteristics of Negro Expression," described it pretty well in 1934 when she argued that

> The Negro is a very original being. While he lives and moves in the midst of a white civilisation, everything that he touches is re-interpreted for his own use. He has modified the language, mode of food preparation, practice of medicine, and most certainly the religion of his new country . . . Everyone is familiar with the Negro's modification of the whites' musical instruments, so that his interpretation has been adopted by the white man himself and then reinterpreted. . . . Thus has arisen a new art in the civilised world, and thus has our so-called civilisation come. The exchange and re-exchange of ideas between groups. (Hurston 1995: 839)

One of the most salient examples of this reappropriation is the way that a word employed solely as a term of defilement was redeployed as a sincere term of endearment. Its global reach, to me, is nothing short of astonishing.

I was in Ghana during the summer of 2007 and one of my favorite hangouts was BusyInternet on Ring Road in the heart of Accra's financial and technology district. BusyInternet is the largest privately owned and operated Internet and communications center in Africa, and it serves as a gathering place for tony urban professionals, creative artists, and competitive entrepreneurs who frequent the establishment to network and socialize online and off. Affectionately known as "Busy," because it is always, it also functions as a veritable *obruni* (white or foreign person) magnet for travelers, college students, and backpackers who desire the Internet bandwidth and connection speeds they have grown accustomed to but rarely need. It is decidedly cosmopolitan, and very, very cool. The steps leading up to the main reception area and cashier teem with a throng of well-dressed young men sporting the very latest in hip-hop fashion. Unabashed yet respectful, they congregate on the steps to check out the ladies who dash quickly by, making their way inside to the banks and banks of workstations. As I was striding up those steps, one handsome twenty-something man, neatly adorned in an Ecko Unlimited tank, Girbaud denims and very white Puma sneakers caught my eye. He made a fist with his right hand and held his arm at a perfect right angle. He then looked me straight in the eyes and said with all sincerity and affection, "Waz up nigga?" Without breaking my stride, I clenched my fist, lightly pounded his fist and retorted, "What's up?" Simultaneously, we both raised our chins one half of one inch. It's a small ritual of solidarity and mutual respect that I have performed thousands of times, mostly in the United States. Usually brother, cuz, or G is the salutation used, but the meaning and intent were identical in this case.

I am fond of saying that "Ghana is the only place in the world where I am considered a rich white man," but this might be changing with the explosion of hip-hop and a realization around the diaspora that the many hues of brown qualify as black in the United States. It took me a second or two to process, but then a flood of questions and concerns took over my thoughts. Did he really know what he was saying, or was he doing what Don Imus purportedly did when he referred to the Women's Basketball team at Rutgers University as "nappy headed hoes" – just reiterating what he thought was acceptable language of the hip-hop generation? Did this young man know the history of its derivative cousin? Was he thinking that this is how a twenty-something man shows respect to a forty-something man in the United States? He *was* very respectful, and clearly just wanted to connect and show a little love to an *obruni*. I thought to myself, "Does he do this with white people?" I had to get my copy-edits out to *Transforming Anthropology* contributors so I did not have time to follow up, but what struck me was how this particular form of inversion has taken on truly global dimensions.

Battle of the Britches

Parents and guardians, preachers and teachers – and evidently town councils – might become a little anxious when their sons and daughters get Chinese characters tattooed on their calves, pierce a body part, or download a few songs from Lil' Wayne, Young Jeezy, or 50 Cent to their iPods. Many adults, however, feel compelled to demarcate a threshold or draw a line between acceptability and unacceptability, respectability and disrespect. The town of Delcambre felt the need to promulgate that line in law. It is a line, however, that is moving all the time within and among race, class, gender, religion, sexuality, and generation.

When the news broke that a new "drawz clause" was tacked on to Delcambre's public decency laws, radio shows, blogs, and newspapers took off with the story, quickly deeming it "the battle of the britches." While it was often couched as "wacky" or off-beat news, some blogs and radio shows seriously addressed issues of racism, discrimination, and civil liberties. Some opponents noted its gender trouble because no one seemed to have a problem with the equally ubiquitous thong peek or whale tail – a bright-colored thong peeking above the popular low-rise pants worn by many women of the same age set. Thongs are sexy and acceptable; boxers are dangerous and indecent. Others, however, saw it as a sensible law that would force kids to pull up their britches and show a little respect.

The ordinance supporters and detractors did not break down along racial lines. Many black people support this type of legislation. In fact, the Virginia House of Delegates passed a similar, state-wide ordinance in 2005, and it was sponsored by Algie Howell, a lifetime member of the NAACP (Jonsson 2007: 1). Although the bill was shot down by Virginia's senate, it fueled activists such as Pastor Dianne Robinson of Jacksonville, Florida. Robinson has waged a "Pull up your Pants" campaign in several black communities, a campaign that prompted this sub-headline in *The Washington Post*: "For Christ Sake, Pull up your Pants" (Steiner 2007). Moreover, it was an African American Councilman, Albert Roy, who introduced the ordinance to Delcambre's legislative body. Although Delcambre's Mayor Broussard did not have much to say regarding the complex and cross-cutting issues his small town weighed in on, the one thing he was certain about was that the ordinance was not racist. He implored that "white people wear sagging pants, too. Anybody who wears these pants should be held responsible" (Associated Press 2007a). Of course, he is right; white kids rock this look too. But was he right that the ordinance was not racist?

In the K-mart parking lot in the northern California town of Grass Valley, I have seen tattoo-covered white kids saggin' as they mill around in their custom 4-wheel drives, tossing back cans of Budweiser. Likewise, I have seen sun-dappled white kids saggin' as they fish for croaker off Bouge Inlet pier on the outer banks of North Carolina. I have also seen tough-talking Hmong-American kids sport this style at the Mall of America in

Minneapolis, and smooth-talking Mexican American kids wearing baggies as they listen to music and chill outside the Los Angeles County Museum of Art. On Duke's campus, there are more white kids who sag than black ones (at least in class), but I am always amazed when I go to my neighborhood convenience store and see young black men who really take this fashion to the extreme.

Pull 'em up, Son

It was a Wednesday evening last June when I stopped by the Town & Country Quick Mart, which is across the street from Hillside High School at the corner of Fayetteville and Cook streets in southwest Durham. It was late and hot; the store was unusually empty. I was making my way up to the cashier when a young boy no older than 15 darted in front of me, slapped some change on the counter, and said simply, "Garcia Vega." As the middle-aged Middle Easterner reached below the counter, the youngster cut his eyes at me. In a particularly bold "it takes a village" moment, I said with a hint of disgust and disappointment, "Pull your damn pants up, Son." This was met with a quick roll of the eyes and an even quicker sucking of the teeth. It was another ritual of solidarity, and ended with us exchanging silent glances; his expression screamed, "Shut the fuck up!" while mine distinctly read, "There should be law against that." But neither of us really meant it. I grabbed my beer, he grabbed his blunt and neither of us said another word.

But then, right then, something happened. My identity and values as a father, uncle, and mentor clashed and contradicted with my identity and values as a teacher, anthropologist, and a liberal. My heartfelt desire to uplift the race crashed down around my hard-won understanding of culture, power, and agency. My background as a liberal anthropologist, who understands the complexity of culture, the power of agency, and the way racism often masquerades under the guise of color-blind neutrality, came in sharp contrast with my personal and pragmatic understanding that the only way black people in the United States can make it *is* by working hard and playing by the rules. Yet at the same time I realize that the American Dream is just a chimerical ideology forged in the crucible of whiteness within the furnace of capitalism. Culture is a double-edged sword that usually cuts both ways and produces a tension between the shackles of tradition and the power of performance. Its relationship to race has always been fraught with racism.

The Quick Mart encounter was a queer and liminal moment, but one that I often experience. It is deeply ingrained with my own psycho-social development, which has always produced second sights, and in many ways driven what I write and the way I write.

I always write for my undergraduate students, and I often have a specific class in mind when I begin to tackle a research project. I want to find ways to demonstrate how the concept of culture is used to advance racism and white supremacy, while it is also used to promote anti-racism and suture solidarity. I rarely find material that I can clearly determine is a case of virtue vs. evil, oppression vs. empowerment, white vs. black. Actually, I seek out historical cases that blur the simple dichotomies students crave so they can neatly package historical moments or movements within pre-defined ideological boxes marked conservative/right-wing or progressive/left-wing and then, given an individual's own political leanings, label the box good or bad. Exploring the history of anthropology within the context of larger movements in the United States enables students to think differently and critically, and it is an apt way of exploding rigid partisan dualities because the actions and attitudes of anthropologists were often difficult to pin down. For example, was Alice Fletcher being progressive or reactionary in 1885 when she wrote in Hampton's *Southern Workman* that "the three things needed by the Indian" were "Land, Law, [and] Education" (Fletcher 1885: 45)? Although she was campaigning for the disastrous Dawes Severalty Act (1887) and favored "civilizing" the Indians, she was identifying common ground with a post-Reconstruction black audience desperately seeking "land, law, and education."

Was Franz Boas being conservative or progressive when he explained that "the Negro problem will not disappear in America until the Negro blood has been so diluted that it will no longer be recognized, just as anti-Semitism will not disappear until the last vestige of the Jew as Jew has disappeared" (Boas 1921: 395)? In 1921, state governments routinely enforced miscegenation laws buoyed by deep anxieties regarding so-called race mixing. This statement was clearly counter-hegemonic and radical, but it demonstrates a blatant disregard for black culture, and suggests that racism was not a problem. The real "Negro problem," according to Boas here, stemmed from nappy heads and darkish skin.

Documenting how culture is used, deployed, and appropriated, as in the case of the baggy pants, involves detailing a messy dialogical process that involves power and history as well as class and generation. In my research and writing, I strive to identify how anthropology as discourse and discipline helped to shape public understandings of race and culture in the US. Although anthropology has always been the authoritative science of race and culture, it has lacked a concomitant attention to racism and structural inequality. Leith Mullings succinctly and perhaps wryly explains, "Although

anthropologists have written extensively about race, anthropological contributions to the study of racism have been surprisingly modest" (Mullings
2005: 669).

Black Power, White Tolerance

Although I cannot claim that I was a part of the Black Power movement
or marched with Martin, I was literally a product of the Black Power movement, being born in the turbulent year of 1966 and, for some reason that
I have refused to find out, given up for adoption. I was raised by a loving
and liberal white family. It was an extended family where the category
"normal" included same-sex and interracial partnerships, and it was
common among my closest friends to have siblings, birth parents or adop-
tive parents who hailed from anywhere in the world. From a young age, I
have always had strong black men who *were* part of the Civil Rights and
Black Power movements as integral parts of my life; they mentored and
guided me and instilled in me that the most effective way to fight racism
was to work twice as hard and expect half as much as my white counterparts. They also taught me to see and understand the complexity, strength,
beauty, and power of African and African American cultures. When I was
calling for the revolution, they persuasively argued that the most effective
way to fight the power was to beat the white man at his own game.

For better or worse, I am stuck with a naive nostalgia for the days when
the most effective way to fight racism was to work to achieve excellence,
work to achieve justice, and work to achieve more responsive institutions
and policies within existing structures of power. In short, I actually believe
that we should strive to make the pillars of democracy stand for all
Americans. I am mindful that this ideology is situated and positioned within
a problematic and deeply flawed rhetoric of racial uplift, betterment, and,
yes, assimilation. Steeped in rather conservative Christian and capitalist
values, it is leavened with equally problematic European aesthetics. Yet, it
is worth noting that racial uplift movements have storied traditions of
working to better the conditions of workers, alleviate poverty, and put the
so-called community before any one individual.

It is, however, the basis for the missionary mentality that assumes the
educated elite know what is best for their less educated brethren. For nearly
two centuries, this ideology of racial uplift has become a successful strategy
of adaptation within the black communities – throughout the diaspora. The
ideology of racial uplift is also the sturdy underpinning for ordinances that
criminalize young men who, for whatever reason, don't want to pull up

their pants, and it becomes party to a particularly pernicious form of racism that hides behind ideas of color-blind respectability on the one hand, and, on the other, shallow claims that this or that policy is not racist because some of the most progressive citizens of the black community support it. Moments like my experience at the Town & Country Quick Mart exemplify what I refer to as the cultural politics of race. Although many might recognize baggy jeans, fashion, structural racism, and even the debate over the infamous n-word as the narrative stuff that might interest anthropologists, one might wonder what this has to do with writing the history of anthropology.

The way I approach writing the history of anthropology, cultural politics has everything to do with it. Since the late nineteenth century, anthropologists have influenced how people in the United States understand race and culture. Likewise, people in the United States have influenced the way anthropologists have studied and theorized culture and race. In fact, the various changes in the way people have understood both race and culture map fairly closely onto the ways anthropologists have studied and theorized those modalities.

That most Americans conceive of culture in terms of a plural noun, and that many view race in social as opposed to strictly biological terms, can be viewed as evidence to demonstrate that anthropology has played a significant role in the way people in the United States – and beyond – understand both race and culture. The very idea that any one individual or social group should or could practice, embrace, preserve, or celebrate a distinctive culture is predicated upon the notion that a particular social group shares a historical view of the world that can be handed down, in part or whole, to subsequent generations.

Reflections and Inflections

In recent decades, anthropologists have scrutinized the concept of culture; at the same time, however, other disciplines, institutions, foundations, industries, media conglomerates and social groups have institutionalized what can rightly be viewed as a skewed but nevertheless anthropologically inflected idea of culture (Fabian 1983; Clifford 1988; Kahn 1989; Abu-Lughod 1991; Trouillot 1991; Visweswaran 1998; Briggs 2002; Williams 2006). For example, people routinely speak of distinctive corporate or campus cultures, while talk-radio pundits speak glibly about the culture inside the beltway – as if members of Congress were the only people living in Washington, D.C. With the advent of the cochlear implant, some who craft cultural expression through writing and signing in deaf communities have decried the end of "deaf culture," prompting the National Association of the Deaf to issue a statement recommending that parents of implanted children "receive education in deaf studies, including deaf heritage, history of deafness and deaf people" (National Association of the Deaf 2000).

For better or worse, the concept of culture as most folks in the United States understand it is tethered to what Charles Briggs described as an epistemological land-grab during a period of history when the discursive terrain of the behavioral sciences was literally up for grabs (Briggs 2002: 481). It is important to note, however, that, despite the way anthropological analytics have been appropriated within popular parlance, anthropologists are not alone. Social psychologists have grappled with the way people use or misuse the term identity, sociologists bemoan the fact that the notion of deviance has been sorely overused, economists no longer hold sway over the compound term "cost–benefit," and historians have always been leery of the way people throw around the word history.

I get the critique about bounded and essentialist ideas of culture, and I am often persuaded by the analysis. Moreover, I understand, oh too well, the downside of essentialism, the danger of viewing culture as stuck and timeless, and I personally understand how a static notion of culture can bleed into ideas of authenticity and give life to a ridiculous line of inquiry that turns on a single question: Is Barack Obama black enough? It is this skewed appropriation of anthropologically inflected ideas of culture that sanctions and authorizes the so-called "Soul Patrol," the self-proclaimed culture cops who demarcate rather narrow boundaries of blackness. Even though this criticism of the culture concept is seductive, I still have to agree with that oft-cited observation James Clifford penned twenty years ago: "Culture is a deeply compromised idea I cannot yet do without" (Clifford 1988:10).

This is a productive tension. It is important to note, however, that post-Boasian notions of culture were articulated and conceived to refute the idea that culture is not a series of stages that went from savagery to barbarism and eventually to a state of civilization. More importantly, the arguments were fashioned in a way that did not dilute or diminish the authority of anthropology as the science of race and culture. Despite the fact that anthropology was no longer a reliable narrator in the narrative of white supremacy, Franz Boas and his students were able to dramatically shift perceptions in the United States regarding culture while maintaining their authority and legitimacy over the science of race, language, and culture. Throughout US history, anthropologically informed concepts of culture have been used to advance civil rights and achieve justice, but they have also been employed to defend segregation and maintain oppression. Many times it is difficult to sort out the intent and intentions from the truth or consequences.

Very little has been written documenting *how* anthropological concepts have been used in the service of political projects (cf. di Leonardo this volume, 1998). One reason that I have chosen to write about this important side of the history of anthropology is to address the paucity. I focus specifically on *how* anthropological concepts, particularly race and culture, have been lovingly adopted by some and disgracefully rejected by others; in each case it is often in the service of a specific political agenda. Although I am interested in the history of theory and institutions, I am simply compelled to uncover and document the many stories that showcase the instances when specific anthropologists or particular anthropological concepts are picked up and used to articulate specific agendas. I have found that these stories are often steeped in contradictions and drip with irony, and almost always have unintended consequences. If I had to summarize the basic question that serves as a framework for my research and writing agenda, it would be: How and why do so-called advocates of specific communities use anthropological concepts of race and culture to advance distinctive political projects?

The Ill Effects of Mind Poison

One of my favorite stories involves the 1918 congressional hearings that debated the use and abuse of peyote. Members of the Society of American Indians (SAI) squared off against anthropologists in a dramatic fight for the future of Native North America. Smithsonian anthropologist James Mooney took the lead and earnestly claimed "that the use of this plant is not an ordinary habit, [and] it is confined almost entirely and strictly to the religious ceremony, excepting that it is frequently employed also for medicinal purposes" (Peyote Hearings 1918: 69).[1] Aligned with the Temperance movement and committed to both racial uplift and the well being of all American Indians, the Society fielded noted author and educator Zitkala-Ša as their chief witness. Zitkala-Ša was a Yankton Lakota and secretary-treasurer of the organization. She lambasted the well-meaning Mooney and went into great detail about the "ill effects of mind poison," calling "peyote,

---

[1]   Peyote Hearings Before the Subcommittee of the Committee on Indian Affairs regarding House Resolution 2614, February 21, 1918, House Committee of Indian Affairs. Subcommittee Chaired by John N. Tillman, Representing Arkansas' Third District, and hereafter cited as PH.

[the] twin brother of alcohol, and first cousin to habit forming drugs" (PH 1918: 164). She reported how she witnessed, first hand, the way some members of her community abused peyote, and she had little sympathy for nuanced explanations of complex rituals. She saw it as a drug, like alcohol, that was destroying certain communities and urged Congress to prohibit it.

As an anthropologist and a defender of the First Amendment, I am sympathetic to Mooney's defense of religious freedom and support of those who practiced complex religious ceremonies as an integral part of their daily lives. To make his case, however, he had to paint the Indian activists as not authentic, not tribal, and not "real" Indians. He was emphatic that "an Indian delegate from a sectarian body or alleged uplift organization is not a delegate for his tribe" (PH 1918: 149). Mooney and other well-meaning anthropologists had a very narrow understanding of what constituted real or so-called authentic Indians, which indeed conformed to rather a limited understanding of culture change, adaptation, and the fluidity of identity.

On the other hand, I also understand how the SAI, a progressive organization that shared a mission similar to that of the NAACP, could be concerned with the use and abuse of peyote. What really fascinated me in this case was how the stake-holders aligned. This one hearing mirrored many of the tensions that emerged between proponents of racial uplift movements and the practitioners of putative traditional practices among Native Hawaiians, American Indians, and African Americans. During the late nineteenth and early twentieth centuries, anthropology and individual anthropologists played various and conflicting roles as attitudes regarding culture changed over time. These roles were as varied as they were ambivalent, but what emerged was a unique and informative racial politics of culture that often pitted progressive white anthropologists and conservative Indian traditionalists against progressive Indian activists and conservative Christian reformers. The political alliances of the early twentieth century are not unlike the racial politics that emerged in the wake of the battle of the britches in Delcambre, Louisiana in the early twenty-first. The cultural politics of uplift and respectability of the nineteenth century do not diverge much from today's countless skirmishes, ranging from debates regarding the misogyny of hip-hop performances to the effectiveness of school uniforms. These debates play out politically in similar and predictable ways. I have studied anthropologists' role in the so-called culture wars throughout the late nineteenth and early twentieth centuries and avidly follow contemporary discussions that turn on the culture concept. I am amazed at how they are still fought with such sincerity and alacrity. The somber fact, however, is that the foundations of many of these arguments are predicated on a lose–lose premise that neither has an impact on institutionalized racism nor ameliorates structural inequality. Seriously, will pulling up one's pants, wearing khakis on the sideline of an NBA game, or quibbling about the phonemic differentiation between an "a" and an "er" following nigg, really influence the number of men incarcerated, the rate of HIV infections, the amount of lead in the water or the cases of early-onset diabetes? No.

One of the biggest ironies of the case of the baggy pants was that the town council passed this new law in a Federal Emergency Management Agency (FEMA) trailer. The township still has not recovered from the devastation wrought by Hurricane Rita, which walloped the Gulf Coast right after Hurricane Katrina decimated New Orleans in 2005, laying bare for the world to see the tenacious and compounding issues of race, racism, and inequality in the United States.

I am perfectly aware that studying the history of anthropology makes an insignificant contribution to the marginal field of history of science. I do not have the immediate, life-saving impact of someone like Paul Farmer. Yet, I still believe my efforts are important for better understanding how racism works. I do so by documenting how even the most progressive social scientists and most thoughtful political activists usually fail to shake loose the noose of racism that constricts and tightens the harder one fights. In the immortal words of India Aire, "There's hope," and I remain optimistic for a better future. Anthropologists, social scientists, and activists have worked together to effect change and fight racism, and have helped to make a better world. It is important to document these efforts too. Anthropologists who strive to be effective change agents must fully understand the limits, but also the possibilities of this crazy field we call anthropology. And that is why I write about it.

References

Abu Lughod, Lila. 1991. Writing against Culture. In *Recapturing Anthropology*. Richard Fox, ed., pp. 137–62. Santa Fe: School of American Research Press.

Associated Press. 2007a. Cajun Town Bans Saggy Pants in Bid to Cover Up "Private Parts." Fox News.Com. June 13. www.foxnews.com/printer_friendly_story/0,3566,281932,00.htm. Accessed September 14, 2007.

Associated Press. 2007b. Louisiana Town Bans Sagging Pants to Avoid Exposing Underwear. Fox News.Com. August 14. www.foxnews.com/printer_friendly_story/0,3566,293209,00.html. Accessed September 15, 2007.

Ayad, Moustafa. 2006. White T-Shirt is Fashion Necessity with a Bad Rep. *Pittsburgh Post-Gazette*. August 7: B1.

Boas, Franz. 1921. The Problem of the American Negro. *Yale Quarterly Review* 10(2): 384–95.

Briggs, Charles L. 2002. Linguistic Magic Bullets in the Making of a Modernist Anthropology. *American Anthropology* 104(2): 481–98.

Christian, Margena A. 2007. The Facts behind the Saggin' Pants Craze. *JET* 111(18): 16, 18, 52.

Clifford, James. 1988. *The Predicament of Culture: Twentieth-Century Ethnography, Literature, and Art*. Cambridge, MA: Harvard University Press.

di Leonardo, Micaela. 1998. *Exotics at Home: Anthropologies, Others, American Modernity*. Chicago: University of Chicago Press.

Fabian, Johannes. 1983. *Time and the Other: How Anthropology Makes Its Subjects*. New York: Columbia University Press.

Fletcher, Alice C. 1885. Land, Law, Education: The Three Things Needed by the Indian. *Southern Workman* 14(4): 45.

Hurston, Zora N. 1995[1935]. Characteristics of Negro Expression. In *Zora Neale Hurston: Folklore, Memoirs, and Other Writings*. Cheryl Wall, ed., pp. 830–46. New York: Library of America.

Jonsson, Patrik. 2007. In Louisiana Town, Wearing Low-Rider Pants May Cost You. *Christian Science Monitor*. June 18: 1.

Khan, Joel. 1989. Culture: Demise or Resurrection? *Critique of Anthropology* 9(2): 5–25.

Mullings, Leith. 2005. Interrogating Racism: Toward an Antiracist Anthropology. *Annual Review of Anthropology* 34(1): 667–93.

National Association of the Deaf. 2000. Cochlear Implants: NAD Position Statement. October 6. www.nad.org/ciposition. Accessed September 17, 2007.

Steiner, Emil. 2007. "For Christ's Sake, Pull Up Your Pants!" Weblog entry. Washingtonpost.com. Accessed April 9, 2007. http://blog.washingtonpost.com/offbeat/offbeat_politics/.

Stocking, George W., Jr. 2001. *Delimiting Anthropology: Occasional Inquiries and Reflections*. Madison: University of Wisconsin Press.

Trouillot, Michel-Rolph. 1991. Anthropology and the Savage Slot: The Poetics and Politics of Otherness. In *Recapturing Anthropology: Working in the Present*. Richard Fox, ed., pp. 17–44. Santa Fe: School of American Research Press.

Visweswaran, Kamala. 1998. Race and the Culture of Anthropology. *American Anthropologist* 100(1): 70–83.

Williams, Vernon J., Jr. 2006. *The Social Sciences and Theories of Race*. Urbana: University of Illinois Press.

6

Stories for Readers: A Few Observations from Outside the Academy

Andrew Barnes

I write with great humility. I do not know the rules of the anthropology insiders, and the few basic ideas I have to offer may be entirely out of place. What I do claim to be is an experienced general reader, part of an audience some specialists seek to reach. The question that first led to my thinking about this topic several years ago was this: Why aren't anthropologists' ideas and insights more often brought to bear in the general public discussion? How can their hard work and clear thought gain greater public currency?

First, let me tell you how to win a Pulitzer Prize (would that it were so simple). Your book, one of tens of thousands published this year, is nominated for the prize. Usually the nomination comes from your publisher, sometimes a friend. Sometimes you may be your own nominator.

The book becomes one of roughly 200, in some categories as many as 400, volumes that will be sent to a jury, usually three readers, mostly academics and newspaper people. The books go out in two large shipments during the year. Picture the size of the box. How do jurors find room to set the books out for consideration?

Clearly, even the most diligent juror will not savor every nuance, or read every word, or even turn every page. How a book rises to the top layer of that overwhelming pile is the question.

To finish describing the Pulitzer process: each jury – there are five for books, as well as music, drama, and of course journalism – comes up with three finalists. All the finalists from all the categories go to the Board, which reads and listens and then convenes each spring at Columbia University for several days of exciting arguments resulting in winners.

To say the obvious, no book is likely to make it through this process, which I am using as a metaphor for achieving wide general readership, unless it is written for those general readers. Tenure books, amplified dissertations, written to achieve academic advancement, are quite a different thing. It is a worthy thing to build the body of specialized knowledge, but it won't move to the front table in Borders, or likely even to the shelf in Borders.

For an author's ideas to become a part of the general conversation, they do have to achieve this broader readership. One factor in this success, I have observed, is to tell stories. Narrative pulls readers along. Tell me what happened next, and how others reacted. How did it smell? What was the parrot's name? Specifics attract reader interest. Abstraction risks boredom.

Another factor: pay attention to the writing. It sounds so obvious, and moreover we all think we are instinctively brilliant writers. Writing, rewriting, editing, accepting the judgments of the few people who will tell you honestly what doesn't work and know what they are talking about – none of this is much fun, or at least I've never thought so. But even though many potential readers will not know why, they will turn away from trite, unimaginative, formula-following writing.

I wrote for newspapers for more than 40 years from the most junior to the most senior positions. My skin never got thick enough to enjoy being told a piece of writing wasn't good enough. But there are no shortcuts. Writing is work and good writing is hard work. If you tell it perfectly, the reader will understand. If you fail in the telling, the reader will start skimming, or go get a beer, and you've lost him.

Writing to an academic standard is different. The norms and conventions of citation determine so much of how you tell your story, and these conventions become ingrained, to the point where the writer often thinks everyone can read that dialect. A lot of us can't, and won't.

Reviews matter. For a book to become widely read, and its ideas to become current, readers have to know about it. Now that I no longer am part of a system that constantly shoved books across my desk I find reviews in the *New York Times*, the *New York Review of Books*, my local newspaper, occasionally National Public Radio to be invaluable.

Your publisher will court reviewers, and you should too. If you know someone, speak to them. It may help and is unlikely to do harm to your cause.

Which brings me to a final point, which to some will seem natural, to some abhorrent. You must accept the need for publicity. There you will be, too early in the morning, being questioned by some guy who clearly hasn't read your book. Moreover, you have only 40 seconds. Smile, and answer the question he should have asked. If you can find another show that will have you, do it again tomorrow. If you don't tell a wide range of potential readers about your book, they won't know about it.

A hugely successful book of a few years ago, Frank McCourt's *Angela's Ashes*, is an example. It's a charming memoir by a guy who just retired as a high school teacher about his mother. How did it get beyond vanity publishing and become part of everybody's awareness?

McCourt writes very well indeed. He tells stories. He misses no opportunity to talk on television and radio in his charming brogue. Irish mothers are also an always popular topic in certain circles. It worked, famously. Obviously, McCourt's success is beyond reasonable hope, but it is worth study.

I don't want to make too much of the Pulitzer Prize but the McCourt book presented an interesting challenge when it came up for consideration. It was in the biography category, and it clearly is a memoir, not a biography. It was up against two excellent conventional biographies. Why did *Angela's Ashes* win? Because it is a beautifully told book of stories everybody finds interesting.

There are many reasons an author seeks wide readership for a book. Fame, advancement, and royalty checks are only the most obvious. My concern that anthropology writing should move from the sphere of specialists to more general discussion is a different one. Too much of our public discussion is superficial. We need more ideas grounded in fieldwork and rigorous thought. It's worth your effort to take anthropology to the broadest possible audience.

II
Creations

7

Writing Poverty, Drawing Readers: Stories in *Love, Sorrow and Rage*

Alisse Waterston

It was a lovely early summer day in June when I drove through Westchester County in the suburbs of New York to visit inmate # 1501964-92-F-78, a poor, black woman named Nora.[1] I parked the car in a lot for visitors at the bottom of a hill at the Taconic Correctional Facility, a medium-security prison across the street from Bedford Hills, the maximum-security prison with greater name recognition than its next-door neighbor. The setting is almost bucolic, with trees and a grassy meadow leading up the hill to the prison gates. Nestled in a far corner of the field are several dozen crude wooden crosses, each with a metal nameplate to mark the name and date of death. Buried there are women who died in the prison, gone unclaimed.

I first met Nora in the mid-1990s at Woodhouse, a community residence at the southern tip of Harlem's west side, the site of my research on women and homelessness for an AIDS prevention study.[2] Nora taught me many things about trust, loneliness, addiction, brutality, self-destruction, generosity, insecurity. From her I learned about relapse: an early sign that an addict is again drinking and drugging is she'll disappear from straight friends and loved ones. "It's hard to catch someone who's running," Nora explained

---

[1] Nora is a pseudonym and this is not her actual prison number. This visit took place on June 3, 2007.

[2] Built on a project designed by research psychiatrist Ezra Susser, my ethnographic research, which extended from 1994 to 1996, was used as a first step in a larger effort to develop an HIV prevention program for a population that had been identified as at high risk for infection. The research was supported by a Center Grant from National Institute of Mental Health (NIMH) to the HIV Center for Clinical and Behavioral Research, Columbia University. My association with the HIV Center coincided with my work as an executive of a private research and consulting firm.

when a woman I was scheduled to interview stood me up, preferring, it seems, the date she had with a crack pipe. As best she could, Nora also taught me about the lure of drugs: "I feel the toke," she cooed, lingering on the thought. "How it feels when it goes down my throat, all through my chest. It's pure pleasure, peace, contentment." Nora puts into words her deepest feelings of loneliness and rage that crack and beer fill up and repress. She puts into words a sentiment I have long felt: "I love all people. But I just don't like most people."

Nora now languishes in the Taconic prison, one of the nearly 70,000 black women locked up in an American jail or prison.[3] Like many in her cohort, Nora has been hit hard by America's attack on its racialized and most vulnerable poor, an assault popularly referred to as the "war on drugs." According to a national prison-reform advocacy group:

> Whether intended or not, a variety of seemingly "race neutral" policies have contributed to growing racial disparity. Due to the intersection of racially skewed policing and sentencing policies, the federal crack cocaine mandatory sentencing laws, for example, have produced highly disproportionate rates of incarceration for low-level offenses. (Mauer and King 2007: 17)

On September 19, 2004, Nora began her four- to eight-year sentence for the "attempted criminal sale of a controlled substance, Class C." She told me it was just another foolish, knuckle-headed, drug-seeking misstep. Back on the street, Nora was looking to get high again when a disheveled white guy came towards her and her acquaintances, asking if they knew where he could make a buy. Nora volunteered. I believe her, recalling how she was always willing to help someone out, run errands for the other ladies at Woodhouse. Of course she had other things in mind too, like getting her cut of the deal, in crack, a little piece of rock she could savor for an extra few minutes. She handed him the drugs, he cuffed her.

"I don't want to die in prison," Nora told me that June day at the Taconic. I realize there's nobody out there to claim her body if she does. I need to be sure she gets my name in her file so I'll get called if she does. It's not an unlikely scenario that she will die. She's got HIV, now advanced to AIDS.

I remember clearly the day I found that out. I hadn't seen Nora or any of the other women from Woodhouse while I was writing *Love, Sorrow and Rage* (1999), needing distance so I could feel freer to write about them. I struggled with the depictions, hoping not to get these wrong. There is a

---

[3]   According to the Sentencing Project, a prison research and advocacy organization, one out of three of the 210,000 women in US jails and prisons are black/African American (Sentencing Project 2007: 2).

part in the book about how Nora and I went to the local clinic so she could get an HIV test. She was so terribly anxious, and so was I. "If I'm positive, I'll live fifteen years, the most," Nora told me in 1996. "If I'm positive, my life is over." But that day the news was good. I was so happy, I couldn't wait to get home and get myself a stiff glass of bourbon, ironically ending the drug chapter with my own yearnings. Months later on a cool autumn morning, I finished writing. I finished the book. A letter from Nora came that very day: "I'm HIV positive," she wrote.

Our Impotence, Our Power

My research, part of a study about AIDS prevention, did nothing to help Nora in that regard. Such impotence! At best, the work seems ineffectual. Worse, it is voyeurism, like so much anthropology of times past.

But I don't really believe that this kind of research and writing is useless, or that it is mere voyeurism. For one, we can't measure our overall efficacy by what happens – or doesn't happen – in individual cases. We might feel sadness and profound sorrow for the suffering of the people with whom we've developed strong bonds in the field, and feel deeply frustrated by our own personal and professional limitations to effect change in the circumstances of their lives. I believe that as social scientists our most important role is to confront power and explain the deep complex of forces and factors that position people such as Nora to become "at risk" in the first place: poverty and structural inequality, the lack of affordable and adequate housing, limited access to preventive health and mental health care, the consequences of institutionalized care, and, on an individual level, the deepest psychological aspects of feeling. For all the Noras, we can reveal with our research and through our writing the totality of their various experiences with homelessness, mental illness, racism, misogyny, and poverty that put them at risk. We can also make clear that under these kinds of social conditions it is a matter of probabilities that a certain proportion will fall to those forces. To expect otherwise is to feign shock, a great political strategy but poor social science.[4]

---

[4] As social scientists, we can "predict" who is likely to suffer and who is not, and should not be surprised when calamity strikes. According to a *New York Times* report, sociologist Christopher Jencks was "surprised" (and then surprised at his own surprise) to see "who got left behind" in New Orleans when the levee broke with Hurricane Katrina (Deparle 2005), a response that seems disingenuous. It brings to mind Captain Renault's famous line in the movie *Casablanca*: "I'm shocked, shocked to find that gambling is going on in here!" he said before picking up his winnings for the night.

To succumb to the belief in our own ineffectiveness is to play into the hands of the worst of distorted political arguments and to provide fodder for furthering our own marginalization. The process is similar to what happens to social programs. Oftentimes, the "failures" or ineffectiveness of such programs have been used by policy-makers and politicians as a rationale for cutting funds even though we need more, not fewer, resources for them.

As I argue in *Love, Sorrow and Rage*, economic restructuring of America's cities over the past thirty years has generated a surplus of poor people. Yet it is the poor who *appear* to be aberrant. Policies and programs designed to address "social problems" seem inevitably to fail. For such a highly developed and sophisticated nation as the US, this dismal track record seems implausible, unless these practices are not failing when outcomes are matched against underlying objectives. We often assume that these objectives are to eliminate poverty, substance abuse, criminality, homelessness, and so on. If the underlying objective is to contain the "surplus" in relatively controlled settings, then current policies and practices do indeed accomplish their mission: some of the surplus find unsteady and poorly paid work in the informal sector, some are warehoused in shelters and prisons, some are intoxicated by illegal street drugs, legal/illegal prescription drugs and legal alcohol, and some have died off in the AIDS epidemic.

The irony is that most social programs (from AIDS prevention programs to institutionalized housing for the homeless) are designed not to effect social change but for maintaining and reproducing a population under existing social conditions. Oftentimes, as programs are developed, root causes of social problems are neglected and generally dismissed as unsolvable. And then, in a distorted and politicized argument, critics decry the programs for not solving the social problem at hand. Programs are often then deemed "ineffective" and funding is further threatened. As these programs struggle to survive, they must move even farther from the deeper, broader causes and provide only fragmented and partial solutions.

For us, the process goes something like this: as solo researchers, we study a social problem, reveal its structural roots and painful consequences for human lives, publish our books and articles on the topic, and feel impotent as the information and insights seem to languish in limbo while the world goes on, still miserable. In our scholarly writings we rarely offer a solution, since that's the purview of applied or practicing anthropology, supposedly a separate endeavor from scholarly practice. We struggle to convince others (funding agencies, even some colleagues) of the importance of this work even though we need more, not fewer resources and more, not less collegial support for it.

For Nora, I believe, *Love, Sorrow and Rage* has been deeply meaningful in a way that can't be measured or seen in the circumstances of her life. She refers to it as "her book," as in "I told the women here [in rehab, in prison, wherever she happens to be] about *my book*," or "So-and-so read *my book* and wants to meet you," or "Can you send me another copy of *my book*?" When the book was published and Nora had read it for the first time, she came to my house for a visit. We sat in my kitchen talking and I was anxious for her response. She was so pleased. She felt important. I'd made her a star! And she was amazed I could "remember" her exact words, the way she told a story. I reminded her of the tape recorder I often had with me and explained about writing fieldnotes, which I did religiously right after our visits. She wrote notes all over the margins of her copy (comments, more memories, annotations) and had only one complaint: Why did I write that she is narcissistic?[5]

I do not know if Nora is, by clinical standards, a narcissist. I do know that she is someone who all her life has been so put down that what seems just self-absorption and self-destruction is a drowning soul trying to breathe, a spirit abused and locked up. Nora's a classic "rubbish person," the expression used by Nancy Scheper-Hughes to describe sufferers of structural violence, the ones "ultimately forced to accept their dehumanized status" (2002: 369; see also 2007). Over her life and early on, Nora learned to swallow many indignities, along the way accepting "fictions as realities about herself," a psychological process identified by Sander Gilman (1988: 3–4).

Nora isn't "some kind of nobody." She is somebody, after all. My book gives public acknowledgment to her humor, her story-telling, her love, her sorrow, her rage.

This understanding directs me to the purpose of my book: to reveal the somebodies behind the nobodies, to make more visible the invisible, to bring to light the human face of poverty and its complex, systemic roots. I have written this book to say and to show that unequal social arrangements are

---

[5] Nora was referring to the section in the book where I noted the psychiatrists could not figure out a diagnosis for her (1999: 31). One week they said she had a borderline personality disorder; the next, she was bipolar; after that, she was narcissistic; and later, just anxious. I came to learn that, at Woodhouse, there were a handful of such "borderline" cases in which the presence of mental illness was uncertain. Because at Woodhouse mental illness was tied to residence eligibility and other bureaucratic concerns, diagnosis was critical for reasons other than the medical treatment of an illness.

implicated in social suffering; ultimately, Nora's sickness is rooted in the "pathologies of power" (Farmer 2003). I have written this book to challenge the privileged to look at the ways in which we are complicit in the suffering experienced by our most vulnerable neighbors.

Nora "doesn't matter" because she's poor, addicted, sick. To be poor in America is first of all to be marked negatively. To be also homeless, mentally ill and drug-addicted is to be thoroughly despised. Captured in stereotype, Nora is emblematic of the social problems plaguing our cities. Any one of her "attributes" signals the pressing social problems of the day. Never mind these are results of a long process of impoverishment; in her manifestation, they now signal disrepute and danger.

Nora matters to me. I had the thought she may come to matter to others, to readers.

Drawing Readers, Imagining Audiences

One of our most important roles as social scientists is to confront power and explain it – explain how social forces become embodied as individual experience, explain how collective cultural fictions (popular and political ideologies) obscure structural inequality and further marginalize the excluded, explain how differential access to material resources and power shape experience, shape social conditions and shape institutional practices. And so there needs to be someone with whom I am in dialogue on these issues, someone to whom these things are being explained. If I am to write a book about Nora, I write in the hopes of drawing readers to a book about poverty in America.

There came a time in the course of this project when I became *ready* to write the book. My professional circumstances were not conducive to such an endeavor; I was not affiliated with the academy, a circumstance both liberating and disappointing. Writing this kind of book would not translate to career advancement in my place of work as it would have had I been on tenure track at a university. In those years, my work life was very schizophrenic; some might consider the conflicts and contradictions a dialectical process. A "practicing" anthropologist by self-definition, I worked with my husband to establish and build a profit-making research business which, as side benefits, provides part-time employment and great, real-life research training for graduate students in anthropology and sociology. It also provided me the time and space to do the work of my heart. I completed my own graduate training in the early 1990s when the academic marketplace was, as now, "difficult," especially for those unable to move elsewhere for a position or those who were North Americanists, doing work "at home." Some among my former graduate student colleagues lapsed into depression or left the field altogether because of dismal prospects for full-time academic employment. I assessed my position within these circumstances and came to this conclusion: I could use the privileges of my situation (including the education I received and the knowledge I gained) to create opportunities, or I could focus on careerist obstacles and be paralyzed. I chose to use the benefits that came from privilege to accomplish multiple goals: make a living and provide for my family, carve out a place for myself in the institutions of anthropology,[6] and do the work that I thought really mattered. Nora.

It took me about two years to do the research, and nine months to write the book. Like many women I know, I learned to be an expert juggler, managing duties, desires, time. I carved out mornings for writing, oftentimes starting at 4 a.m., a practice I learned as a graduate student working a couple of part-time jobs and raising a child. I've always found before daybreak a quiet time, when nobody or nothing else is making demands, my mind fresh and awake.

I write, in part, for myself, since the process helps me think things through. It's what writers mean when they say, "I write in order to know what I think." Don DeLillo said that in a *Paris Review* interview (Begley 1993), Lily Tuck said it after winning the Pulitzer for her novel *The News from Paraguay* (Finn 1994), and Paul Farmer said it in his 2005 "Anthropology off the Shelf" remarks:

> I would say that writing books allows me to think. That I think with my hand. I have met people who are able to think without careful preparation, without writing things down carefully. I am, however, not able to do that. I have to work things out by writing. And it's been ever thus for me.

But that's not all. I wrote *in dialogue with* an imaginary interlocutor, my colleagues in anthropology, especially those with a critical, political-economy perspective and those interested in urban poverty issues in North America, including the US. I had a yearning to be a part of my discipline, and to make a meaningful, scholarly contribution even as I often found myself tired of presenting conference papers where everyone in the room shared similar views, interests and concerns, and we never seemed to get beyond that point.

---

[6] Specifically, I became very active in the American Anthropological Association (AAA) and the Society for the Anthropology of North America (SANA), an AAA section.

I also wrote *for* an imagined audience, to speak *to* a category of reader drawn from my mind's eye, personified in the mothers of my young daughter's friends. I'd met them at swim and dance class, or in the neighborhood, the local park and school, the kind who, at best, can muster up sympathy for the poor, but who are just as likely to have disdain for them, especially the likes of Nora. I've heard these mothers talk, the remarks they can make ("Black children are uneducable," said a former local high school chemistry teacher. "My child's paying the price for schooling illegal immigrants," commented a mother of an elementary school child who happened to be struggling with his own school work; she deflected his "failings" onto an easy target who, in this mother's view, costs her big taxpayer bucks and takes attention away from her deserving child). As much as I get tired of chatter among like-minded scholars, this kind of talk is pernicious and can have all too real effects.

I wanted to *talk back to* those mothers of my daughter's classmates who believe it when the tabloid press, some popular politicians and social scientists depict *other* women as undeserving and disreputable. I wanted to refute their belief that Nora is wretched, bizarre and amoral, that she is nothing more than a victim of her own or her family's moral failings, that she is a social burden, with no clear productive role.

But that's not all. I longed to write this book as a small tribute to the women who are its subject.

Writing Poverty: Challenges and Confrontations

I might want to talk to or be in dialogue with a set of imaginary readers, but I knew it would be a hard sell to get them to listen, to pay attention, to read. First there's the problem of the subject matter. "Some might consider this an unpopular subject," I wrote on the first page of the book, "no one wants to know about poor women . . . no one wants to read about poor women." I suppose that's an understatement if there ever was one, although I can't help but disagree with it. I still believe that people yearn to understand and solve the human crises that surround us, crises driven by poverty, inequality, and structural violence, and manifest in crime, disease, addiction.

The very thing that keeps some people away from learning about poor women is the very thing I would like them to see and understand. Poor people are hidden from view; people who are not poor don't necessarily want to get too close or discover that poverty is *not* rooted in poor people's "sloth and sinfulness." For my imaginary mother-readers, getting intimate with Nora might too easily touch on a sense of vulnerability they may feel, even among those who seem economically secure. Nora, along with her housemates in Woodhouse, symbolizes that which they fear, a process I describe on the pages of *Love, Sorrow and Rage* (1999: 18–21) as the ideological armature so central to the reproduction of poverty in the US. The "cult of individualism," "the doctrine of self-help through work," these days considered a moral truth, helps consign the poor to the dustbins: hard work will pay off; poverty signals laziness. "Any class below the most securely wealthy [is] insecure and deeply anxious," Barbara Ehrenreich claims, speaking for most Americans. "[We are] afraid of misfortunes that might lead to a downward slide." We have learned from the cult of individualism, however, that any reversal can be overcome by inner strength and hard work. The doctrine, then, adds to our anxiety another layer of fear: "a fear of inner weakness, of growing soft, of failing to strive, of losing discipline and will" (Ehrenreich 1990: 15).

From Ehrenreich's perspective, whether "looking down toward the realm of less, or up toward the realm of more, there is the fear, always, of falling" (1990: 15). Something must be done with the fear to make it bearable. Sander Gilman finds a clue in the need for society to identify the "other": "We project this fear – the fear of collapse, the sense of dissolution – onto the world in order to localize it and, indeed, to domesticate it. For once we locate it, the fear of our own dissolution is removed. Then it is not we who totter on the brink of collapse, but rather the other. And it is an-other who has already shown his or her vulnerability by having collapsed" (1988: 1).

Like Nora. For my mother-readers, Nora represents everything they fear, and the proof they are whole, safe, healthy, sane, not like her – different, destitute, diseased or mad (Gilman 1988: 271–2). Nora is an icon. *Love, Sorrow and Rage* threatens to make her real, to humanize her, the very thing my mother-readers don't want to face.

My intention was to reveal Nora's humanity, to demonstrate to these mother-readers that Nora's worries, desires and concerns are not so very different from their own.

Nora's intention, I believe, was to let us know she knows how all this works. She knows exactly where she fits into the scheme of things.

I would try, then, to write an engaging narrative combined with critical poverty theory together in one book. My reading of the most widely cited popular literature on poverty revealed two specific attributes of these writings: they offer a compelling read and are extraordinarily atheoretical. For example, in the Pulitzer Prize-winning *Rosa Lee: A Mother and Her Family in Urban America* (1997), journalist Leon Dash provides a vivid and moving description of one family (not necessarily representative of poor people in America), with no context for why Rosa Lee and so many of her children fare as they do, and no critical reflection on "the underclass," a concept and term he uses liberally. In the mid-1980s, journalist Nicholas Lemann helped put the term on the popular culture map with his widely disseminated series, "The Origins of the Underclass" (1986a, 1986b). Lemann leaves the "fact" of the "underclass" unexamined; what he "explains" is unquestioned, and unquestionably assumed to be a self-sustaining culture. Accounts such as these may put a human face on poverty but fail to take the discussion outside of the "dysfunctional" people and their equally "dysfunctional" cultural life ways. These may be more palatable for my mother-readers, but are, in the end, what Micaela di Leonardo calls "fake ethnography," distorted representations of the poor in inner cities (1994: 6; see also 1998: 112–27).

There is value in writing compelling stories, though, a knack journalists seem to have over anthropologists. In the same year that Lemann published his series on poverty for *Atlantic Monthly*, Mary Pratt challenged anthropologists, "How, one asks constantly, could such interesting people doing such interesting things produce such dull books?" (1986: 33; see also Agar 1996: 5). There is no single answer to Pratt's question. At times, complicated ideas require using more difficult language – words, phrases, sentences – because these are best able to capture the complexity the author hopes to convey. Other times, authors choose difficult language when more straightforward prose would serve better. In those cases, it seems authors are looking to *sound* intellectual, or mask a simple analysis or limited bit of information behind impenetrable language. Oftentimes the strategy works, since it fits well with the academy's own prejudices and what it privileges.

Not affiliated with a university, I was in a good position to break out of the rote academic expectation. I was free to write the book I wanted. Unlike many other scholarly works, mine would privilege the deeply personal and the intimate, not dismiss these aspects as irrelevant. Without them, the women would appear to be as emotionally impoverished as they are materially dispossessed, a distortion that can also lead to theoretical vacuity and suspect political conclusions.

I chose to emulate the story-telling style of journalists who write so vividly and sometimes movingly about poverty. I would try to write good stories – the women's stories, Nora's story – give good care to my words, and readers might come, I reasoned. More challenging was how to "write theory" at the same time, and still draw mother-readers to the book. I had become (and still am) tired of reading about "the pathological, irresponsible inner city," plastered on the nightly news and reproduced in journalistic articles or books given front-page reviews in presses with very high rates of circulation. For my own work, I refused to write about poor women without making clear the ways in which external social and political forces have their effect on what happens to them. My task was to somehow expose "the mechanisms of structural violence" and "the machinery of political economy" (Farmer 2003) for an audience likely to feel threatened by this explanation of poverty in America.

Writing Poverty: Style and Strategy

There came a moment in the course of this project when it was time *to write* the book. There were hundreds of pages of fieldnotes in electronic format which allowed me to easily pull out quotations and stories by key themes: experiences with poverty, homelessness, work, the institutional setting, drug and alcohol use and abuse, sexual violence, mental illness, AIDS, family and interpersonal relationships, sexuality, race, gender, and food. These general themes form the main portion of the book, an ethnographic narrative in twelve chapters.

My narrative strategy was clear and specific, though it was not easy to accomplish. There would be two aspects to the narrative, the women's stories and my analysis. I started with the women, literally closing myself off from most of the world to stay intimately connected to them – their own words and powerful stories, and our relationships – the heart of the book. I made every effort to stay true to their own descriptions of their experiences and our conversations together, the only tribute I could offer them.

After many months, the ethnographic description was complete. I had written a novel-like account, hoping to convey what it is like to live on the streets, and how it feels to lose your mind, about the taste of crack cocaine and the sweetness of friendship. The narrative was uninterrupted by overt analysis even as I had consciously inferred it as part of the description. There were small moments that dropped hints of meaning. There is the reference to aspidistra, a resilient plant known for its ability to endure neglect, a stand-in for the women that also graced the dayroom of the community residence (1999: 43). There is the description of our first meal together, the women and I, a bland supper with iceberg lettuce and Shake 'n' Bake, mentioned at the close of "Home, Some Place," the book's first chapter that describes their paths to homelessness, a brutal condition that has itself become naturalized and normalized, an American way of life

(1999: 41). I portray myself, furiously scrubbing the kitchen when a new resident meets me, the anthropologist, researcher, writer, and neurotic person fixated on hygiene, suggesting the line between "normal" and "abnormal" is awfully blurred, an analytic theme of the book (1999: 201).

I wanted to link individual life stories with larger social, political and economic processes, but do so in a way that did not intrude on the stories, and did not overwhelm or turn away my mother-readers or the women I write about who would read the book. The solution was to gently weave my commentary at key moments in the story, and place a concise social analysis in a prologue. By means of this structure, readers would hear the women's voices, without mine interrupting with abstractions, yet my theorizing about the women's experiences would be there up front, requiring readers to step over it to get to the story.

Drawing Readers: The "M" Word

There is a rich body of literature on poverty that refutes false and mean-spirited stereotypes and provides rigorous explanation for the social suffering we see in the wealthiest, most powerful nation in the world. Yet these works receive little public attention; the best of critical poverty theory rarely enters the public conversation. While many Americans are familiar with Herrnstein, Murray and D'Souza, how many have heard of Brett Williams, for example, or even Charles Valentine from many decades past?[7]

Our own reticence is part of the problem. We shun publicity and rarely utter the "m" word (marketing) lest we violate certain unwritten rules of the academy. Publicity and marketing constitute the sin of self-promotion, taboo activities for a true scholar. But from now to eternity we can stamp our feet opposing the circulation of false images and uncovering the systemic workings of political economy, but if no one is listening, *reading*, who cares?

---

[7]   It's maddening that the vast anthropological literature on poverty is ignored at the same time that distorted images of the field continue to be reproduced in the public sphere (see di Leonardo, this volume, 1998). For example, in a June 2007 *New York Times* article, Alex Beam reviews Robert Frank's new book, *RICHISTAN: A Journey through the American Wealth Boom and the Lives of the Rich.* Beam, writing about Frank's information-gathering approach likens *RICHISTAN*'s author to an anthropologist in the Amazon Basin who "goes native," then arrogantly asks, "Look out the window. It's Pooristan. Hmmm. I wonder who lives there. And will anyone be writing a book about them?" Had Beam done his homework, he'd find out we have, and done so as ourselves.

To draw readers, I realized, I would have to lure them to *Love, Sorrow and Rage*, and take an active role in marketing this book. Publishing my first book had taught me about the importance of the look of the cover, whether or not the book is available in paperback, the cost. The first time around I let things fall as they may; when released, my first book was an expensive, hardcover volume with a nondescript jacket.

This time it would be different. Virginia Schofield's beautiful art graces the cover. I have admired Virginia's work for years, and her painting "Comadres," fits so well with the theme and setting of the book. I also requested of my publisher that it be released in paperback, even though many academics consider this "unprestigious"; hardcover first, paperback later, apparently holds higher status value. For me, everything about this book – its look, its feel, its cost, its content – would be designed to appeal, to be accessible.

I had ambitious publicity plans, with little payoff. I tried it all: from Oprah to *American Ethnologist*, from postcard mailings to press releases. My mother even hand-delivered a copy to Charles McGrath, then editor of the *New York Times Book Review*, who also told her by phone he had my book on his desk (where it stayed, apparently). I had stiff competition, however. *Love, Sorrow and Rage* was released the same time as *Monica's Story*, Ms. Lewinsky's memoir. While *Monica's Story* filled tables at bookstores throughout New York City, a single copy of *Love, Sorrow and Rage* could be found on the fiction shelf at the 14th Street Barnes and Noble (a good thing, I suppose). In the end, sales and reprints have been average for a scholarly book, with about 2000 copies sold in two reprints.

I've had rewarding moments with *Love, Sorrow and Rage*: notes from colleagues and students, some lovely reviews, a reader on the subway. There was also a mother-reader, the mother of my daughter's friend, who read it once and then again, drawn, she said, to the women, and by a yearning to understand, I like to think.

In truth, I have no way of knowing the impact of this book, or if it has any at all. It's no longer in my hands. What remains are Nora's wise words, her gift to me: "The book, the book, the book," she once admonished; "the really important thing is – you've come into my life and I've come into yours."

References

Agar, Michael H. 1996. *The Professional Stranger: An Informal Introduction to Ethnography*, 2nd edition. San Diego: Academic Press.

Beam, Alex. 2007. Lifestyles of the Rich. *The New York Times Book Review.* 10 June: 8.

Begley, Adam. 1993. Don DeLillo on the Art of Fiction. *The Paris Review* 128 (Fall).

Dash, Leon. 1997. *Rosa Lee: A Mother and Her Family in Urban America.* New York: Plume Publishers.

Deparle, Jason. 2005. Broken Levees, Unbroken Barriers. *The New York Times.* 4 September: A1.

di Leonardo, Micaela. 1994. *Gender, Race, and Representation: Neighborhood Shift in New Haven.* Paper presented at the annual meeting of the American Anthropological Association, Atlanta.

di Leonardo, Micaela. 1998. *Exotics at Home: Anthropologies, Others, American Modernity.* Chicago: University of Chicago Press.

Ehrenreich, Barbara. 1990. *Fear of Falling: The Inner Life of the Middle Class.* New York: HarperPerennial.

Farmer, Paul. 2003. *Pathologies of Power: Health, Human Rights and the New War on the Poor.* Berkeley: University of California Press.

Finn, Robin. 2004. A Life Knocked Off Balance by National Acclaim. *The New York Times.* 30 November: B2.

Gilman, Sander L. 1988. *Disease and Representation: Images of Illness from Madness to AIDS.* Ithaca, NY: Cornell University Press.

Lemann, Nicholas. 1986a. The Origins of the Underclass [Part 1]. *Atlantic Monthly* 257 (June): 31–53.

Lemann, Nicholas. 1986b. The Origins of the Underclass [Part 2]. *Atlantic Monthly* 258 (July): 54–69.

Mauer, Marc and Ryan S. King. 2007. Uneven Justice: State Rates of Incarceration by Race and Ethnicity. *The Sentencing Project.* July. http://sentencingproject. org/Admin/Documents/publications/rd_stateratesofincbyraceandethnicity.pdf. Accessed September 10, 2007.

Pratt, Mary Louise. 1986. Fieldwork in Common Places. In *Writing Culture: The Poetics and Politics of Ethnography.* James Clifford and George E. Marcus, eds., pp. 27–50. Berkeley: University of California Press.

Scheper-Hughes, Nancy. 2002. Coming to our Senses: Anthropology and Genocide. In *Annihilating Difference: The Anthropology of Genocide.* Alexander Laban Hinton, ed., pp. 348–81. Berkeley: University of California Press.

Scheper-Hughes, Nancy. 2007. The Gray Zone: Small Wars, Peacetime Crimes, and Invisible Genocides. In *The Shadow Side of Fieldwork: Exploring the Blurred Borders between Ethnography and Life.* Athena McLean and Annette Leibing, eds., pp. 159–84. Malden, MA: Blackwell Publishing.

Sentencing Project. 2007. Women in the Criminal Justice System: Briefing Sheets. *The Sentencing Project.* May. www.sentencingproject.org/Admin/Documents/ news/womenincj_total.pdf. Accessed September 10, 2007.

Waterston, Alisse. 1999. *Love, Sorrow and Rage: Destitute Women in a Manhattan Residence.* Philadelphia: Temple University Press.

8

Write-ous Indignation: Black Girls, Dilemmas of Cultural Domination and the Struggle to Speak the Skin We Are In

Signithia Fordham

"She writes like a (Black) girl." I hear these words and I am immediately emotionally engaged – or is it enraged? My write-ous indignation – my power to voice my viewpoint and to transform the world we share – is linked to the act of creating a counternarrative that I sometimes jokingly refer to as "paper babies."

Paper babies. They gum up my life, spilling out of my dedicated home office onto every available surface. They escape their nooks and crannies and land on the microwave, the plant stands, and the credenza. They over-load my small cottage, finding their way up and down the stairwell. My paper babies' displacement is ubiquitous, like my own. In various stages of gestation, they perch haphazardly on my dining room table and occupy the seats of the chairs; they saunter onto the kitchen counter and dribble into my sunroom. Their most disconcerting migration is into my bedroom. We start out every evening with a great sense of joy and anticipation. Sometimes my paper baby (occasionally there are multiple births) is a newborn that I cannot stand to leave unattended because it was a gift from another writer. Sometime it is a text I created the night, week, month or year before. Paper babies crowd into my bed and into my head and I agonize every day over who to remove and who to keep for another day.

Paper babies – both the many I consume and the few I have (re)produced – are the bane as well as the blessing of my existence. Indeed, now that I think about it, their visible proliferation was responsible for ending my last relationship. He, who like me is an academic, could not abide coming to my home and seeing all the books and papers. It reminded him too much of the fact that he should be working. He wanted a woman whose greatest ambition was to take care of him – exclusively. He wanted me to cook those good Black girl southern dishes and then make love to him until the moon blacked out.

Above all, I want to see my counternarratives – my paper babies – grow up, leave home, and make their way in the world. My desire to make my writing at one and the same time accessible to people outside the discipline and acceptable to the powerbrokers within the discipline is the most critical issue I face. In striking contrast to typical academic practice, I try to create texts that use concepts and principles that are widely known (as opposed to unknown) in the (Black) community and expand their meanings – for example, "acting white." This task often paralyzes me with indecision and frustration. I see the pen, broadly defined, as the academy's Uzi, the most powerful weapon of human civilization, the instrument that can be used to enslave, to grant freedom, and everything in between. Like Zora Neale Hurston and Margaret Mead, I want the potentially transformative power of anthropology known and valued by readers who are not anthropologists. I want my writing to be seriously consulted by journalists, marriage counselors, teachers, preachers, and the omnipresent churchladies – to name a few.

Ironically, now that I have obtained a modicum of visibility as an academic, what Claude Steele (1992, 1999) calls "stereotype threat" compels me to fear the power of my own voice. If I write in the skin I am in, I worry that I will reinforce the dreaded and demeaning stereotype: "She writes like a (Black) girl." Admittedly, while writing like a Black girl is not inherently deformative or inappropriate, the hegemonic power and control of mainstream editors and publishers often stymie this counternarrative out of deference to the presumed sensibilities of a predominately White readership.

Write-ous indignation, then, is the metaphor I use to describe both my current dilemma as a professional anthropologist and my reaction to the cultural, racial, and gendered displacements I involuntarily embraced in school. Displacement refers to the seemingly benign underground hostility that is inevitably embedded in the domination of existing cultural practices, social relationships, and political ideologies in academic institutions. I begin with my childhood experience of the writing process.

Like my ancestors before me, I did not experience these cultural, racial, and gendered displacements as some kind of fragmentation of my identities as a culturally Black person, a Black girl, and/or an unhyphenated

American. Rather, as they were then socially constructed, each aspect of my identity was a separate and all-encompassing entity. Yet I intuitively knew that my academic survival was wholly contingent upon my unconditional acceptance of the dominant set of norms and cultural practices, including a political and educational ideology that explicitly validated my stigmatized status. As an imagined unfragmented Black person, my displacement was readily sanctioned by school officials. Indeed, my timid schoolgirl attempts both to be academically successful and to retain my imagined unhyphenated Black and female identities, to be the unreinvented, unrepentant me, were repeatedly blacked out, erased by a system whose liberal creed, ironically, compelled me to engage actively in my own socially mandated displacement.

Nowhere was this blackout more apparent than in how my schoolmates and I were required to write. Narration, the academic benchmark used to judge the adequacy of our presumed or compulsory transformation, was highly stylized and formulaic. Writing in our native voices – regardless of the circumstances or our level of sophistication – was either erased or repeatedly edited by our teachers and other school officials to fit a preexisting template. We were compelled to write not only in "the standard" (Fordham 1999), using the dominant version of the English language, but in the voice sanctioned by the school, regardless of who we were, what the nature of the subject matter, and what our life experiences might have been. Narrating out of voice – outside our lived experiences – was obligatory, yet almost impossible to do. I found this task particularly daunting and painful. The only way that even a conformist like me could become academically successful was to write as if I were only "accidentally" Black and "accidentally" female. My worldview and my writing were expected to be indistinguishable from those of any other person on the planet. After all, as Americans, we all attended the same schools and were taught the same narrative forms by the same teachers – at least they seemed interchangeable. I shamefully admit that as a high school student, in order to complete difficult writing assignments (e.g., what were the three most important causes of the Civil War?), I often pretended to be White and (fe)male. This self-initiated displacement, this out-of-body experience, promoted my academic success but invariably left me shivering in the shame of my self-duplicity. Writing out of voice – that is, as if I were not Black and female – meant never bringing into the classroom or the school anything that remotely resembled what I had learned and valued either as a female or a Black person in the community. This stricture meant never "writing like a (Black) girl" and never acting like, interacting like, or speaking like the Black people I loved and lived with on a daily basis.

As a female, African American child who desired to achieve academic success, I learned to make self-alienating choices that promoted my academic performance but, at the same time, perhaps unwittingly reinforced my displacement. My classmates and I were continually watched, our images filtered through the lens and the pens of White sensibilities. Beginning with the claim that Christopher Columbus had discovered America and the notion that Black families had been destroyed by enslavement, the most powerful and abject images of African Americans – slaves, three-fourths human, sharecroppers, colored, Negroes – were sewn into the official texts of the nation and routinely duplicated in newspapers, on television, in books, magazines and other sources that shape what Benedict Anderson (1991) labels the "imagined community." Was there space in this imagined America for Black people out of place? Because both written and visual images of the national body are not neutral, the official White gaze has always appeared to be stuck on raping, raging against, and rapaciously consuming Blackness. While Black folks have consistently dreaded the power of these White images, as was the case for me and my childhood friends, Black people's write-ous indignation has, until very recently, been widely ignored, masked under the claim of orality: African Americans are an oral rather than a writing people. Indeed, prior to the epiphany I experienced during my work at Capital High (Fordham 1988, 1993, 1996; Fordham and Ogbu 1986), I erroneously assumed that contemporary Black children were no longer constrained by the narration obstacles that mutilated the dreams of my generation.

When I was in school, it was widely understood that we could not write what we thought, either in form or substance. As African American school children we generally agreed on two basic facts: (1) Christopher Columbus could not have discovered America since the American Indians were already here; and (2) African Americans did not have a matriarchal family structure. Patrick Moynihan's (1965) infamous government-sponsored assertion notwithstanding, matriarchy, or rule by women, is not the same as matrifocality, families centered on mothers. We children knew that as well as any anthropologist. Nevertheless, in the school context, most African Americans of my generation did not publicly dispute these claims in our written academic assignments, at least not if we wanted to get a good grade. Like our White classmates, we were taught how to critique an author's writings and to disavow emotionality. Adding insult to injury, we were also taught to internalize the claims made against us as Black people. Our only other option was to refuse to do the assigned written work, as Corey did at Capital High (Fordham 1996) – "I don't do no book reports" – and opt to fail academically. This displacement, this disengagement, was at the core of our academic lives and made school so utterly frustrating, unrewarding, and unfulfilling.

I grew up keenly aware of the marginalization and limitations of my social world, especially in school. Reading became my escape from hypocrisy, the primary way I managed the stresses of gender and racial oppression. My relatives' *National Geographic* and Margaret Mead's books powered my nascent belief that anthropology and anthropologists could make something of the claim that "no condition is permanent." Even for a young impoverished Black girl, these paper babies reinforced both my perception of the power of the pen and my fear of the written word, especially as it related to the life conditions of people of African ancestry in America. How could this knowledge be translated into writing that was liberatory rather than alienating?

Throughout my own years in school, as well as in my later participant-observation of high schools, I saw that Black students were unable to write in our own voices, to tell our unique stories. Our academic efforts were subverted. Our academic performance reflected the evolution of our fear: we came to fear our own writing, and to fear that what we wrote would further distort our lived reality. Indeed, given the choice of being misrepresented in blackface or blacked out, most of my generation opted for silence. Being erased or blacked out, we reasoned, was preferable to being misrepresented. Nevertheless, the then dominant blackface constructions stuck to us like ill-fitting garb, compelling us to silence and the masked fury most of us grudgingly endured. Moreover, because these predatory images of Blackness were constructed and propagated primarily through written documents, our fear of writing ourselves was matched only by our fear of what was already written about us. This pervasive fear ran like a river through our individual and collective psyches. As school-aged children, we literally feared the power of the pen; the weapon used to document and officially black out our community's claims to modernity, to a life outside enslavement, even to civilization. The rapacious hegemony of the pen, coupled with our unanimous absence from involvement in the construction of our own self-images, blacked out our dreams.

Historically, African Americans have been powerless to construct, to control or even to interrupt the reigning images promulgated and propagated by the dominant culture. Unable to create our own images, we have opted to live outside the White constructions that have repeatedly marked our lives. Our narration began and in some instances continues to be an "out of body experience." My generation's self-constructions were deeply at odds with the dominant images sanctioned in the official representations of Blackness. As a young adult who grew up hearing the refrain, "We shall overcome," I erroneously assumed that the constraints my generation endured were no longer Black children's social reality. I became intensely aware of how intractable and persistent this problem is for contemporary African-descended people during the Capital High study.

The Third Rail of Duplicity: "Acting White"

My personal history of gender and racial displacement, dropped into the vortex of anthropology's unrelenting postmodern debates about writing culture and the politics of representation, combined with an engaged praxis in the public sphere to influence not only my write-ous indignation regarding cultural texts but also the "paper babies" I construct. For most anthropologists, "going native," as it is widely known and occasionally practiced, is "BFF" – brief, frustrating, and fraudulent. Ideally, "going native" is an effort to convince the population we are studying that as outsiders, anthropologists, we respect and honor their way of life. Both parties – the anthropologist and the natives – realize that the anthropologist is "acting," pretending to be a member of the group he or she is studying in order to achieve his or her research goals. We and they realize that this is a temporary guise or mask and that going native or becoming an "authentic" other is not an option. Neither party expects the anthropologist to be indistinguishable from or become one of them – permanently.

Among African Americans "acting white" is tantamount to going native, with similar, although much more ominous results. As the exemplar of "going native" in the African American community – not just the school context – "acting white" is the third rail of duplicity, the sociocultural space where the individual is at risk of losing his or her Black identity and becoming, inadvertently, a raceless or an identity-less exile in both the Black and White communities. In going (or becoming) a native, the African American seeks to embody an all-American image, usually linked to a Eurocentric image with white skin, blue eyes, and blond hair.

In my earlier work, I chose to study "acting white" in a school setting because it is the one remaining obligatory American institution, a space where the values, mores, and practices imagined to be connected to the larger society are historically salient. Moreover, it is a culturally mandated space that I share with the generation I am studying. As an anthropologist whose specialty is North America, I seek connections in order to make what is so taken for granted, so well known, unfamiliar. Making the familiar strange is one of my primary objectives. I remembered my generation's schooling experience and the burden of "acting white." So I undertook the research that became *Blacked Out: Dilemmas of Race, Identity, and Success at Capital High*. Conducting the fieldwork was challenging and enjoyable; formulating the thesis generated a level of intellectual excitement I had never known. But writing the book was among the most difficult things I was ever called upon to do.

After many fruitless struggles and dead ends, I was ultimately able to write *Blacked Out* by slipping in and out of a gender-specific, historical Black voice. By reclaiming my lost childhood voice and merging it with the voices of the students at Capital High, I was able to confront the lies of my childhood and manage the pervasive fear that connects the lives of two or more generations of people of African descent in America. These two generations – mine and the cohort of students at Capital High – share a parallel sociocultural location, despite the decades separating our child-hoods. This location, which not only carries a deep collective memory but also evokes present pain, cemented the students' doubts about whether I could be trusted to tell a Black story.

My respondents' fears were partially confirmed when the first published article based on the research, "Black Students' School Success: Coping with the Burden of 'Acting White'" (Fordham and Ogbu 1986), was discussed in the *Washington Post* and other major media. The response was as if I had suddenly touched the third rail of Black life in America; the debate was non-stop in popular culture and to a lesser degree in academia. If my goal was to initiate a discussion outside the academy, this was (and remains) my shining moment. In the ensuing years, this debate has included my counternarrative voice.

What I came to realize early on was that these media were not interested in helping me promote the counternarrative I was proposing: that is, how and why Black adolescents achieve academic success. Instead, they inverted my narrative to highlight the students' failure, often mocking their efforts to avoid "acting white" and transforming it into a marker of Black inadequacy. This initial response to my work became fixed in the public imagination, remaining unchanged even after some media sources modified their earlier assessment in the wake of the publication of the book. Jolted by the upside-down interest in my work and the presumed power of my voice, I now struggle to create paper babies that are culturally organic but immune to misinterpretation. Determined to white out the black-out of Black students' academic success, I now realize that the subject of my research, Black adolescents' academic performance, was what attracted the attention of an audience outside anthropology. What and how I wrote about students' success was almost beside the point. *Blacked Out* has been hotly debated, not because the writing and analysis are so compelling, but because the topic it engages is so controversial. National media attention paid to my work ultimately distorted its findings to fit the dominant images of African American youth.

Publishing to Perish

Indeed, the fear evoked by the perception that I was and am "a body out of place" engaging in "write-ous indignation" was implicated in the entire process of getting *Blacked Out* published. As a discipline, anthropology has relied historically on reporting the strange practices of remote peoples. In many ways my ethnography promotes a similar pattern of consumption, even though it is situated in America: it is, unfortunately, often read as promoting the consumption of the homegrown Other. When some segment of the academic and publishing complex needs to promote diversity or Otherness, I am the resident *du jour*, though only temporarily.

When I managed to slither through the obstacle of finding a publisher, my progress was stymied at the very next rung of the ladder. I remember my short-lived happiness when, after collecting enough rejection letters to paper my bedroom wall, I received the acceptance letter and contract from the University of Chicago Press – though not until I had agreed to revise every chapter. Soon thereafter, I was notified that my contract at the university where I was then employed was not going to be renewed. I was devastated, for I had naively assumed that by obtaining the publishing symbols that protected my academic colleagues, I, too, would be rewarded. I was never so wrong. My write-ous indignation, even when sanctioned by a prestigious publisher, earned me unemployment. For a large segment of the academic and publishing establishment, Black bodies are still bodies out of place. The smell of fear is everywhere.

If the implicit presumption of efforts to enhance the educational achievement of Black youth is that in order to be successful academically they must become culturally extinct by write-ously forswearing all practices that make them – as they perceive it – Black, I can report that this effort has been a colossal failure. Supporting an academic process that compels Black youth to white out their Blackness by embracing the official cacophony of lies that the dominant social system propagates will continue to be met with the drop-dead silence practiced by earlier generations of Black students and by the write-ous indignation rampant among the students I describe in *Blacked Out*. Yes, I know. Every other immigrant group (and most of us are immigrants) had to learn English and give up many of the old ways that they embraced prior to coming to America. This is a specious, though quite prominent, argument. Contemporary Americans whose ancestors were enslaved speak a version of English and, because enslavement compelled our mothers and fathers to forswear their indigenous lifeways, most of us have no collective memory of our African cultural practices. Consequently the idea of giving up old-world practices is not applicable to the situation confronting contemporary African Americans. Rather, it is the practices that have emerged in the wake of contact (what Ogbu [1982] describes as "secondary discontinuities") with those whose ancestors enslaved us that are massacring the achievement efforts of contemporary African Americans. Moreover, since these cultural practices appear to have their genesis in the unique kind of dehumanization that is the Black American historical and cultural experience and, more centrally, these practices owe their origin to this history, the educational system's insistence that these children act as if they are a people without a history of dehumanization continues not to be efficacious.

As a professional anthropologist, I believe a group's sense of belonging – the shared conviction that this is who we are; this is where we belong – fuels their passion, inspires them to achieve. In striking contrast, their sense of inappropriateness – this is not who we are; this is not where we belong – subverts and/or undermines all efforts to motivate them. Black history – merged, of course, with my personal narrative – replays in my memory and influences what and how I write.

Counter(narrations) and the Public Sphere

The determination to claim a space in American public discourse for a viewpoint that comes from my position as Black and female is an integral part of my quest for justice. In an effort to practice writing as a form of social activism, I submit op-ed pieces for publication by well-known newspapers and magazines. Most never even acknowledge receiving my work, though I have had several pieces published, including in the newspapers of the city where I currently teach. I have noticed a significant imbalance in the consideration my work receives, depending on whether it highlights race or gender: writing that highlights race and is gender-neutral meets with a greater degree of acceptance. I offer a few examples to demonstrate this pattern.

A local paper repeatedly requested that I write about the Capital High study, although the research was completed more than 20 years ago. I do not complain about the longevity and continuing relevance of this work, but only about the misrepresentations of it that continue to circulate. The editors eagerly sought an article about the idea of Black students' academic performance and the "burden of acting white." I finally agreed, unable to convince them that my more recent research in a local high school about gender-differentiated achievement and competition between Black and White girls was more relevant. I made what turned out to be a futile effort to shift the narrowly constructed meaning of "acting white" in the popular media.

> Was Rosa Parks guilty of "acting white" that day in Montgomery when she refused to give up her seat to a White man who boarded the bus? When the other Black passengers did not initially support her because she was upsetting the imposed and customary order of race relations and they feared White reprisals against the whole Black community, were they responsible for the insult to her dignity? . . . Most reasonable people would agree that, like the Black people on the bus with Mrs. Parks that day, the less successful Black students are not the major obstacles to the elimination of the Black/White achievement gap. Like every Black person on the bus that day, all African American students are victimized – regardless of their academic performance – by social policies and educational practices that challenge their humanity and aspirations. How ironic that in the current debate about the Black/White academic achievement gap, we overemphasize the influence of students who are not doing well academically on the performance of Black students who are successful. At the same time, we fail to examine the configuration of power on the bus and underemphasize the power of the social configuration of the school, especially racialized academic tracking and teachers' low expectations of Black students' academic performance. Twenty years ago, I concluded that academically successful students at Capital High were compelled to "cope with the burden of 'acting white'." After reviewing what has been written about the schools that most American students of African ancestry attend today, I am convinced that my earlier research was not seriously flawed and that the notion of "acting white" is still very much "a black thing" (*City Newspaper*, February 8, 2006: 10, 14)

Again, some readers missed the point. Both denial and misunderstanding were among the readers' responses, including the claim that "acting white" was the same thing as being smart or a nerd.[1] Others argued that because

---

[1]   Benjamin Nugent (2007) addressed an issue that I found both baffling and fascinating at Capital High: the students' reluctance, even resistance, to define high academic performance as the embodiment of nerdiness. Using the work of another professor, Nugent concludes that the language practices of some white kids in California have cast 'nerdiness' as an exclusive, "hyperwhite" identity. Nerds are not rejecting the "hegemonic" appropriation of "trends in music, dance, fashion, sports and language . . . often traceable to an African-American source." Instead, they are promoting a sort of linguistic apartheid. "[B]eing a nerd has become a widely accepted and even proud identity," but it is not one to which even the highest-achieving African American students may lay claim.

I did not include Americans who do not identify as either Black or White but as of "mixed race," the theory was useless.

In striking contrast, in a piece that highlights both race and gender as important social categories, I sought to connect the current contest for the Democratic presidential nomination with a debate that took place in the mid-nineteenth century.

In many ways, the upcoming presidential primary battle between Hillary Rodham Clinton and Barack Obama parallels a more distant debate between the iconic abolitionists and suffragists Frederick Douglass and Susan B. Anthony, both of whom lived a portion of their lives in Rochester and are buried in that city's Mount Hope Cemetery.

Although the Douglass/Anthony feud occurred in the mid-1800s, some of the issues they fought over are relevant to our time. At the heart of their conflict was the question of which struggle was a more important priority: the women's rights movement or Black Americans' struggle for equality. . . . The official emancipation (1863) of African Americans unraveled the Douglass/Anthony alliance, not because their quest was unsuccessful but – at least partially – because of its success. . . . Fueled by the cry for the end of slavery and full citizenship for African Americans (males), Douglass strongly supported the passage of the 14th and 15th Amendments. Anthony did not. She not only disagreed with her former comrade, she was furious that he did not share her view. . . . Paradoxically, Anthony's failure to win white women the right to vote before Black males led suffragists to seek reinforcement of the subordination of Black and other non-white females by compelling them to embrace the subordination she and the other suffragists were fighting to escape. . . .

As with the Douglass/Anthony alliance, a contest between a Black man and a white woman (still) has the potential to consume all the oxygen in the room. Although unacknowledged, race and gender have always been central issues in who gets to seek the presidency. Clinton's and Obama's efforts to expand the pool are likely to be seen by some as threatening. (Unpublished document)

This commentary was not accepted by the *New York Times*, perhaps because it raises an issue so explosive that editors do not wish to expose it in their pages. The paradox is that a prestigious publisher, Oxford University Press, has "been there, done that" in the book *White Women's Rights: The Racial Origins of Feminism in the United States* (1999) by Louise Newman.

My most recent unsuccessful effort to publish a counternarrative was in response to Don Imus's attack on the "nappy-headed hos" at Rutgers

University. My indignation was so profound that I had to force myself to revisit the self-initiated displacement that was so familiar during my pre-professional schooling. For several weeks, I struggled with an essay that I thought of as a response to what I identified as the Imus debacle. I began by telling the story shared by an anthropology colleague, a professor at a predominately white university, who repeatedly observed some Black female students entering a fraternity house with a sign in the window that said: "Hos Get In Free."

> Why, she wondered, would girls enter a building with a sign in the window that denigrated them – unconditionally? Why wouldn't they boycott such a sexist campus space, she asked? ... African American women (and many other women) are rewarded (marriage, motherhood, protection, etc.) for the acceptance and maintenance of the double-layered male domination sewn into the very fabric of the American social structure. As racial and sexual beings, Black women are subsumed into the Black male category; as Black females we are masculinized, deemed "nappy-headed hos," only partially eligible for membership in the dominant (white) female category. (Unpublished document)

This submission was rejected as well, even though it was written about a timely subject and met the formal criteria for correctness. Regrettably, unlike what our teachers told us, more is demanded of a writer than proper grammar and subject matter that engages the reader. Couching the text to fit the sensibilities and expectations of the perceived audience trumps everything else. Subversive arguments do not get a hearing.

(Counter)narration, then, is what I use to try to decenter the hegemonic practices that mutilated my generation's childhood and the children and youth of today. Although carefully crafted both to embody my scholarly training and to limit the discomfort of an assumed mainstream audience, my paper babies are inevitably smeared with my interlocking cultural, racial, gender, and socioeconomic indignation.

The question remains: how do we promote a kind of anthropological text that lives off the shelf, that is read and debated rather than consigned to a space with the spines stiff and the analysis not widely known? How do we, contemporary anthropologists, make anthropology the embodiment of the power of the pen?

We need an anthropology that considers not only the exotic Other but also the homegrown Other. We must do so by interrogating familiar American practices and by communicating our discoveries in a language that does not reinforce the marginalization and stigmatization of the subject position from which we speak.

The power of the pen has structured every aspect of my life. But, even as an academic, I am no exception; it shapes the lives of most Americans, including those who are pushed out of the public school system. As a Black girl, my formative years were framed by the paper babies created by others, the history books that told me and every other Black school child that I was a descendant of a people who were rightfully and abjectly enslaved. According to these authoritative sources, we were intellectually inadequate, lazy, incompetent, and undeserving. Whether portrayed as natively inferior or, in a liberal version, as degraded by our environment, we were perpetually subject to others. Moreover, it was not just skin color that worked against my humanization; my gender identification interlocked with my racial ascription in ways that intensified the impact of both. "Writing like a (Black) girl" had real consequences for me. As a voracious reader and a lifelong student, I have had these racial and gender images reinforced repeatedly from multiple written sources. The pen is the most powerful weapon of human civilization, the instrument that can be used to enslave, emancipate and everything in between. In writing anthropology off the shelf, fear of the power of my own voice is erased and writing like a Black girl is no longer tinged with stereotype threat. Like everyone else, I am able to create paper babies that tell my truth. My truth is then in a position to interact with other truths in the universe.

Finally, if the goal of the development of anthropology off the shelf is not simply to promote the creation of paper babies but their rapacious consumption, then my write-ous indignation will be rewarded and "writing like a (Black) girl" will not be in vain.

References

Anderson, Benedict. 1991. *Imagined Communities: Reflections on the Origins and Spread of Nationalism*, rev. ed. London: Verso.

Fordham, Signithia. 1988. Racelessness as a Factor in Black Students' School Success: Pragmatic Strategy or Pyrrhic Victory? *Harvard Educational Review* 58(1): 54–84.

Fordham, Signithia. 1993. "Those Loud Black Girls": (Black) Women, Silence, and Gender "Passing" in the Academy. *Anthropology and Education Quarterly* 24: 3–32.

Fordham, Signithia. 1996. *Blacked Out: Dilemmas of Race, Identity and Success at Capital High*. Chicago: University of Chicago Press.

Fordham, Signithia. 1999. Dissin' "the Standard": Ebonics as Guerrilla Warfare at Capital High. *Anthropology and Education Quarterly* 30: 272–93.

Fordham, Signithia. 2005a. "Signithia, You Can Do Better Than That": John Ogbu (and Me) and the Nine Lives Peoples. *Anthropology and Education Quarterly* 35: 149–61.

Fordham, Signithia. 2005b. Race and Identity. *Rochester Democrat and Chronicle*, December 12: 11A.

Fordham, Signithia. 2006. Was Rosa Parks "Acting White"? *City Newspaper*, February 8: 10, 14.

Fordham, Signithia and John Ogbu. 1986. Black Students' School Success: Coping with the Burden of "Acting White." *Urban Review* 18: 176–206.

Moynihan, Daniel Patrick. 1965. *The Negro Family: The Case for National Action*. Washington, D.C.: United States Department of Labor, Office of Policy Planning and Research.

Netsky, Ron. 2006. Acting White. One professor studies the fight between identity and achievement. One student copes with it. *City Newspaper*, February 8: 10–13.

Newman, Louise. 1999. *White Women's Rights: The Racial Origins of Feminism in the United States*. New York: Oxford University Press.

Nugent, Benjamin. 2007. Who's a Nerd Anyway? Someone Very, Very White, for One Thing. *New York Times Magazine*, July 19: 15.

Ogbu, John. 1982. Cultural Discontinuities and Schooling. *Anthropology and Education Quarterly* 13: 290–307.

Steele, Claude M. 1992. Race and the Schooling of Black Americans. *Atlantic Monthly* 269(4): 68–78.

Steele, Claude M. 1999. Thin Ice: Stereotype Threat and Black College Students. *Atlantic Monthly* 284(2): 44–7, 50–4.

9

Writing Truth to Power: Racism as Statecraft

Arthur K. Spears

Introduction

With this writing, I am concerned with storytelling about racism. In this case, the story involves my coming to the idea of putting together and publishing an edited volume, *Race and Ideology: Language, Symbolism, and Popular Culture* (Spears 1999). Racism reveals itself in this story, and the story exposes that racism is everywhere. I experienced this racism as a rather comfortable academic involved in the process of academic publishing. It seems difficult to compare this experience of racism with, say, lynching. Nevertheless, we must still acknowledge that both are related not only to the phenomenon of general racism but also to the more fundamental, underlying societal organizing principles that determine access to economic assets and political clout. Racism in publishing and lynching, even though different in the pain they are wont to produce, are nevertheless of a piece, part of the same macro story.

One axiom underlying this writing is that white-supremacist racism is institutionalized in the United States (Fanon 1968 [1961]; Blauner 1972; Spears 1999). Note here that white-supremacist racism is the only kind that is significant on a global scale, both historically and today. I use the term *racism* in reference to social hierarchies, constructed on racial categories, which regulate access to power and wealth. These hierarchies are oppressive ranking structures that self-reproduce and may become ever more important in a societal system as the linkages and functions of the hierarchy become more tightly interwoven and critical to the maintenance of power–wealth configurations.

In a mature, racialized state, the US, for example, racism has become the pillar of statecraft, as it pertains to the nation-state and its empire. It must be made explicit that where racism is institutionalized, it is state-craft. Conversely, in the mature, racialized state, statecraft is racism, where statecraft is defined as the pursuit of the interests of the ruling elites, and where *interests* is defined as power–wealth, if we may adapt Morgenthau's concept (1962). In our current world, this is the only prac-tical definition of statecraft, even granting that statecraft is subject to popular anti-statecraft. Racism cannot be disentangled from the pursuit of interests. Observe, additionally, that the US is the world's pre-eminent nation and empire and also the world headquarters of racism. It is where we find racism, not to mention capitalism and Gramscian hegemony (Gramsci 1971 [1929–35]; Spears 1999) in its most extreme and advanced form (Spears 1999).

Since racism is institutionalized, we expect to find it in all institutions – in all (US) endeavors involving a distinctive complex of purposeful social actions, carried out according to rules and/or guidelines concerning time, manner, and place. In this social science sense, the term *institution* applies not solely to imposing edifices with bureaucrats toiling away inside, but to all distinctive complexes of social actions as just described – including everything from sports bars, basketball, and hip-hop to lynching and rape. Associated with institutions, as we all know, are rites of initiation or guide-lines for entry (gatekeeping writ large), rituals, and symbolism, along with typically distinctive ways of speaking, discourses, vocabularies, epistemolo-gies, ethics, and aesthetics. In other words, US institutions are racialized, not to mention gendered, classed, sexualized, ethnicized, age-d, whether in categorical (all or none) or quantitative terms.

Some of the institutions I have just mentioned may seem unqualified to be designated as such, but further thought provides justification. Lynching, for example, does involve aesthetics – scales of appropriateness and suitability in the form and texture of objects such that they may induce pleasure in their intended perceivers. Excluding lynching from the purview of a theory of aesthetics would be nothing more than an ideological maneuver in the service of white-supremacist racism (even recognizing that some whites have been lynched; again, social science deals with the categorical and the quan-titative). All of this is to say that we must include the consideration of horrors as they may relate to all of our intellectual constructs, lest our intellectualizing be reduced to triviality in the service of a state- and soci-etally promoted, restricted gaze. We must also include the never-ending suc-cession of career-diminishing indignities, for example those produced by the publishing industry, that are also essential ingredients in the saga of racism.

Concept to Publication: A Microethnography of Racism

Race and Ideology (hereafter *R&I*) was not written for tenure, as one colleague and "friend" assumed. She told me when I mentioned the idea of sending it to her press for consideration, "Oh, you should send it to a university press for help with tenure." A charming, white, left-leaning progressive, her assumption that I did not have tenure related to some of the book manuscript's discussions – and to the curious fact that even today, with my graying hair and older self, I am still persistently thought to be a student as I make my way around CUNY campuses.

As it actually happened, in the 1980s I thought it would be highly desirable for an anthropology department to offer a course focusing on race and racism (as well as gender, ethnicity, class, and other categories that cannot be absent from any profitable discussion of race/racism). My training is in linguistics; in fact, I had no formal anthropological training outside of linguistics. Consequently, I thought it would have been most appropriate for one of our cultural anthropologists to teach the course. To my mild surprise, there were no takers. I decided to teach the course myself, since over the years I had done a lot of reading on the subject.

In preparing to teach the course, I searched for just the right textbook, since I do not like reading packets – too unwieldy and, I have often suspected, an unnecessary waste of paper. I found no textbook that I considered suitable, notwithstanding the availability of many readers that others might consider adequate. I needed a book that clearly laid out the principal issues connected with racial categorization and racism and that clearly articulated these issues with those relevant to gender, ethnicity, class, and sexuality. I did not expect any book to deal adequately with this last topic, even though I do feel that understanding sexual iconography is essential for understanding the functioning of racism from a symbolic standpoint (oppressed groups are at once hypersexualized and desexualized). I was surprised that none of the candidates for the main text were acceptable. All offered either no or inadequate definitions of *race* and *racism*. All definitions of *race* ignored the fact that race categories are not all based purely on phenotype (observe that some US blacks look as "white" as any white person). In other words, books produced in the US, some of them intended as textbooks, had no definition of *race* that could handle US realities.

At that late date – in the early 1980s – the fact that a number of the textbooks gave only a few sentences' mention to the notion of institutional racism was nothing short of astounding. All labored stereotypes and individual prejudices, as though these phenomena have a life of their own, rooted in individual experience, having sprung Topsy-like out of the unnamed ethers that magically produce racial formations.

I did not have time to write a textbook, but decided to pull together an edited volume with contributions from grounded scholars who would get at the heart of things. I would provide a full introduction to frame the book. Since I saw the book as one for my students, I asked all contributors to avoid using jargon. All of my colleagues complied, as did my students who contributed two chapters (theirs were not jargon-filled to begin with).

I should say something about the student-contributed chapters. These were from two of my undergraduates who had written term papers for a course I teach on television and film. Like most of the students at the time, these were older and savvy, excellent students who had not gone straight through school to get their bachelor's degree. In their term papers, the two students analyzed narrative products for the screen in terms of how they reproduce and speak to dominant ideologies. They were assisted in this task by prepublication drafts of the introduction to *R&I*. Their chapters required significant editing, but it was primarily to make their tone closer to that of the chapters submitted by academic colleagues.

The finished manuscript was, as intended, *"an emancipation-oriented treatment of race/racism as illuminated by the concept of ideology"* (Spears 1999: 16, emphasis in the original). As editor, I made sure the book:

1. presented jargon-free discussions;
2. provided adequate definitions of key concepts such as *race* and *racism*;
3. underlined crucial linkages among all types of oppression, with examples;
4. historicized and theorized racism; in other words, it made clear how sociohistorical processes converge to birth racial formations and affect their evolution;
5. emphasized the role of the mass media, education, and religion in reproducing racism;
6. pinpointed the role of racism's functioning in implementing divide-and-conquer strategies against all working people – whites, blacks, and others;
7. clarified racism's root purpose of assisting in the maintenance of unequal access to wealth and power;
8. stressed the critical role of ideology in racial systems generally and in US society specifically, where oppressive ideologies are internalized by their victims to an extent unseen elsewhere today in the world or in the past; for the first time in human history, oppressed people are on the

whole not aware of their own oppression, so narcotized are they by the vapors of their ideational environment;

9. gave due attention to the interplay between ideology and coercion.[1]

The key statement in the book, upon which hangs its uniqueness and defining orientation, is that "America cannot be America without racism." Institutionalized to an extent seen in no other society, racism in the US is such a rooted phenomenon that without it, the US would be unrecognizable, a distinctly new thing with fundamentally different operating principles. As I state in the Introduction, "This should not be seen as a cause for despair, but as a call for sober pragmatism and solid work for change" (Spears 1999: 12).

One interesting outcome of producing the book was that it compelled me to think about race and racism within the context of political theory, and to provide at least preliminary answers to questions such as: Is racism basically about the maintenance of white privilege or the maintenance of power, essential for reproducing inequality? Is racism the only "regime maintenance imperative" (a requirement for a ruling elite to maintain power), and if not, how does it interact with other imperatives? Are there regime maintenance strategies that could be substituted for racism in the US? Is it possible for the US ruling elite to truly entertain the possibility of eliminating racism? "America cannot be America without racism" provides the answers.

Additionally, strategies and processes that have emerged more clearly in the US and the rest of the wealthy, highly developed world since the publication of *R&I* indicate that my assessment was correct. Note, for one, that the rampant increase in inequality in the US has been accompanied by a subtly coded but very real increase in the racialization of American social and political discourse (since the "thawing" of racialization in the 1960s and 1970s). I have only to point out the "Southern strategy" of the Republican Party, whereby Southern (and other) whites are, in coded

---

[1] I pay tribute to Eleanor "Happy" Leacock (Sutton 1993), who was department chair and my anthropology tutor when I first joined the Anthropology Department. Any theoretical adequacy that my work on race and racism may have today is due significantly to long conversations with her and the readings that she handed to me, both of which jumpstarted my understanding of the gender, race, class triad. Her husband, James Haughton, through his grounding in theory and political activism, provided a strong praxis bookend to Happy's mainly but not solely theoretical one. I must also mention Faye Harrison, Pem Davidson Buck, and Lee Baker, who all provided me with important feedback on the manuscript. Pem and Lee also contributed chapters.

language, promised that blacks and other people of color will be kept in their subordinated place if Republicans are in power. Note also how ruling elites in Western Europe are increasingly racializing their populations, pitting them against one another, so that they too may enjoy the kinds of soaring corporate profits and inequality with immunity that American ruling elites have produced in making critical use of racist politicking. The immunity to backlashes against inequality comes from focusing the attention of white majorities on racialized interlopers (Arabs, Muslims, guest-workers, and so forth) threatening to stamp out their beloved traditions and parasitize national economies, when not stealing jobs from "real" citizens. In France, for example, Nicolas Sarkozy got himself elected president in May 2007 by injecting calculated amounts of racialized immigrant demonizing in order to steal enough thunder from the far right contender, Jean-Marie Le Pen, to beat his major challenger, the Socialist Party's Ségolène Royal.

One of the features of *R&I* that I am most proud of is that it clearly laid out, before the fact, what made possible George W. Bush's "selection" as US president in 2000 (even though Democrat Albert Gore won the popular vote), acceded to by a supine Democratic Party: the corrupt American political process, riddled with vote fraud. One year before the election, I wrote, "[M]any Americans have been historically and continue to be disfranchised by means of the voter registration process, economic debilitation, strategic voting machine malfunctions, and vote-tally fraud"; witness "[t]he 'breakdown" of voting machines in black neighborhoods in New York City during Jesse Jackson's presidential campaign" (Spears 1999: 38).

Getting It Published

The volume complete, I sent the manuscript to the press that eventually did publish the book. I received a letter of rejection, though the manuscript had not gone through the peer-review process. I received no official explanation for the rejection. Unbeknownst to me at the time, an academic colleague who was on the editorial board felt that something was amiss; namely, that the book was rejected because of its candor – its straightforward, objective calling of things what they are, calling them by their name, and letting the chips fall where they might.

The astute colleague on the editorial board came up with a plan. Since the manuscript had not been reviewed, she arranged that it get two reviews, one by someone considered a leading figure in anthropology and linguistics. Both reviews were positive and strongly supportive. The great white father had spoken; the editor then gave the go-ahead for the project.

However, the story did not continue uneventfully to its conclusion. I noticed that the copyedited manuscript I had submitted on computer disc later came back to me with a number of errors and typos – mysterious and inexplicable. I corrected them all and returned the manuscript, only to receive galleys later that still had a few errata, one of them a howler that had somehow been introduced into the text. Upon inquiring into the matter, I was assured that there was still time to correct the errors, and that it would certainly be done. I sent at least a half a dozen e-mails to verify that indeed the errors had been removed and was assured that they had been – only to find them still in the text when I received published copies. Talks with the press's staff concerning remedies led nowhere.

I went on with my career and scholarly writing. The awful inaccuracy was not mentioned in any book review; all of the reviews that I have seen have indeed been positive. Most have been flattering. The whole episode gradually came to occupy a place somewhere in the back of my mind when, as fate would have it, I happened to run across an article in the *Chronicle of Higher Education*. The "Careers" section caught my attention just as I was about to throw the issue away. The attention-getter was a front page article titled "Understanding Academe, Authors, and Editors" (Toor 2007). In one passage the writer speaks of "nasty authors" and how they can easily find their work sabotaged. I wondered, was I a "nasty author"? Though persistent when issues arise, I have always intuitively followed the advice Toor gives for getting the best support and results from press staff, including, quite importantly, lower-ranking ones who can do a lot to help authors. By the time I read the *Chronicle* article, I had also heard reports of unreflectively racist behavior with the manuscripts of nonwhite authors, particularly when these authors have submitted work highly critical of American society or its institutions. These and other considerations have led me to wonder if my book was sabotaged because it speaks ugly truths to a many-tentacled power.

One senses that there is a strong impulse for those who feel themselves to benefit from the status quo or to be part of the establishment to appoint themselves as gatekeepers charged with turning away texts that do not hew to the party line regarding the American Dream and America's putatively superficial imperfections. One does see in many arenas a penchant for the powerless to identify with power, obediently accepting the wages of whiteness, maleness, and other statuses.

References

Blauner, Bob. 1972. *Racial Oppression in America*. San Diego, CA: HarperCollins.

Fanon, Frantz. 1968 [1961]. *The Wretched of the Earth*. Trans. C. Farrington. New York: Grove.

Gramsci, Antonio. 1971 [1929–35]. *Selections from the Prison Notebooks of Antonio Gramsci*. Ed. and trans. Quintin Houre and Geoffrey Nowell Smith. New York: International Publishers.

Morgenthau, Hans J. 1962. *Politics among Nations: The Struggle for Peace and Power*. New York: Alfred A. Knopf.

Spears, Arthur K. 1999. Race and Ideology: An Introduction. In *Race and Ideology: Language, Symbolism, and Popular Culture*. Arthur K. Spears, ed., pp. 11–58. Detroit: Wayne State University Press.

Sutton, Constance, ed. 1993. *From Labrador to Samoa: The Theory and Practice of Eleanor Burke Leacock*. Arlington, VA: Association for Feminist Anthropology/American Anthropological Association.

Toor, Rachel. 2007. Understanding Academe, Authors, and Editors. *Chronicle of Higher Education*, Section C: Careers, May 4: C1, 4.

10

Remembering Octavia

Sharon Ball

Asking Octavia Butler to join us at the New Orleans meetings in 2003 was a hopeful but wildly extravagant gesture. Our topic was "Anthropology off the Shelf for the 21st Century," and we sought speakers who wove the stuff of culture into riveting fiction and compelling social commentary. Sharon Ball, former cultural desk editor at National Public Radio, was a master of the craft; as a journalist she knew what we needed and as a friend she was willing to travel from D.C. for our panel. We weren't surprised by Octavia's quick understanding of what we were after, but her good-natured willingness to join us was a stunningly generous gift. The second gift came when we saw them together, two long-distance "telephone friends" who clearly relished the chance to share a podium. An expectant crowd of anthropologists came to hear writers talk about writing, and they were not disappointed.

Unlike our other three panels, however, this one was designed as a con-versation – electrifying in its moment but not preserved through formal remarks or papers. And by the time we began to assemble this volume, Octavia Butler had passed away. Sharon marked their participation in our dialogue with this adaptation of "Eye on the Stars, Feet on the Ground," a tribute to her friend which originally aired on NPR's All Things Considered. *– MDV and AW*

Every month or so from August 2001 to March 2006, Octavia Butler and I talked on the telephone for never less than two hours at a pop. We had our last conversation about three weeks before her death. The loss of an award-winning science fiction writer was news and I heard about it on the radio.

I was at work one afternoon, half-listening to NPR's *Talk of the Nation*, when I heard Neal Conan say, "We have word that science fiction writer Octavia Butler has died . . ." The words exploded in my head and I heard nothing else for a while. I sat frozen, holding my breath. Then I broke into tears, sobbing and sniffling like a much younger human. A colleague from the office next door appeared in the doorway to ask what was wrong and, like an idiot, I pointed to the radio and choked out, "Octavia . . . Octavia's dead!" Uncomfortably, he mumbled something sympathetic, fidgeted for a moment, then retreated to his office. I got up from my desk and closed the door, still sobbing. Then I did something that Octavia would have labeled just plain silly. I picked up the telephone, punched in her home number, and waited for Octavia's answering machine to play the tape of her deep, oddly muffled, androgynous, amused voice.

That compelling voice had always aroused me – not sexually, exactly – but viscerally, down deep where mind and body conjoin. There was a feeling of being held close but from a great distance. The voice was both earthy and otherworldly, a combination that defined her writing and managed to get under my skin from the first encounter.

You could say that Octavia and I met through *NPR News* in Washington, D.C. That's where I was working in the early 1990s when a copy of her new novel, *Parable of the Sower* (1993), came across my desk. The book was just another advance copy seeking air time. But the unusual dust jacket caught my eye. It featured a thoughtful-looking, brown-skinned woman. I skimmed the publisher's blurb about the award-winning, African American woman author and felt embarrassed that I knew nothing of her work. I started scanning the first chapter and "came to" three chapters later when the phone rang, jerking me out of an apparent trance. I had never considered myself a science-fiction fan, but *Parable of the Sower* knocked me out and kept me up most of that night.

The story left me feeling itchy and disturbed. The book's heroine, Laura Olamina, is a young, black girl who is afflicted with a crippling "delusion" of hyper-empathy. Olamina, as she is called, literally feels other people's pain. She also feels their pleasure. But in the book's crumbling, violence-saturated, future America, pain is dominant. Olamina cannot hurt another human being without sharing the experience. She cannot see someone shot without feeling the bullet tearing through her own flesh or witness death without collapsing from the sensation of dying herself. Olamina is a visionary leader forced to hide her vulnerability from the robbers, murderers, rapists, corporate thugs, religious zealots, and desperate others who would use it to enslave her and "sharers" like her. After finishing *Parable*, I set out to read everything that Octavia E. Butler had ever written.

Octavia understood how easily people could turn on you, how deeply imbedded is our need to feel superior to others. Virtually all of her books and stories explore this idea in one way or another and her heroines –

always black women with heart and guts – must always deal with the consequences. In real life, Octavia talked often about the "schoolyard bullies" in Pasadena where she grew up, who "pounded" her for being tall, dark-skinned and different. We are all afflicted, to one degree or another, with the need to lord it over others and we know it by many names such as racism, misogyny, xenophobia, nativism. In all of her stories – but particularly in her series *Dawn, Imago* and *Adulthood Rites*, collected in the volume *Lilith's Brood* (2001) – Octavia advances the notion that we are hierarchical by nature, an intelligent species genetically hardwired to figure out ways to claim superiority and exert power over others – even to our own destruction. The matter-of-fact, almost non-judgmental way the idea is presented spoke to me, to my life-long struggle with ambition, ego, mistrust and fear. It feels as true to me now as it did 15 years ago and remains oddly comforting. We are what we are, but we have the power – the intelligence – to resist. But will we? Octavia's stories offer no easy answers.

Over the years, I bought and gave as gifts paperback sets of the *Dawn–Adulthood Rites–Imago* series. It's a saga about a race of space aliens, a tall, African American woman named Lilith, and their corporeal partnership to reverse the self-inflicted near-extinction of human beings on Earth. Whether tentacled Oankali or two-legged Earthling, the people Octavia created feel familiar, true to life. No matter how far out in space or how far back in time or how far gone in mind and body, these people are as real – sometimes horribly so – as the breathing being that sleeps within or beside us. Octavia's people are as real as she was.

We met in person for the first time in the late 1990s, when she came to Washington, D.C. to give a lecture at the Hirshhorn Museum. There was that voice, soft and strong, telling funny stories and offering straightforward advice about the key elements of a writing life: Research; Realism; Description; Details; Family Stories; Serendipity; Persistence; Go on Learning; Walk the Ground You Want to Write About; Write Your Passion. As you see, I took notes. Afterward, I stood in line with the other excited fans to get an autograph. When my turn came, I babbled stupidly that I just loved her work and I, too, always intended to write. At that point, she looked up and said, not unkindly, "Well, you'd better get to it!" and she smiled right at me. It was a great day.

A year or so later, I decided to pitch an essay idea to Octavia, through her agents. At the time, I was cultural editor for *NPR News*. As part of the network's coverage of the upcoming United Nations Conference on Racism (which America's first black Secretary of State, Colin Powell, chose to boycott), I thought it would be interesting to ask a writer to imagine a world in which racism did not exist. It turned out that Octavia E. Butler was a big public radio fan and she accepted the commission. The fan in me freaked out a bit when her agent gave me her home number in Seattle. But I concentrated on the work and Octavia proved to be a rarity in my professional experience – sane, low-maintenance, creative, unpretentious, professional, direct, unsentimental, genuinely kind and a whole lot of fun. Her segment aired on NPR's *Weekend Edition Saturday* with Scott Simon, and afterward, I called to finalize our business arrangements and to thank her for the opportunity to work with her. We ended up talking for hours.

In the years since that first conversation, we clocked weeks of phone time. I could feel it in my bones when it was time for a talk with Octavia and that's when my phone would ring or I would find her voice on my answering machine, or I would pick up the phone and call Seattle. We talked about politics and the state of the world, family, friends, our bodies, her work, my job, men, women, black folk, white folk and every color of folk in between. She never mentioned the MacArthur "genius" grant awarded to her in 1995. We talked about her grandmother's place out in the California desert, my daughter's trials and triumphs, her cousin's stroke, my mother's knee surgery. In fact, while I managed my mother's recuperation in Ohio, Octavia sent me tapes of the BBC's original *Hitchhiker's Guide to the Galaxy* to keep me entertained. I still listen to those hand-labeled dubs from her vast collection of dependably low-tech audio cassette recordings.

Octavia loved it that people loved what she wrote. She did not pretend to be bored with celebrity or annoyed by admiration. In 2002, we were both in New Orleans to participate in "Anthropology off the Shelf in the 21st Century" during the American Anthropological Association's Centennial Meeting. When our work was done, we went exploring together and found an African American bookstore. And yes, there on the shelf was *Kindred* (1979), Octavia's now classic novel about a modern, middle-class black woman who is snatched backward in time and into slavery. As Octavia examined the display, the two black women behind the counter recognized her. They squealed with pleasure when she confirmed that indeed, she was Octavia E. Butler – the writer. She stood pleased and calm, as the women ran around grabbing up copies of *Kindred* for Octavia to sign. Her pleasure in the moment warmed everyone in the room.

Octavia traveled a lot to speaking engagements at colleges and writers' conferences. She was a careful eater and traveled with her own provisions. Sometimes Octavia complained about her struggle with writers' block brought on by medication for a heart condition, which was caused by the high blood pressure that ran in her family. She told hilariously graphic stories about medicinal side effects. But there was nothing funny about her decision to destroy a novel she had managed to complete despite her writer's block. She dismissed my outrage by saying in her matter-of-fact way, "Well, it just wasn't any good." About this time, she started thinking and reading about vampires and for my birthday that year, she mailed me three paperback vampire novels – rollicking reads that were part of Octavia's research for her final novel, *Fledgling* (2005).

Octavia E. Butler was a traveler who did not drive. Until her health interfered, she walked and rode city buses. She let others pilot the planes, trains, automobiles and Amazon River boats that took her where she wanted to go. She told me once that she tried to learn to drive during her late teens, but found the experience confusing and dangerous for others. Driving disagreed with the way her mind worked, so she gave it up as a waste of time and adopted other ways of reaching her destination – here on earth and out there in the vast reaches of her imagination. Unlike most of us, Octavia always knew what she wanted to be. As she wrote in 2001: "I am a 53-year-old writer who can remember being a 10-year-old writer and who expects someday to be an 80-year-old writer. I'm also comfortably asocial – a hermit in the middle of Seattle – a pessimist if I'm not careful, a feminist, a black, a former Baptist, an oil-and-water combination of ambition, laziness, insecurity, certainty and drive." Octavia was right about everything except her allotment of time – just 58 years.

For a while after she passed, I kept calling her number. For a time, the answering machine would pick up. I would listen to her voice and hang up. Later, the phone would just ring and finally, a computerized voice told me that her number had been disconnected. Now, when I feel that itch to talk to Octavia, I read something she wrote and I remember the promise she made as we ended each of our conversations: "I'll be talking to ya." And in the way that mattered most to her, she still does.

References

Ball, Sharon. 2006. Octavia Butler: Eye on the Stars, Feet on the Ground. National Public Radio, March 4. 2006. www.npr.org/templates/story/story.php?storyId=5245686. Accessed August 27, 2008.

Butler, Octavia E. 1993. *Parable of the Sower*. New York: Four Walls, Eight Windows.

Butler, Octavia E. 2000. *Lilith's Brood*. New York: Warner.

Butler, Octavia E. 2004. *Kindred*, 25th Anniversary Edition. Boston: Beacon Press.

Butler, Octavia E. 2005. *Fledgling*. New York: Seven Stories Press.

11

Believing in Anthropology as Literature

Ruth Behar

> *When I sit down to make my stories I know very well that I want to take the reader by the throat, break her heart, and heal it again. With that intention I cannot sort out myself, say this part is for the theorist, this for the poet, this for the editor, and this for the wayward ethnographer who wants to document my experience.*
>
> Dorothy Allison, "Believing in Literature"

My editor asks me gently, she knows I might take offense.

"Would you consider allowing us to omit that line from the blurb, where it says your book is a work of cultural anthropology?" Trying to reassure me, she adds, "The rest of the blurb is wonderful. We'll use it prominently on the back cover. But since we're marketing the book as a trade book, we need to reach the general reader, and any reference to an academic discipline is a turn-off. They say it's toxic. They've done studies. I strongly advise we make the cut."

Mind you, my book is being published in a small edition by a university press, not in industrial quantities by a commercial publisher. You won't find it for sale at Wal-Mart. But these days even university presses keep a nervous eye on the bottom line, especially when they're trying to market a book that's about a somewhat sexy topic. My new book, *An Island Called Home* (2007), is about Cuba. And Jews. The combination is exotic enough that it might attract some interest beyond the academy. That is why my editor would have me forgo the gorgeous line of endorsement that makes me absolutely ecstatic, the line that describes my book as "cultural anthropology that rises to the level of great literature."

This blurb makes me happy because I've been telling students for years that the writing we do as cultural anthropologists, what we call "ethnography," *is* a form of literature, a unique variety of "creative non-fiction" that has yet to be taught in Master of Fine Arts programs. At the same time, I've let them know about the huge fear of good writing in anthropol-ogy – the assumption being that good writing has a scary tendency to be precious, to be too full of itself, to be self-indulgent (always a no-no in anthropology), to be a distraction from the pressing reality at hand that needs to be analyzed rigorously and unselfishly. It is as if a stringent work ethic got established in anthropology from its earliest days, disdaining the idea that ethnography as a literary form could be a source of pleasure. Good writing became associated with frilliness, with caviar, champagne, and dark chocolate truffles. The mission of ethnography required that we sacrifice such bourgeois privileges and get down and dirty with the natives. A certain moral righteousness ordained that we not spotlight the ethnographer car-rying out the work, but rather those heroic people at the margins of history and capitalist development who could be assisted in their quest for cultural survival through our attention, activism, and publications. Ethnographic writing had to be as pure, unadorned, and unscented as Ivory soap, and go in and get the job done.

Even with such restrictions, there have always been ethnographers who have shone as writers and whose artistic longings have poignantly risen above our second-fiddle genre. I've also been telling students that we need to take our writing seriously and learn the art of ethnography from the master writers in our field – among them Ruth Benedict, Zora Neale Hurston, Claude Lévi-Strauss, Barbara Myerhoff, John Gwaltney, and Clifford Geertz. It was Clifford Geertz (2000) who characterized ethno-graphic writing as "thick description" and famously portrayed the Balinese cockfight in ornate language that laid out its fictions and metaphors, not to mention its complex politics.

Geertz was admirably talented, prolific, and creative. But he didn't exist in a vacuum. He couldn't have done the work he did if there hadn't been a tribe of writers disguised as anthropologists who, like him, had found ways to reinvent the genre of ethnography by brilliantly mixing together travel stories, memoirs, biographic vignettes, and cultural analysis, all in the service of creating vivid accounts rooted in fieldwork, the rite of passage which consists in spending stretches of time interacting with other people to learn how they find meaning in the world.

Some members of this tribe of writers have traveled far away, as did Claude Lévi-Strauss (1992), who went into the jungle regions of Brazil and wrote with deep existentialist angst about the "sad tropics." Others returned home, as did Zora Neale Hurston (1990), going back to Eatonville, Florida, to examine her own town through what she called the "spy glass" of anthropology. The destination isn't what makes their writing sparkle. It's the way these authors ponder the question of how people think about belonging *someplace*. It's the detail and sensuality with which they evoke an elusive *beingthereness*. It's the degree of honesty and fearlessness they bring to their meditations on the purpose of their own journeys.

Aware of this history that precedes me in anthropology, I proudly say to my editor, "My book is a work of cultural anthropology. Why should I hide it?"

And she, "You're going to scare away readers. They're going to think it's a textbook, the usual standard fare in anthropology. Boring stuff."

Now what I feel is shame. I feel exposed, shorn of a great and wonderful illusion, like the emperor finding out the truth about his new clothes.

Forget what I've been telling students for years. What I've been telling them is a fancier version of what I've been telling myself. As a young woman I'd wanted to be a writer, but I became a cultural anthropologist. Anthropology seduced me. I was a child-immigrant from Cuba and irresistibly drawn to the topics that anthropology adores – identity, culture, displacement. How could I not be enamored of the passport that anthropology gave me to travel, to spend long periods of time abroad in Spanish-speaking countries, including back in Cuba, as a voluntary exile? I figured I'd find my way as a writer eventually by studying anthropology.

It's taken a while, but I tell myself I *am* a writer. I do cultural anthropology *as a writer*. I feel I'm part of an anthropological tribe of wannabe writers, some of them heartbroken, some of them not. Clifford Geertz's early ambition was to be a novelist, but he gave up the dream for anthropology and wrote in a marvelously witty *New-Yorkerish* voice as an anthropologist. I don't think he had any regrets. Ruth Benedict penned poems that were so clichéd they're best allowed to retreat into oblivion, but she wrote with memorable lyricism about Native American Pueblo cultures. I think she did have regrets about giving up poetry; she felt so uncomfortable about also wanting to be a poet that she published her poems under the pseudonyms Ruth Stanhope and Anne Singleton.[1] Only a handful of anthropologists have gained distinction as anthropologists and creative artists, most notably Zora Neale Hurston. For the most part, I believe it is repressed, or sublimated, artistic longing that feeds the creative spirit in anthropology.

By wanting to scratch out the line that tied me to my chosen field, my editor reminded me of a reality I hadn't wanted to face: no matter how hard I might try to turn cultural anthropology into literature, the majority of people out there, including some very well-educated folks, aren't going to see things the way I do. For these potential readers, to say you're a cultural anthropologist is *a turn-off*, or at best an invitation to a conversation

[1]   I discuss Ruth Benedict's poetry in Behar 2008.

in which they ask, *Oh, so what have you dug up lately?* and in which you try to let them know you're not Indiana Jones. *No, I don't go digging for bones or pots or ancient civilizations, I simply talk to people and write about how they see the world.* Before you've finished your tale, your companion's eyes are glazing over with boredom.

For better or for worse, my kind editor doesn't want to hurt my feelings. She's given up trying to convince me to erase the line about my book being a work of cultural anthropology. It's going to be printed on the back cover. Call me naive, call me a hapless dreamer, but I'm going to cling to that line, which tells me my efforts haven't been in vain, that the decision I made long ago wasn't totally foolish. I'm going to cling to that line because it lets others know I come to my writing via cultural anthropology. Whether they like it or not, I found my voice slowly, painfully, writing my way into and out of anthropology. That's the truth. It would be a lie to pretend otherwise.

Like Dorothy Allison, who studied anthropology in New York before giving it up to become a fiction writer, I too want "to take the reader by the throat, break her heart, and heal it again" (1994: 180). I too believe in literature, believe in the power of the written word to do good work in the world. And through my work, I've been trying to make myself and others believe that anthropology can also be a way of doing literature.

So I am delighted, at least initially, when I receive an email message from a Latino anthropology student in New York, who writes, "After reading your book, *The Vulnerable Observer* [1996] you have given me a greater appreciation for all the sacrifices that my mother and many other Latinas have made for their families. You have greatly inspired me, as a Latino, and I know that once my sister reads your book, she will also be inspired." He then goes on to say, "I was confused about whether or not anthropology was to be my road. I had doubts that I would be an effective anthropologist since the gringos dominate the field. Yet after reading your book ... and reading more on indigenous anthropologists and historians ... I have realized that this is my destiny." He thanks me and signs himself "a brother of Colombian background."

When I get messages like this, I am amazed that a complete stranger has found something in my writing that speaks to him. I had not envisioned a young man, a young Latino, as a reader of my book. I am extremely moved that he took the trouble to look me up and write me warm words of praise and solidarity.

At the same time, I worry. My readers frequently seem to find things in my writing that I didn't know I had put there. I try to think, in this case, about what exactly I said in my book that would have led my reader to be grateful for the sacrifices his mother and other Latinas have made for their families. I mean, I don't mind that this is a message he took away, but as far as I can remember, I never discussed specifically the issue of Latina self-sacrifice in my book. So I worry about how it is that meanings, even meanings we approve of, get inscribed in our texts independently of our will as writers.

But this is not the only or even the main reason I worry. I worry for yet another reason. What worries me more is that something I have written has inspired another person to want to enter the field of anthropology. I know it is heretical to say this. After all, it would seem that the aim of anthropologists, who seek to write books that readers will want to pull off the shelf, should be to entice would-be disciples to join our discipline. But I worry, I worry sincerely, about the burden of responsibility I feel when I am told I have inspired someone to pursue anthropology. I worry because I do not consider my work to be representative of what most anthropologists consider anthropology. I worry about my lack of a sense of authority in this discipline where I reside, still uncertainly, often disloyally, and sometimes, I feel, illegally. Who am I to dare to lead others into my anthropology? What if my anthropology is a flimsy raft that won't deliver my trusting reader to a safe harbor? What if my reader, depending on me, doesn't make it to the other side?

I worry because I know that even though anthropology has changed in the last few decades – changed to the point where some of us can say out loud, as Virginia Domínguez (2000: 361–93) recently has, that what we need to pursue in anthropology is a "politics of love and rescue" – it really has not changed all that much, not enough yet. I don't tell my Latino reader this, but I think to myself that maybe he was right to be apprehensive about the gringos who dominate the field. Most efforts to bring emotions and feelings, including love and gratitude, into our work are likely to be dismissed as "feminine sentimentality."

I worry that my published words are too utopian, that they will not protect my reader from the sharks and stormy currents that lie ahead. I worry that I have shooed away his quite legitimate fears, which he ought to continue to take seriously, so he will be ready to swim, or at least, float, if the raft he has found in my words gets torn apart in midstream.

It is not just this lone Latino reader I seem to have encouraged to join me on my humble raft. Messages keep arriving, usually via email, like secret notes in bottles thrown to the sea, the messengers unsure whether I will receive, let alone reply to their request for . . . well, for what exactly? I think what they're requesting of me, those readers who write to me, is simply that I acknowledge and support their desire to be the kind of vulnerable observers they wish to be.

Let me cite two other email messages regarding *The Vulnerable Observer* that came to me from women readers. One reader, whom I later met while she was visiting Ann Arbor, wrote, "I know you probably get tons of emails telling you this, but even in the early stage that I am in, it speaks so much to feelings I have about so many things. I am in the process of deciding what career path I am going to take and how much of what I believe corresponds to what anthro is (should be?). For example, I am an African-American woman, I have received Orula and Los Guerreros [Santería deities]. I could never imagine studying my own *ile* [Santería house] and I feel as though I would be invading if I went into another as a 'scientist.' I, or at least my ancestors, have been the 'other' and I have a really hard time with separating myself from the people/things I want to study. Yet, on the other hand, I want to know and learn and it is personal in the sense that I want something that is very dear to me to be portrayed accurately, not sensationalized." Another female student of anthropology, who doesn't reveal her background, writes, "I have grappled with the sterility and short-sightedness of Anthropology, so much so that I have seriously considered abandoning it altogether. Thank you for renewing my faith in living and learning as an honest human being. I now feel that I can explore Anthropology without the veil that hinders me both creatively and intellectually. I am greatly looking forward to the progression of the field as you and others with your bravery are acknowledging the multifaceted eye."

My vulnerable writing produces, or seems to call forth, a vulnerable reader, a reader I am helpless to save, a reader who follows me at his or her own risk. What my vulnerable readers want is to do intellectual work that will not alienate them from themselves or from those whom they seek to understand and eventually write about. In me they feel they have found a guide, even though I have issued a warning in my book to follow me only if they don't mind going places without a map.

But maybe I shouldn't worry so much about my readers. If they've found my writing, if they've taken the time to let me know my writing has meant something to them, they've probably already thrown away their map.

When I think of my own progression as a writer, I believe I have gone from trying to write for my teachers to trying now, in the most recent phase of my work, to write for my mother so I could write for the world.

My mother is the only reader I ever see in my mind when I'm writing. Even though I'm fluent in Spanish, I do most of my writing in English, and my mother's English, even after 45 years in the United States, is still heavily accented with the Cuban Spanish that is her native tongue. She didn't go to college and never read a book or had intellectual aspirations while I was growing up, but for the past 30 years she's been in an academic environment as an administrator of diplomas at New York University, a job from which she will soon retire. I am very aware that I had to turn away from my mother in order to become the person I became. But I suffer bouts of imposter syndrome. My father made sure I learned to type at the age of ten. Sometimes I fear that I too was only meant to be a secretary.

My mother reads much more now than she used to. She reads the *New York Post* and *Vanidades* and an occasional Danielle Steele novel, but when she hungers for stories, she turns to her favorite *telenovelas* on Spanish television. My writing she will read religiously, the writing I tell her about and show her – I've become more cunning as I've grown older, hiding writing from her that is too revealing about our family and that I know she won't like, or writing that is too revealing of my feelings and divulges secrets I'd rather she didn't know. For example, I hope she won't read this. I certainly don't plan on showing it to her. Not that there's anything here that would offend her. I just need to know that I'm writing something she could read, but won't read. How absurd this must seem. Writing remains so fraught for me. It is fraught with the desire to please my mother and my shame about my mother and my shame that I'm ashamed. Will my mother be able to read what I write? I hope so and I dread it at the same time.

My first book was my dissertation, *The Presence of the Past in a Spanish Village* (1991). I look back at it now with a mixture of embarrassment and sorrow. Embarrassment because the theoretical perspective was limited, the writing uninspired, and the vision of who might read the book terribly narrow, terribly untrusting of the possibility that anyone beyond the specific field of Spanish village studies would ever want to read the book. And sorrow because I knew much more than I was capable of writing at the time about the people who shared their lives with me, and now it is too late to tell those stories; they are gone, and the anthropologist I was then, the anthropologist who heard those stories and could have told those stories, is also gone.

The odd thing was I thought I was writing for my teachers, but in fact I was writing for an image, a mirage, of what I assumed to be proper academic work, as I see my own students doing now. I recall my teacher James Fernandez candidly saying to me, when I turned in my dissertation, that he had expected me to produce something much more literary, something much less canonical. I had his permission to do the creative writing I so much wanted to do, but the weight of the academy bore down on my shoulders. I wrote a book that, as far as I'm concerned, failed me and failed my informants. But this book got me tenure in anthropology at the University of Michigan. It was the only book I'd written when I was blessed to receive the MacArthur Foundation "genius" award.

As I was contemplating how to write about the experiences I'd had in Spain, I read John Berger's *Pig Earth* (1992) and loved it, loved the way it reached deep into the everyday mud, wine, cows, sheep, and desire of European peasants. But to have written a book like Berger's required a degree of courage, security, and self-confidence, not to mention writing skill, I did not yet have. I was trying then to find my voice in and through academic anthropology, for which Berger's book wasn't an acceptable model.

By the time I was ready to write my second book, *Translated Woman* (1993), I knew that I didn't want to repeat the mistake of writing a book that disappointed me. I wanted to produce a book that took more risks, a book that didn't seek approval, a book that was naughty, a book that would be rigorous, feminist, engaged with issues of anthropological storytelling, while at the same time being emotionally compelling. And yet with this book as with my first, I knew at the time that there were options that would have made the book more accessible to a wider audience, and that, more importantly, would have plumbed its literary potential, and again I didn't pursue those options out of fear of rupturing my ties to the academic world.

One of the first readers of an early draft of my manuscript was the writer Sandra Cisneros and she suggested I take Esperanza's stories and completely reshape them, mixing and matching sentences from here and from there in her narrative, blending Esperanza's stories with my own fictional elaborations, and creating my own version of her tale in the style of a testimonial novel. At the time I couldn't follow this suggestion, tempting though it was. I felt I had recorded a life history in a certain order and in a certain voice and in a particular historical moment and that it was important to maintain its integrity as far as possible, even if Esperanza's story was going to have to be highly edited in order to be readable as a book.

While I couldn't turn Esperanza's story into a novel, the strategy I finally used combined a novelistic and a scholarly voice. The book begins with Esperanza telling her story with few interruptions from me. Only the categories of "rage" and "redemption," which I used to structure her story, reveal my presence as a storylistener. I kept Esperanza's story in the order she told it to me and added no fictional elaborations. But I did edit her words to highlight the dramatic punch of her story. This part of the book, readers tell me, does read like a novel. It is the part of the book, certainly, that my mother enjoyed most. The book then proceeds to an account of my relationship with Esperanza. There I explore her life as a marketing woman and the comical way in which I traipsed after her during her trips to the city to sell fruits and vegetables from her plastic buckets. In the last section, I move to a series of feminist, historical, and autobiographical interpretations of her story. I wrote this section knowing I wanted *Translated Woman* to be read and discussed in the academy.

I am sure my mother skipped over most of my interpretive ruminations, with the exception of the concluding autobiographical chapter of the book, "The Biography in the Shadow," which addressed the clashes I'd had with my father in wanting to become an intellectual, and pained her and my father in ways that I came later to regret. In that chapter, which some readers love and others detest, I explored the wrenching process by which I came to be an educated, privileged woman scripting Esperanza's story into my book. It was a mere 20 pages, but this chapter proved to be the most controversial part of the book. In Deborah Gordon's eloquent words, it was there that I dared to address "the difficult position of women in the academy who reap the rewards and still want to criticize the very system that has rewarded them so generously."

Both *Translated Woman* (1993) and later *The Vulnerable Observer* (1996), a collection of personal essays about my ethnographic experiences in Spain, Cuba, and the United States, are books I think of as having one foot in the academy and one foot outside. They are located uneasily between the world of scholarship and the world of creative non-fiction, not entirely satisfying the requirements of either, yet hoping for joint citizenship in both.

When I think about my basic criterion – will my mother be able to read what I write? – I realize I didn't fulfill my goal in these books. Although they're largely devoid of jargon and other forms of exclusionary writing, they were still written for my teachers, in other words, responding to the internalized presence and pressure of the academy, even now that I am a teacher myself and should feel more free to change the rules. Thinking of myself as writing for my mother has allowed me to move my writing beyond what was permissible in the academy. But it isn't easy to balance for long periods of time on the one foot that's standing shakily outside the door of the university that provides my bread and butter.

When I was a young woman, I wasn't confident enough to call myself a writer. That felt too presumptuous. But I could say I was an anthropologist who wrote. The writing was being done for a higher purpose – to elucidate the stories of those who didn't have access to the written word and to publishing. This made it possible for me to write. I was a scribe, putting down on paper other people's stories for posterity. It was only as I grew older and more confident that I started wanting to be a writer who also put her own story into the text of other people's stories. I was ready to stand on my own two feet. Without the crutches that anthropology had given me when I was wobbly.

More and more, I dare to think I can call myself a writer, plain and simple. But I can't forget that I took up the pen for the same reason all anthropologists do: because we care passionately about the worlds that others inhabit and not just about our own small worlds. Of course, writers of literature claim to feel the same way, even without obtaining degrees in anthropology. The difference is that anthropologists would be booed out of the discipline if any of us attempted to do what Nathan Englander just did in his new novel, *The Ministry of Special Cases* (2007), which is set in Argentina – spend ten years writing about a place he only visited once for a weekend before beginning the writing. To be taken seriously, anthropologists must visit the places they write about, not once, but over and over. Our imaginations are in service to real communities we know firsthand and to real journeys we've taken across land and sea. And this isn't a bad thing at all, so long as we know how to spin a tale about all that we've witnessed.

I know I have said that ethnography at its best is just another form of creative non-fiction, but I still often think that one day I will have to stop being an anthropologist in order to write stories that can truly be called literature. For reasons I myself don't fully understand, I keep putting off that day. I guess anthropology continues to seduce me. Or maybe, like a turtle, I've created an anthropology that I can carry on my back, an anthropology that I can live in and also hide within. At the same time, I feel that I have yet to do the writing I was put on this earth to do. Maybe that sounds pessimistic, but I feel it's optimistic. Knowing I still have more writing to do keeps me going, keeps me returning yet again to the blank page.

I would love to believe that my latest effort at writing as a cultural anthropologist "rises to the level of great literature." I know it doesn't. I wish it did. Still, I'm grateful for this generous overstatement that will be on the back cover of my book. Thanks to my editor's warning, I'm prepared to lose numerous potential readers, who will return the book to the shelf as soon as they see it's a work of cultural anthropology. But I pray there will be some readers who will take the book off the shelf and try to imagine for a moment, along with me, that anthropology has all the potential to inspire a story that takes you by the throat and won't let you go, a story perhaps worthy of being placed on that mighty pedestal we call literature.

116   *Ruth Behar*

References

Allison, Dorothy. 1994. Believing in Literature. From *Skin: Talking about Sex, Class, and Literature*. Ithaca, NY: Firebrand Books.

Behar, Ruth. 1991. *The Presence of the Past in a Spanish Village: Santa María del Monte*. Princeton, NJ: Princeton University Press.

Behar, Ruth. 1993. *Translated Woman: Crossing the Border with Esperanza's Story*. Boston: Beacon Press.

Behar, Ruth. 1996. *The Vulnerable Observer: Anthropology that Breaks Your Heart* Boston: Beacon Press.

Behar, Ruth. 2007. *An Island Called Home: Returning to Jewish Cuba*. New Brunswick, NJ: Rutgers University Press.

Behar, Ruth. 2008. Between Poetry and Anthropology: Searching for Languages of Home. In *Arts-Based Inquiry in Education: Foundations for Practice*. Melisa Cahnmann-Taylor and Richard Siegesmund, eds., pp. 55–71. New York: Routledge.

Berger, John. 1992. *Pig Earth*. New York: Vintage.

Domínguez, Virginia. 2000. For a Politics of Love and Rescue. *Cultural Anthropology* 15(3): 361–93.

Englander, Nathan. 2007. *The Ministry of Special Cases*. New York: Knopf.

Geertz, Clifford. 2000. *The Interpretation of Cultures*. New York: Basic Books.

Hurston, Zora Neale. 1990. *Mules and Men*. New York: Harper Perennial. [1935]

Lévi-Strauss, Claude. 1992. *Tristes Tropiques*. New York: Penguin. [1955]

III
Receptions

12

Walking in Zora's Shoes or "Seek[ing] Out de Inside Meanin' of Words": The Intersections of Anthropology, Ethnography, Identity, and Writing

Irma McClaurin

> *Words got a hidden meaning. . . . Most people is thin-brained. They's born wid they feet under the moon. Some folks is born wid they feet on the sun and they kin seek out de inside meanin' of words.*
>
> Zora Neale Hurston, *Mules and Men*[1]

I count myself among that generation of Black anthropologists and writers strongly influenced by Zora's example. I cannot say that I followed Zora's path consciously. Nor can I say for sure now whether it was Zora who brought me to Florida to teach anthropology at the University of Florida,[2] or whether it was the warm weather, and the fact that azaleas bloom madly in the spring, and the Spanish moss drips off the oak trees lending a delicate beauty to the Florida landscape. I can only say that now, having read her letters to Langston [Hughes], having perused her handwritten and typed manuscripts, her spirit walks with me.

Irma McClaurin, *Belle Lettres: "Dear Langston, Love Zora"*

---

[1] Cited in Burrows 2001.

[2] I was an Assistant Professor at the University of Florida from 1995–9. I became the first African American faculty member to receive tenure and promotion to Associate Professor in 1999. I served as the first director of the Zora Neale Hurston African Diaspora Research Project during this time, and resigned from the University in 2005.

Tracing Zora's Footprint

I vividly recall reading Zora Neale Hurston's *Mules and Men* on my first road trip from Massachusetts to South Carolina in 1974. I had just pub-lished my second book of poems, *Song in the Night*. Somehow, reading Zora seemed the right thing to do, as we passed long hours in the car. Her language and vivid ethnographic descriptions kept us amused, and prepared us for the many instances of interesting and out-of-the way places and people we would encounter. Ordinary. Yet not.

At the time, I knew Zora only by her literary reputation. Little did I know how embedded I would become in her other life as an anthropologist. I was not prescient and could not have foretold how much she would become intertwined in my future.

Thirty-four years later, I once again turn to Zora as my muse in writing this essay. Her dualistic life – anthropologist and writer – has served as a paradigm for me to follow as I navigated my way from a literary back-ground and a career in educational administration to become a card-carrying anthropologist. It was Zora's vision of ethnography as a genre and her ability to use the ethnographic data she collected to inform her literary creations that captured my attention, and made it possible for me to believe that not only could I cross over from the humanities into the social sciences, but that the tools I carried with me would be of value in my new environment. There is no better example of how Zora linked ethnographic observations and anthropological analysis with literature than every-one's favorite novel, *Their Eyes were Watching God*, first published in 1937.

Zora's creation of a strong-minded, independent woman who ultimately eschews cultural conventions in the choices she makes about life and love can be directly traced to her observations on women and gender construc-tions in her ethnography, *Tell My Horse*, published the following year (1938). Zora actually wrote the novel while conducting fieldwork for the ethnography. Additionally, she drew upon her other ethnographic research in the south, using the actual events of the 1928 hurricanes and subsequent floods in Florida[3] as the final setting for Janie's transformation into a truly independent soul.

---

[3]   The flood and aftermath that Janie and Teacake face are referenced in an article by Luigi Monge. The abstract states: "This study focuses on the five known African-American topical songs dealing with the two hurricanes and ensuing floods that took place in Florida in the summer of 1928."

The novel is reflexive as it presents us with a heroine who is not unlike the independent researcher/writer Zora; it is also observant and draws upon the rich data Zora collected on social position and stratification of women in the Caribbean, specifically Haiti and Jamaica. At the start of the novel, Janie, the protagonist, is somewhat passive in her own life, and is admonished not to challenge the status quo by her grandmother who speaks the most powerful line in the novel – the black woman "is de mule uh de world." In making that statement, the grandmother seemingly casts Janie's fate in the tradition of being subordinate to men, marrying because that's what women do, and being required to give up daydreaming. Through the grandmother's acquiescence to her own fate as a subordinated woman, we come to understand that some women are constrained by gender conventions. But the novel does not stand on conventionality. The reader is invited to follow Janie's life and observe the choices she makes. From Janie, who challenges her grandmother's attempts to enculturate her, we learn about resistance, human agency, and how some women actually defy gender conventions. Because of the novel's ethnographic richness, we also gain insight into the life ways of black rural folk, the role of community in shaping social roles and social compliance, and how small communities react to natural disasters such as floods and the accompanying challenges they bring to faith, hope and love – decades before Katrina.

These literary and anthropological, or autoethnographic, elements of Zora's writings anticipate writing trends in anthropology now often associated with scholars such as Ruth Behar (*Translated Woman*, 1993) and James Clifford (*The Predicament of Culture*, 1988), and also predict the debates about identity, representation and writing articulated in *Writing Culture* (Clifford and Marcus 1986) and *Women Writing Culture* (Behar and Gordon 1996). The missing element in the historicization and discussions of these now not-so-new ethnographic trends has been, and continues to be, Zora's omission as a significant contributor. If James Clifford 1988 and Vincent Crapanzano 1980 can be invoked as forefathers of new directions in ethnography, then Zora surely has earned the right to be positioned alongside Ruth Behar and Trinh Minh-Ha – as female and feminist progenitors of innovations in ethnography and as warrior women unafraid to cross literary and anthropological borders simultaneously.

In my first ethnography, *Women of Belize: Gender and Change in Central America* (2000a[1996]), I wrote about observing the same complexities and contradictions of gender constructions that Zora captured in her writings, both literary and ethnographic. Zora builds the character of Janie by revealing her private musings that ultimately conflict with her grandmother's beliefs about what it means to be a woman and marriage.

[Janie] was stretched on her back beneath the pear tree soaking in the alto chant of the visiting bees, the gold of the sun and the panting breath of the breeze when the inaudible voice of it all came to her. She saw a dust-bearing bee sink into the sanctum of a bloom; the thousand sister-calyxes arch to meet the love embrace and the ecstatic shiver of the tree from root to tiniest branch creaming in every blossom and frothing with delight. So this was marriage! Then Janie felt a pain remorseless sweet that left her limp and languid. . . . "Ah wants to see you married right away." . . . Somebody done spoke to me 'bout you long time ago." . . . "Nanny, who – who dat been askin' you for me?" "Brother Logan Killicks. He's a good man, too." . . . The vision of Logan Killicks was desecrating the pear tree, but Janie didn't know how to tell Nanny that. She merely hunched over and pouted at the floor. (1990[1937]: 10–11, 12–13)

Witnessing Gender through Life Histories

In choosing the life history method, which relies upon a narrative structure, like Zora, I was able to elicit from Belizean women their innermost thoughts about their lives, their gender roles, and the cultural contradictions with which they grappled on a daily basis, all the while drawing upon the best biographical and autobiographical traditions in literature and dialogic, reflexive and autoethnographic traditions in anthropology. Reflecting some years later on the use of life history as a methodological strategy, I wrote this explanation:

> I think both feminist and indigenous scholars who are interested in document-ing, *salvaging* – that is, rescuing from waste, destruction, and invisibility – the richness of the past and the nuances of the present, have efficaciously used narrative in their diverse configurations of life histories, testimonies, autoeth-nographies, memories, and memoirs as a precise and rigorous methodological tool. (McClaurin 1999)

Is it effective? Let me respond with the following letter from a reader. In 2002, I received an unexpected "review" of *Women of Belize* in an email. I do not believe I have ever received such a compelling justification for why it is important to write in ways that move our communication beyond the scholarly constraints that have shaped most academic writing, and truly get at what Zora called "de inside meanin' of words." This reader's letter serves as a caveat and a reminder of what Caroline B. Brettell calls the "the politics of audience reception – of how ethnography is received and interpreted not only by anthropological colleagues and the general public, but also, and most especially, by those who are the subjects, directly or indirectly, of anthropological investigations" (Brettell 1996: 3).

Dear Professor McClaurin,
    Please excuse my intrusion into your web space. I was born in Belize and although I have lived in the United States for 31 years, I still think of myself as a "Belizean." I want to thank you for the invaluable gift you gave me in the form of your book, "Women of Belize: Gender and Change in Central America." Currently, I am a third year doctoral student in the School of Nursing at ——. I plan to conduct my dissertation study in Belize and evaluate Belizean women's vulnerability for HIV infection. Your book has proven to be a valuable tool in writing my dissertation.
    Also, it has touched my personal life in a manner that I find difficult to express in writing. As much as I wanted to believe that I was different from women in Belize because I have lived in The [*sic*] U.S. most of my life, reading your book made me feel as though I was looking in a mirror. I did not realized [*sic*] the extent to which living in our ethnic enclaves in the US had perpetuated our culture. There is no difference between us (Belizean women in the US) and them (women in Belize), except in our minds and geographic locations. There will never be any true difference until our eyes are opened to the reality of our existence. Then and only then will we become forever changed.
    As I read the book, my first response was anger – How dare you expose us? After reading your book, I felt naked, revealed. I experienced emotions similar to those described by victims of rape or incest. I felt ashamed and dirty but relieved that the secret was out and, miraculously, you understood and was [*sic*] compassionate. It was as though I had been found not guilty and by extension all Belizean women were declared innocent. I want to thank you for your gift, "I am forever changed." Needless to say, you will be cited extensively in my dissertation. In the future, I hope I will be able to apply my knowledge and experience [*sic*] to help my sisters in Belize in their struggle for autonomy. Thank you.

The significance of this letter for me as anthropologist/ethnographer/ writer is its demonstration of the power our words have to represent and to shape how the world sees a particular place, a particular group of people, or an individual. Whether we are writing for or against culture, we have taken upon our shoulders an enormous responsibility that is beyond any allegiance we might owe to the academy or any desire for tenure. We hold in our words real people's lives.

Another compelling aspect of this reader's comments that I pay attention to is her articulation of the strength of narrative not only to tell individual stories, but in doing so to implicate readers such as herself in ways that provoke an epiphany that their own life course is not altogether different from the lives rendered in the ethnography they are reading. For this reader, and for others regardless of their origins, W*omen of Belize* compels "bearing witness"[4] to the social reality that *real* women's lives are messy, contradictory, and still in process even as they tell their life stories – and that we are all somehow connected by history, circumstances, gender, our relations to racial systems, and other dimensions of society and culture.

> When I traveled around Belize talking to women of different ethnic groups . . . , I believe it fair to say that some of the women viewed me as "different." I think they saw me not as better, but certainly different, because I had left my children and husband to come and do what I wanted to do. . . . One question we all pondered, despite the differences in our personal circumstances, was whether we as women could ever acquire the requisite freedom to fulfill our own desires. This is not just a woman's question, but a human one. We all feel the need to assert our individual desires at one time or another in our life cycle, yet as social creatures, we are always constrained by societal or community rules, obligations, and expectations. The reality of these constraints may limit our ability to fulfill our desire but in no way diminishes the desire. (2000a[1996]: 13)

Upon finishing the book, some readers have inquired, "What has happened to Zola, Evelyn, and Rose?" Their question brings into relief the strong connection ethnography establishes between reader and subject matter that is a crucial point of engagement. In ethnography, readers care because, as they engage in the details of a real person's life, someone who is not unlike themselves, they shift into that space of the "vulnerable observer," of which Ruth Behar speaks so eloquently. It is also this intersection that embodies the most powerful aspect of anthropology – its capacity to take specific examples and generalize about the human condition. These are also some of the gifts that Zora contributed to anthropology through her folkloric studies, and through the plays and novels she wrote based upon her fieldwork.

---

[4] In the mid-1980s, the late James Baldwin made an arrangement with the University of Massachusetts Amherst to teach every other year. I was privileged to attend his lectures, host him as a guest in my home, and photograph him at these lectures and private events. Publicly, and privately, Baldwin often spoke about how his writing served as a "witness" to the social injustice black Americans faced. In the series of photographs I took of Baldwin lecturing, there is one I have titled "Witness."

Reclaiming Zora from the Shadows of Anthropology

More recently, in an essay entitled "An Autoethnographic Approach to Black Feminism" (2001),[5] I have turned to Zora and positioned her as a black feminist *ancestor* in recognition of her value to the history of anthropology and ethnography. I do so for several reasons. But the most significant is that I wish to re-enshrine her in the canon of interpretive and reflexive anthropology. While there are still debates about the validity of canon formation, in practice we continue to create canons every time we cite the same ethnographers or use their books as "classic" examples of past, present, and cutting-edge anthropology. There is also a feminist canon that has not been as inclusive as it could be, and so those of us who have been relegated to its margins must draw attention not only to ourselves, but to the totality of exclusions that mar feminist history and canon formation. Today, I do not think it too assertive to state that Zora languishes in what I call "the shadows of anthropology."[6]

I wish to bring Zora into the centerfold of anthropology because I think her perspective on what it means to be a "native" anthropologist and her ethnographic methodology were clear innovations in the field at the time; moreover, her perspectives and her rich ethnographies still resonate with many of us today who grapple with these issues under the rubrics of "native" or indigenous, reflexive, and interpretive anthropology. Zora drew upon the best of the black intellectual tradition, which anthropologists such as St. Clair Drake claim as part of their genesis. She used literary conventions as a way to engage the public. She truly understood what she called "de inside meanin' of words." And she sought to leverage their power to tell the stories of those who populated the turpentine camps and citrus camps; though underpaid and economically impoverished, Hurston found them rich in oral traditions of story telling, music, and language formation.

Zora was not always consistent in her scholarship; however, she was an inclusive ethnographer sensitive to the important contributions of

---

[5] This essay appeared in my edited collection, *Black Feminist Anthropology*. In 2003, the collection was named a *Choice Magazine* Outstanding Academic Title.

[6] I am currently working on a bio-history (biography + history) of Zora entitled *Zora Neale Hurston: In the Shadows of Anthropology*. For my other writings on Zora, see References. My discussions of Zora's contributions are archived and available for listening at: National Public Radio: http://wamu.org/programs/kn/01/08/09.php, http://wamu.org/programs/kn/02/04/26.php and Florida Humanities Radio (http://wmfe.convio.net/site/News2?JServSession Idr012=iey4q0r0y4.app13b&news_iv_ctrl=1081&page=NewsArticle&id=6279). Accessed August 27, 2008.

dispossessed women and blacks to culture and society. In this respect, her work predates the grounded approaches of feminist scholars such as Michelle Rosaldo and Louise Lamphere, Florence Babb, Helen Safa, and Connie Sutton, but is very much rooted in what St. Clair Drake termed "salvage anthropology" as reflected in his own work and the works of the late Montague Cobbs, Vera Green, John Gwaltney, and many others. In some respects, with her interests in language, culture and biology, and their intersections, Zora anticipated the new vanguard of African-descended scholars who use bio-cultural, intersectional, and political-economic approaches to interpret the life ways and cultural histories of African-descended people throughout the African diaspora, as represented by Johnnetta B. Cole, Lynn Bolles, Angela Gilliam, Faye V. Harrison, Cheryl Mwaria, Karla Slocum, Terry Weik, Michael Blakey, France Winddance-Twine, Theresa Singleton, and myself. And there is of course the next generation who extend the boundaries and border crossing of the scholarship of black anthropologists even further: Dawn Elissa Fischer, Kevin Foster, David Simmons, Sybil Dione Rosado, Kimberly Eison Simmons, Deborah Thomas, George Jackson, Antoinette Jackson, and Tracy Rone, to name a few. These are, of course, only examples; there are many more African, African American, Latino, Native American, and other indigenous scholars in the field today than when Zora began.

Walkin' Zora's Walk and Talkin' Zora's Talk: Anthropology and Literature

One good example of how I see myself walking in Zora's shoes is my inclusion of the poem "A Mother's Day Blessing" in *Women of Belize: Gender and Change in Central America*. Like Zora, who used Langston Hughes's poetry as an opening to conversation in the field, I used my own poems to introduce myself to members of the community in Belize. It was a Belizean community worker, veterinarian, and writer, Ludwig V. Palacio, who suggested that I write a poem based on local images that would be both familiar to Belizeans and accessible to others. He felt some of the images in my poems were very American-centric, and might get "lost in translation" – his comments were not unlike those that Zora shared with Langston about which of his poems "worked" and which failed to resonate with her audiences in the citrus and turpentine camps.

While I was not consciously thinking about Zora at the time, certainly her use of dramaturgy as a medium for presenting ethnographic findings was a mechanism for "translating" data into forms that could reach multiple audiences. The poem was a success in Belize, published and posted at places where women congregated, worked, and shopped. I also sent a copy to a colleague, Sue Hyatt, who was doing fieldwork among working-class women in England. She shared the poem with them, and wrote to ask if they could read it at an upcoming conference and publish it. Multiple audiences, public engagement: Zora was the precursor and my role model.

A Mother's Day Blessing
Bless the mothers of Back Street, Queen Street,
Main Street, and all the streets that crisscross the corners of "Lemongrass"
    Town and Toledo District;
Bless the mothers soothing and cuddling their crying babies;
Bless the mothers up at 5 A.M to wash clothes and bake bread;
The mothers who don't eat so their children can be full;
Bless the mothers who walk the hot streets and dusty roads in the midday
    sun to sell tamales, bread, and tarts;
Bless the mothers who keep watch from dusk to dawn, without sleep, when
    their child has fever;

To you, the Village women twisting straw into baskets for a few dollars so
    your children's lives will be easier;

To you, the learned women who speak Garifuna, Mopan, Ketchi:
ancestral languages that must not be forgotten;

To you, the dancing women whose feet teach us
rhythms of joy, happiness, and forgetfulness from life's troubles;

To you, the crying women who mourn babies, youths, and husbands:
dead from malnutrition, diseases, alcohol, drugs, and bad luck;

To you, the praying women who only have God to comfort you in hard
times;

To you, the hopeful women who dream of a better life for your daughters;

To you, women all, mothers all
in Lemongrass, in Toledo District,
in Belize, Central America;

To you, women and mothers everywhere:

We say thank you.
With every breath we take,
with every pleasure or pain that we feel,
we say thank you for giving birth to us
for guiding us throughout the years
with love and generosity.

We say Bless You.
        (1996: 40–1; used with permission of Rutgers University Press)

My appreciation for Zora continues to evolve, to such an extent that I
intend to write a book about her "living in the shadows of anthropology."
In doing so, I reclaim her for those of us who are exhausted from the battle
we do constantly in this discipline to prove ourselves worthy of attention
through citations, invitations to present at capstone conferences, and inclusion in books that establish the history and canon of anthropology and
ethnography. Years ago, I wrote that for me "Zora Neale Hurston . . .
stands a woman before her time, testing and blurring boundaries, and
infusing social science with creativity and vision" (McClaurin 2000b: 18).
I think that statement is still true today.

Lost in Translation: The Current Dilemmas of Academic Writing in Anthropology and Elsewhere

Having established that writing is central to anthropology, probably more
so today than in Zora's time, it is ironic that it is the one "skill" we do not
teach. I am mystified how we could expect students to transform the ethnographic data they collect into brilliant dissertations and ethnographies
without training. I make this critique having completed a Masters of Fine
Arts, a professional writing degree comprised of hours spent in writing
workshops. I have served as editor of *Transforming Anthropology* and as
a member of the *Feminist Studies* editorial board. I have worked as a free-
lance journalist, attended numerous writing workshops, and operated my
own consulting business in which I was a speech writer for scholars and
for Dr. Cora Christian,[7] the first woman to enter the governor's race in the
US Virgin Islands in 2003–4. I have also designed and implemented writing
workshops at the annual meetings of the American Anthropological Association and the Caribbean Studies Association.

Throughout my career as an editor, I have witnessed some of the most
turgid writing submitted for publication by scholars known and unknown.
I am shocked by the lack of creativity, poor command of word choice and
grammar usage, and weak syntax. This is especially surprising to be found
among anthropologists where one would expect better, since the discipline
became preoccupied with "writing culture" as early as the 1980s (Marcus
and Fischer 1986; Clifford 1988; Behar and Gordon 1996). At that pivotal
moment, which also marks the emergence of greater reflexivity in ethnography, and a movement towards an interpretive anthropology (Geertz 1973;

---

[7]   Cora Christian is a medical doctor and the sister of the late Barbara Christian, black feminist literary scholar.

see also Marcus and Fischer 1986), one would expect that our methodological training of graduate students would also shift.

It has not. While courses on reflexivity and anthropology, life history methods, and analysis of past and present ethnographic styles abound, there are virtually no courses on "how to" write this new ethnography as part of our formal core graduate or undergraduate curricula. We have analyzed the "new" ethnography to death. Beginning with the dialogic in Vincent Crapazano's *Tuhami: Portrait of a Moroccan* (1980) and fast forwarding to James Clifford's classic essay, "On Ethnographic Authority" (1988 [1983]), published three years later, anthropologists became preoccupied with the shift in what the literary world calls "point of view," followed by critiques of the omniscient narrator, à la Evans-Pritchard in *The Nuer*, from scholars such as Geertz (1988), and finally settling into first-person voices, captured by Ruth Behar's *Translated Woman* (1993). The ethnography of Esperanza's story as told to Behar, and the latter's "biography in the shadows," which chronicles her own story of transformation, are both powerful because of their first-person, and somewhat confessional, perspectives. Yet despite a surge in books that document the importance of narrative and writing in anthropology – most recently Behar's brilliant collection of essays, *The Vulnerable Observer* (1997), and those mentioned previously: Clifford's own eschewing of ethnographic authority, Clifford and Marcus's canonical collection, Behar and Gordon's response to and feminist critique of Clifford and Marcus, the well-attended writing workshops at the annual American Anthropological Association meetings, and the various articles on writing and anthropology that have surfaced in *Anthropology News* over the last two decades – there have not been any radical changes in the content or structures of the majority of undergraduate or graduate programs in anthropology as they relate to writing.

As a matter of course, if writing is acknowledged at all as important, it is usually "outsourced" to the English department or a writing program, as was the case at my former institution, the University of Florida. Certainly, having "something" in place is better than nothing at all, but this approach has its own flaws. First and foremost, not all English departments know how to teach writing, and the type of instruction usually provided by writing programs is more focused on the mechanics, rather than style and content. Moreover, English departments and writing programs are rarely equipped to guide social science graduate students through the nitty-gritty of formulating interesting arguments and descriptions using the data they've collected and the rich experiences they've acquired through participant observation. The graduate students I encountered at the University of

Florida who had bothered to enroll in such courses were left frustrated that the instructors were "clueless" about the traditions of ethnography and completely unaware of the range of audiences whom an anthropologist might wish to reach.

I addressed this contradiction in "Publishing in the Academy," an essay I published in *Anthropology News* in 2002. I posed the following question: "Given the emphasis anthropology places upon writing, why have we paid so little attention to it in our training of graduate students?" We are in the same state of affairs as the proverbial shoeless shoemaker and the chronically sick doctor.

> We recognize that without good method, the researcher could acquire poor or insufficient data, and so we provide courses in ethnographic methods. Similarly, we understand that all data are filtered through particular paradigms, theoretical frames or approaches, and so we teach about the history of the various theories that have informed anthropology. Having provided students with a foundation in theory and method, why do we stop short of giving them guidance in how to write good, sound, clear, and coherent ethnography? (2002: 42)

I concluded by calling for a "renewed commitment to teaching writing." In this charge I also threw down the gauntlet to my colleagues who grade papers with the normative "B" and do little more than provide a check mark as a poor substitute for comments.

> [We must begin] . . . to pay greater attention to *how* ideas are communicated – whether there are any good ideas at all. It compels us to move beyond simply placing a check mark on the paper to show we've read it, but to provide critical, substantive commentary. This should hold true whether the final grade is an "A" or a "C." Even good writers need to know precisely "what" about their writing is effective. (2002: 43)

I am forever grateful to Ralph Faulkingham of the University of Massachusetts Amherst, who taught me this; even with a grade of "A," he always provided thoughtful, reflective feedback about what was significant in my writing. Throughout my training in route to becoming a card-carrying "born-again" anthropologist, I was encouraged to write and think outside the normative box – to challenge myself and engage the new theories and ideas that were just breaking the surface of anthropology in the late 1980s. My decision to use a life history method as an ethnographic strategy was encouraged and supported by my University of Massachusetts dissertation committee: the late Sylvia H. Forman, trained as an applied anthropologist,

Ralph Faulkingham, trained as an economic anthropologist, and Robert Paynter, an archaeologist. I also worked with Anna Tsing, who was just beginning to explore the possibilities of the new approaches to ethnography. All were more than willing to step outside their comfort zones and suspend their roles as authoritative figures who might easily have demanded that I write in a conventional style. Instead, they queried my stylistic choices, organization, use of certain structures, different strategies for integrating my analysis with my interviews, my reflexivity, and more. They encouraged me to seek out models among the new directions that anthropology was taking. We debated ethnographic authority, and what relinquishing such authority might mean for a "native," black woman, feminist, anthropologist, writer.

Such discussions have informed my own teaching and the way I dialogue with those graduate and undergraduate students under my temporary guidance. Have I been successful in pushing the envelope further than where the discipline stands? I hope so, but the proof of the pudding is in the taste, and thus the proof of my success will reside in the experiences that my students carry forth with them after taking leave of me. Following my own departure from the University of Florida in December 2004, one of the students in my undergraduate course, "The Literature of Ethnography," wrote the following:

Fall semester of my senior year I elected to take a course titled "The Literature of Ethnography." . . . The first day of class, I was stunned. Not by her man[ner] or personality, but by her syllabus. It wasn't terrifying, but it was as challenging as I once had expected college to be. We had a paper due the second class. NO professor ever assigned a paper due the first week of class. She did. She wanted to get a feel for our writing ability as well as our level of education in anthropology.

I came to class with what was usually an "A" paper, spit out in an hour while doing three other things, and she gave me a "C." The entire paper was written up in red. She embarrassingly laughed and asked us to excuse her using the color red, as it can feel demeaning. She must have spent an hour on each paper. I had no idea how to react. I have always been an "A" student, never working hard at it. It was extremely humbling.

By the third paper, I was improving. My thought process for anthropological literature was changing dramatically. My writing surpassed what I never even knew existed. I would spend . . . hours on a three-page paper to make it as strong as I possibly could. . . . She challenged every anthropological theory I'd learned. She created this world of thought we never knew existed. She taught me that anthropological theory was about challenging what you know, or think you know, and the very root of that is challenging in itself.

... I edit everything I see now. Nothing is ever good enough. Unchallenged thought processes as well, are never good enough.[8]

These words make me aware that I am one of those *blessed* to be "born wid they feet on the sun" and able to "... seek out de inside meanin' of words." And so, it is with the most profound sense of modesty and humility that I claim to try to walk in Zora's shoes. In doing so, I recognize that in relation to her career as a writer and an anthropologist, I am still an infant. Only time will tell, and of course more writing, whether her shoes will ever fit properly.

Acknowledgments

I would like to thank my writing mentors who, at different points along my journey of life, offered me criticism and wisdom and expressed a profound belief in my ability to become a good writer: my second-grade science teacher, Carolyn Reid-Wallace, Chinua Achebe, Sonja Sanchez, the late Andrew Salkey, Pat Salkey, Ralph Faulkingham, Kesho Scott, Johnnetta Cole, France Winddance Twine, my children (Malik, Antonio and Zena), my mother Bennie Brown, my sister Reece Bell, and of course, myself. I am still in the process of becoming.

References

Behar, Ruth. 1993. *Translated Woman: Crossing the Border with Esperanza's Story.* Boston: Beacon Press.
Behar, Ruth. 1997. *The Vulnerable Observer: Anthropology that Breaks Your Heart.* Boston: Beacon Press.
Behar, Ruth and Deborah A. Gordon. 1996. *Women Writing Culture.* Berkeley: University of California Press.
Brettell, Caroline B., ed. 1996. *When They Read What We Write: The Politics of Ethnography.* Westport, CT: Bergin & Garvey.
Burrows, Stuart. 2001. "You heard her, you ain't blind": Seeing what's said in *Their Eyes were Watching God.* http://findarticles.com/p/articles/mi_qa3643/is_200107/ai_n8958530/pg_7. Accessed January 23, 2008.
Clifford, James. 1988 [1983]. On Ethnographic Authority. In *The Predicament of Culture: Twentieth-Century Ethnography, Literature, and Art*, pp. 21–54. Cambridge, MA: Harvard University Press.

---

[8]   Sarah A. Smith graduated with honors from the University of Florida in 2005; she is currently pursuing both a Masters of Applied Anthropology and a Masters of Public Health at the University of South Florida. She continues to write vigorously. Used by permission.

Clifford, James. 1988. *The Predicament of Culture: Twentieth-Century Ethnography, Literature, and Art.* Cambridge, MA: Harvard University Press.

Clifford, James and George Marcus, eds. 1986. *Writing Culture: The Poetics and the Politics of Ethnography.* Berkeley: University of California Press.

Crapazano, Vincent. 1980. *Tuhami: Portrait of a Moroccan.* Chicago: University of Chicago Press.

Evans-Pritchard, E. E. 1940. *The Nuer: A Description of the Modes of Livelihood and Political Institutions of a Nilotic People.* Oxford: Clarendon Press.

Geertz, Clifford. 1973. *The Interpretation of Cultures.* New York: Basic Books.

Geertz, Clifford. 1988. Slide Show: Evans-Pritchard's African Transparencies. From: *Works and Lives: The Anthropologist as Author*, pp. 49–72. Stanford: Stanford University Press.

Hurston, Zora Neale. 1990 [1935]. *Mules and Men.* New York: HarperCollins.

Hurston, Zora Neale. 1990 [1937]. *Their Eyes were Watching God.* New York: HarperCollins.

Hurston, Zora Neale. 1990 [1938]. *Tell My Horse: Voodoo and Life in Haiti and Jamaica.* New York: HarperCollins.

Marcus, George E. and Michael M. J. Fischer. 1986. *Anthropology as Cultural Critique: An Experimental Moment in the Human Sciences.* Chicago: University of Chicago Press.

McClaurin, Irma. 1999. "Salvaging Lives in the African Diaspora: Anthropology, Ethnography and Women's Narratives." *Souls. A Critical Journal of Black Politics, Culture and Society* 1(3): 25–39.

McClaurin, Irma. 2000a [1996]. *Women of Belize: Gender and Change in Central America.* New Brunswick, NJ: Rutgers University Press.

McClaurin, Irma. 2000b. *Belle Lettres*: "Dear Langston, Love Zora." *FlaVour Magazine.* November.

McClaurin, Irma. 2001. *Black Feminist Anthropology: Theory, Politics, Praxis, and Poetics.* New Brunswick, NJ: Rutgers University Press.

McClaurin, Irma. 2002. "Publishing in the Academy." *Anthropology News* (February): 42–3.

Minn-Ha, Trinh. 1989. *Woman, Native, Other: Writing Postcoloniality and Feminism.* Bloomington: Indiana University Press.

Monge, Luigi. 2006. Their Eyes were Watching God: African-American Topical Songs on the 1928 Florida Hurricanes and Floods. *Popular Music* 26: 129–40.

13

Off the Shelf and into Oblivion?

Catherine Kingfisher

Single mothers on welfare comprise a pariah group in many western cultures. They are regarded as the "undeserving," as opposed to the "deserving," or "working" poor, because their parenting labor is not counted as work. Accordingly, they are constructed as parasites and free-loaders, as undisciplined and unwilling to defer gratification or contribute to society, and, in some cases, as promiscuous or otherwise immoral. In a very real sense, such women represent the Other to what both Goffman (1963) and Foucault (1977) referred to as *normals*. As Smith noted in her work on the naturalization of poverty (1990), they are non-persons who set the parameters of proper personhood; they stand outside of and thus delimit the boundaries of ordered society.

My intention in writing *Women in the American Welfare Trap* (1996a) was to intervene in this situation. I employed two strategies in this regard. The first was to tell stories, or rather, to allow the women to tell their own stories. I believed, as did the women with whom I worked, that if people could somehow connect with poor women, they would come to recognize their essential humanity and, thus, their worthiness and deservingness. It was a matter of thinking that if people just stopped long enough to *listen*, if they could allow themselves to *hear*, if they could relate to what it's like to struggle to feed one's child, or to what it's like to have to bury a child, or if experiences of public humiliation resonated with their own experiences, then they would be unable to sustain the negative valence of "welfare recipient." The large volume of vignettes and conversations included in the book serves not only the theoretical purpose of documenting social construction in action, but also the political purpose of making *present* the lives, experiences, and essential humanity of poor single mothers on welfare.

In writing the book, I was nevertheless aware that, however sympathetically their lives were presented, however poignant their stories, welfare mothers could still be cordoned off in a separate, "non-normal" category by even the most compassionate reader. I thus employed a second strategy of intervention, which consisted of placing poor single mothers on welfare in the same category as a more "worthy" group of individuals, that is, welfare providers. Insofar as they are constructed as hard-working, contributing members of society, welfare providers, or street-level bureaucrats, are regarded as *normals*, and are accordingly awarded full personhood.

Welfare providers are an appropriate group to associate with recipients because they share a number of attributes and situations with their clients. They tend to be women. They tend to be mothers – or at least this was the case in my research site. Significantly, providers are located about as close to the bottom of the welfare hierarchy as one can get before becoming a client; indeed, some of the street-level bureaucrats with whom I worked had received welfare at some time in their lives, or had relatives who had. In a very strong sense, providers feel *they* are a pariah group, as evidenced by their low levels of pay and the lack of recognition they receive from colleagues and supervisors.

There were good theoretical reasons as well for focusing on this alignment. Welfare providers and recipients are in structurally related positions in US society; together, their situations reveal a lot about gender, motherhood, and work in our culture – and about the construction and policing of the boundaries between the deserving and the undeserving, between persons and non-persons. The possibilities of political alliance stemming from recognition of their similarities, as analyzed by Frances Fox Piven (1984), for instance, are also highly relevant, and are accordingly addressed in the book.

In employing this literary strategy of alignment I was, in a sense, emulating the welfare recipients with whom I worked, who often preferred to refer to themselves as welfare *mothers* rather than *clients* or *recipients*. This discursive move allowed them to appropriate and deploy the positive meanings attached to *mothers* as caring, responsible and morally pure, and thereby partially offset the negative valence of *welfare* – a classic anti-stigma strategy of the kind outlined by Goffman (1963). In combining ethnographic analysis of these two groups of women (a rarity in the literature, to the best of my knowledge), I was simply attempting to extend recognition of the connections between them to include *readers*, in the hopes that the worthy side of the provider–recipient coupling might help mitigate the supposed unworthiness of the other side.

Of course, in writing *Women in the American Welfare Trap*, I wanted to make a case for providers, as well as for recipients. Welfare providers are an oppressed group of workers, beleaguered, like many street-level bureaucrats, by unrealistic workloads, responsibility without authority or resources and low status in the bureaucratic hierarchy. They are also often mothers trying to juggle paid and domestic labor, and in this case, paid work that was not handsomely remunerated. One aspect of this constellation of factors is the well-known hostility that welfare providers often express in their relationships with clients, which is the one area in their work lives where they can exercise any autonomy. My point, very simply, was that both providers and recipients suffer.

I had two audiences in mind when writing the book: policy-makers and practitioners, and undergraduate students. I felt that I could not simultaneously target practitioners in social welfare and advanced graduate students in anthropology, because their discursive universes are so dissimilar. It was possible, however, to simultaneously address practitioners and undergraduate students – which is not a slight to either, but an attempt on my part to match discursive and conceptual repertoires as closely as possible. And working with the great American assumption of "the more the better," I felt that targeting undergraduates in a number of disciplines – not only in anthropology, but also in sociology, political science, and social work – meant reaching more people, and thus providing wider circulation for the women's stories.

Targeting Audiences

There is no such thing as "pure," atheoretical or amethodological data; I felt strongly that both policy practitioners and undergraduates needed to be given explicit access to how the data were produced and to the theoretical frameworks employed in generating and interpreting those data. But I also felt that neither policy practitioners nor undergraduates would be particularly enamored of anthropological theory or method as stand-alones. Therefore, instead of having separate sections or chapters called "theoretical framework" and "methods," I chose to interweave theory and methods throughout the text. I did this on a strictly need-to-know basis, raising theoretical and methodological issues in accessible language and only when they became relevant, in the same way that I raised questions in conversations with research participants only when they were topically and contextually appropriate (Briggs 1986). "Theory," Stuart Hall writes, "is always a detour on the way to something more important" (1997: 42). One could say the same about methods, which are not just free-floating techniques to produce particular kinds of data, but techniques based on specific theories about how the social world operates. Theory and method are clearly not irrelevant, and both have a place in my work, but a place that reflects their roles as tools in the service of making understandable, sensible, reasonable, and *human* the lives of poor single mothers on welfare and welfare providers. And for those more directly interested in theory and method I provided two offerings: an appendix to the book, in which detailed transcripts of process as well as the content of conversations are presented and analyzed; and an article in *Discourse & Society* (1996b) that plays more explicitly with structuralist and post-structuralist theories of agency.

I coupled these published materials with face-to-face efforts to dissemi-nate my data and interpretations. I began by approaching the Governor and the Director of Social Services in the state where I had conducted the research. In my naïveté, I wanted to convince them that welfare grants needed to be increased and provider workloads decreased. Given that the Department of Social Services was undergoing restructuring at the time, and that I was able to secure only *five minutes* with the recently elected Governor, I was not surprised that neither individual was terribly receptive to what I had to say, although I wondered if their lack of enthusiasm was an artifact of the restructuring, of an inability on my part to present my case in palatable terms, or of some combination of the two. In the end I sent a copy of *Women in the American Welfare Trap* to the administrative gatekeeper in the Department of Social Services who had awarded me access to the welfare office in the first place. I never heard back from him and have no idea what he did with the book.

The situation was somewhat different in Aotearoa/New Zealand where I taught women's studies for six and a half years. In this small country, where everyone knows what everyone else is doing, I was quickly invited by the government's Social Policy Agency (SPA) to present my work. I decided to alter my approach from the one I had followed in the US in two ways. First, I made a decision to decouple providers and recipients for this particular audience. Because providers are more "deserving" than recipi-ents, I speculated that an emphasis on the former alone might be more palatable to policy analysts, and thus focused in my presentation exclusively on the (unofficial, unsanctioned) street-level policy-making activities of providers, underscoring the negative circumstances, and often negative content, of their policy production. By this time, I had begun to wonder if aligning providers and workers might be politic in relation to some audi-ences and impolitic in relation to others. The message of my presentation was that providers were overburdened by heavy caseloads, and that their considerable expertise was unrecognized and therefore unutilized. These conditions were in need of amelioration, the result of which, I argued to SPA analysts, would be a happier and therefore more efficient and productive workforce. Although an emphasis on providers alone undercut my efforts to decrease the stigma suffered by "undeserving" welfare recipients by associating them with their more "deserving" sisters, and while my deployment of the language of efficiency and productivity represented a capitulation to dominant discourses, I reasoned that policy-makers might be more willing to make the lives of providers (as opposed to recipients) easier, and that if they did so, this would in turn make the lives of recipients easier. A key point of my book was that providers' negative policy-making was an artifact of their location in the welfare bureaucracy. If this could be changed, I thought, so might the content of their policy-making practices.

The second change I made was procedural in nature, and consisted of playing audiotapes of research participants' conversations for my audience. Playing the tapes was a way of bringing the women to life; it also created a space for audience participation in analysis, insofar as listening to the tapes generated brainstorming sessions around how to interpret what was occurring in participants' lives and how to think about the implications for policy. It is not clear to me whether the greater receptivity of the New Zealand audience reflected my focus on providers in and of themselves, the enticement of listening to the women's conversations on tape, or the fact that my data were from the US and not from New Zealand, which meant, perhaps, that audience members could engage with the implications of the data without feeling directly attacked by them. Although I was never sufficiently arrogant to imagine that my work would effect changes in the situation of welfare providers in Aotearoa/New Zealand – a situation remarkably similar to that in the US with regard to the status and decision-making powers of providers – policy-makers received what I had to say positively and with great interest. That provider caseloads were, in fact, cut considerably after the election of a Labour Coalition government in 1999 prompts my continued efforts.

In response to the interest of the analysts at the Social Policy Agency, I decided to publish an article in a journal that policy practitioners might be more likely to read if they did not have the inclination to read the book. As in my presentation, I focused on the everyday policy-making of street-level bureaucrats. "How Providers Make Policy: An Ethnographic Analysis of Everyday Conversation in a Welfare Office" (1998), published in the *Journal of Community and Applied Social Psychology*, is very much oriented to the concerns of policy formation and delivery, and draws explicitly on the discourse and literature of policy administration.

In the process of crafting the same work for academic audiences and for policy-makers in the US and Aotearoa, I learned valuable lessons about both bringing data to life for an audience and speaking in language to which an audience can relate. Coupling *Women in the American Welfare Trap* with written and oral materials that targeted different readers and audiences provided the means to invite a wide range of publics to engage with the work.

Working in a Local Community

If my goal in writing *Women in the American Welfare Trap* was to reach a wide undergraduate and policy practitioner audience, my goal in more recent work on homelessness in Canada has been to engage (in addition to an academic audience) a very small target audience in a very particular context. On sabbatical in fall 2002 and planning to continue my local work with welfare mothers, my attention was captured by the crisis that erupted when the only homeless shelter in town was closed by the local health officer, engendering a heated controversy over where to put the new shelter and how to deal with the presence of the visibly homeless in what is known as the "downtown core" – six to eight blocks of cafés, shops and a park. Given my long-standing interest in the construction and negotiation of pariah status, I put my research on welfare aside to explore instead how the homeless were being constructed by the (housed) public in general, and by those involved in making decisions about services for the homeless in particular. I first focused my efforts on Social Housing in Action (SHIA) – a city-sponsored group of 80 community members interested in housing and homelessness. In addition to reviewing documents produced by SHIA, I interviewed 28 members of the sub-committee most closely involved in selecting the location and program operator for the new shelter. I placed equal emphasis on a second group: the public at large, or, rather, those members of the public who were sufficiently exercised about the homeless and homelessness to attend and speak at one of two City Council public hearings on the matter. In my analysis of audio-taped interviews and video tapes of the public hearings, I focused on the production of the homeless as "Others" who needed to be evicted from the "downtown core," the heart of the city, and reformed into proper persons fit to occupy social space. Specifically, my analysis traces (1) the discursive production, via indexicality and omission, of an unmarked categorization of the homeless as male Aboriginal[1] addicts, and (2) the destructuring, individualizing influences of official discourses of "diversity" – both within a framework that

---

[1] I use this term interchangeably with Native, which, in this context, was the preferred appellation among both Natives and non-Natives.

underscores the metaphorical borderland between the homeless and the housed as a site for the cultural production of notions of proper personhood and sociality.

My research resulted in two academic publications: an article in *American Ethnologist* (2007a) devoted to analyses of destructured understandings of homelessness and the discursive production of an unmarked categorization of the homeless as Native addicted men; and a chapter in an edited volume on neoliberalism (2007b), in which I focus on how the "downtown core" was reconfigured as a neoliberal space of productivity and consumption via the eviction of the non-neoliberal – the homeless shelter and its residents, along with their improper practices and ways of being. Constructions of the homeless as (Native) Other, and the location of the new shelter on the other side of the tracks from the "downtown core," I argued, recapitulated the historical treatment of Natives in the area.

More relevant to my discussion here, however, were my efforts to share what I had learned about how "we" (the housed) construct "them" (the homeless) with precisely those who were engaged in producing such constructions, and to point to the impact of such constructions on decision-making processes. As I struggled with how to present my data to members of SHIA, City Administration and the public at large, I began to realize, in the most practical sense possible, the importance of what my mentor, Frederick Erickson, had suggested many years previously, which was to distinguish among four audiences: those for whom the data will be no news, but good news; those for whom the data will be no news, but bad news; those for whom the data will be news that will be positively viewed; and those for whom the data will be news that will be viewed negatively. Specifically, I learned that bad news is best sandwiched between good news, and that the worst news of all is news that is no news but bad news, simply because energy has already been expended in keeping it in the closet. The key, of course, is to present things in such a way that they can be heard and taken in, a goal anthropologists also pursue in the classroom when teaching about topics such as racism, colonialism and gender inequality. With this in mind, I set out to write a report for SHIA and the City, which I would also use as the basis for a public presentation.

I followed three strategies in writing the report. The first was to enlist the help of a research officer on campus who specialized in writing for off-campus consumption. Paul Sparrow-Clarke took my report and changed it considerably, inserting multiple section headings, adding an executive summary, and altering the language to make it more accessible to non-academics – in other words, he rendered it portable (Strathern 2004: 17) from one organizational structure, the University, to another, City

Administration. Instead of referring to "metaphorical borderlands" and "othering," for example, language is straightforward and key findings are listed in an executive summary.

In addition to transforming an academic paper into a "report" for non-academic consumption, I had to address the issue of "bad news." In this case, the bad news was not new news, since everyone knew that "homeless" was code for addicted Native man (otherwise it would not have functioned as an unmarked category). Thus my second strategy concerned framing. First, I situated the unmarked categorization of the homeless as Native addicted men in historical and social context. Not only was this ethnographically appropriate, but it also served to deindividualize the problem, and thus avoid threatening (and possibly shutting down) members of the target audience. Second, I framed the destructuring, individualizing features of discourses of "diversity," as they were deployed in this context, in relation to the unimpeachable good intentions of the architects of such discourses and, in particular, to unintended outcomes. I hoped to accomplish this framing by inserting an additional section into the report. Here is an excerpt of the section I titled "Some notes on learning about 'us' ":

> This study focuses on "us" as opposed to "them." While most research on homelessness concentrates on the homeless themselves – who they are, why they are homeless, what their experiences are, and what they need – this research concentrates on the *housed*. While an analysis of "us" as opposed to "them" may make some readers uncomfortable, it also provides an opportunity for "us" to reflect on the impact of our thinking (and especially our assumptions) on the well-being of the homeless.

I also wrote that "social problems such as racism reside in social systems, not in individuals," a statement I found difficult to make, since I see racism as both structural and individual. In this sense my strategy here might be considered capitulation, but I see it as a strategy to get in through the back door. My emphasis on the social was not about letting people off the hook, but, rather, about giving them a view of how their individual behavior reflects historical, social patterns rather than simply their individual "badness." It was about finding a workable hook, one that would draw people in rather than alienate them.

My final strategy was to downplay my expertise in deference to that of members of SHIA:

> This study was not intended to produce specific policy recommendations, but rather to explore how the housed think about the homeless, and how this thinking might influence or relate to current policy. I have expertise in neither

policy analysis nor policy construction *per se*, but rather in analyzing the *cultural contexts* of particular policy orientations. I see my role as providing information that policy-makers can use as they see fit.

My goal here was to counteract the stereotype, no doubt also common in other small university towns, of academics as elitist snobs who think they know everything.

In my presentation to SHIA, which was open to the public although not terribly well attended, I repeatedly emphasized the *social*, the *historical* and the *unintended*, but I coupled this framing with clear data on the production of the unmarked category of the homeless as male Aboriginal addicts, complete with scientific-looking slides of frequency counts of references to the homeless in the public hearings. In other words, I didn't stop at the framing, but used it as an entry point (some might say it was a sucker-punch) into my key points: that racism is rampant in Lethbridge and that policy ignores structural issues and remedies at the peril of actually worsening homelessness. My suggestions that policy-makers pay attention to local sensitivities about race and poverty and always keep in mind structural issues when engaged in planning and programming followed directly from these points. Although there is no way to know if my report will have any substantive, long-term positive impact, two items are worth noting. The first is that during the discussion period after my presentation, one audience member (accompanied by enthusiastic nods from a few other audience members) thanked me for "finally talking about race" in a town in which people avoided speaking directly about Aboriginal issues for fear of either recapitulating negative stereotypes or being accused of racism. The second is that my report has since been posted on SHIA's web site. The cynic in me reads the latter move as an easy out – why not instead set up a task force to devise specific recommendations on the basis of my findings? – but at least the report wasn't buried.

Conclusions: Anthropology versus Social Cause Marketing

I would like to conclude with some reflections on audience, and on one of the key stumbling blocks encountered when trying to present a particular culture to members of that culture: the "so-whatness" of the kinds of data that anthropologists produce. In analyzing the social construction of reality, we inevitably analyze the most mundane of activities, such as everyday talk and institutional arrangements that are taken for granted. How do we present this so-what data so that readers/audience members can apprehend not as commonsense or natural, but as socially constructed, and therefore contingent and only one possibility among many? If there is a key so-what that runs through my work, it is possessive individualism – the assumption that persons are, naturally, autonomous, independent, entrepreneurial utility-maximizers. Indeed, a great deal of welfare reform and interventions in homelessness are based on the claim that the poor and the homeless are deficient as persons. Such assertions are based on the often unspoken assumption that *full* persons are, as I've already stated, independent utility-maximizers. This is clearly a historically and culturally specific construction of the person, but to many it seems unremarkable. And it is precisely this commonsensical notion of the person that informs the well-intentioned desires of many to help the poor enter "mainstream" society and that permeates current discourses of "inclusion."

My agenda here, accordingly, is twofold: to show people how other people's "negative" behavior may, in fact, make good sense in its contexts of occurrence, and to show people in the "mainstream" how their own behavior is arbitrary and historically and culturally contingent. The first is best achieved by that old anthropological tool of the trade, contextualization. The second is more difficult, because this is where one encounters the "so-what," or, rather, "*of course* (it's only *natural)*, and so what?" My most common strategy for dealing with this is to juxtapose our common-sensical notions of the person with those constructed by other cultures or by our own culture in the past. This kind of cross-cultural and historical comparison – another anthropological tool of the trade – is, I think, quite effective, although I have learned from my classroom experience that its effects may take some time.

My final reflection concerns one of the most potentially problematic aspects of developing strategies for addressing different audiences. My fear here concerns the superficial yet notable resemblance between anthropological endeavors to gauge audience and participate in discussions of what needs fixing and how, and the "social cause marketing" discourse of Management, which resurrects notions of social engineering. An anthropological sensibility to nuance, context and complexity will hopefully lead to productive (rather than patronizing and arrogantly manipulative) engagements with various knowledgeable insiders, but we need to remain vigilant in this regard. The only way to encourage audiences to treat others (here, welfare recipients and the homeless) with respect is to treat them with respect, rather than as objects to be manipulated.

In the end, of course, there is no way to measure in any direct way the impact of my efforts to reach wider audiences. It would be highly useful to target research toward answering the kinds of questions posed recently by Marilyn Strathern in *Commons and Borderlands* (2004: 14–18): How does knowledge move from one community to another? How is it rendered portable? How is it deployed in different organizational structures? What happens to particular communities in the wake of knowledge travels? And what kinds of communities are created via such travels? Systematically tracing the processes associated with the production and travel of knowledge would allow us to determine whether our ventures off the shelf are leaps into oblivion or jumps to places that may someday prove beneficial.

Acknowledgments

Thanks to the late Gay Becker for her insightful comments as discussant in the "Anthropology off the Shelf" session in which the first version of this paper was presented, to Barbara Rylko-Bauer for her responses to an earlier version of the paper, to Paul Sparrow-Clarke for helping me in my work with SHIA, and, above all, to Maria Vesperi and Alisse Waterston, for their tireless work in organizing all the "Off the Shelf" sessions and putting together this volume.

References

Briggs, Charles. 1986. *Learning How to Ask: A Sociolinguistic Appraisal of the Role of the Interview in Social Science Research*. Cambridge: Cambridge University Press.

Foucault, Michel. 1977. *Discipline and Punish*, trans. Alan Sheridan. New York: Vintage.

Goffman, Erving. 1963. *Stigma: Notes on the Management of Spoiled Identity*. Englewood Cliffs, NJ: Prentice-Hall.

Hall, Stuart. 1997. Old and New Identities, Old and New Ethnicities. In *Culture, Globalization and the World System: Contemporary Conditions for the Representation of Identity* (rev. ed.). Anthony D. King, ed., pp. 41–68. Minneapolis: University of Minnesota Press.

Kingfisher, Catherine. 1996a. *Women in the American Welfare Trap*. Philadelphia: University of Pennsylvania Press.

Kingfisher, Catherine. 1996b. Women on Welfare: Conversational Sites of Acquiescence and Dissent. *Discourse & Society* 7(4): 531–57.

Kingfisher, Catherine. 1998. How Providers Make Policy: An Analysis of Everyday Conversation in a Welfare Office. *Journal of Community and Applied Social Psychology* 8(2): 119–36.

Kingfisher, Catherine. 2007a. Discursive Constructions of Homelessness in a Small City in the Canadian Prairies: Notes on Destructuration, Individualization, and the Production of (Raced and Gendered) Unmarked Categories. *American Ethnologist* 34(1): 91–107.

Kingfisher, Catherine. 2007b. Spatializing Neoliberalism: Articulations, Recapitulations and (a Very Few) Alternatives. In *Neoliberalization: States, Networks, Peoples*. Kim England and Kevin Ward, eds., pp. 195–222. Oxford: Blackwell.

Piven, Frances Fox. 1984. Women and the State: Ideology, Power, and the Welfare State. *Socialist Review* 74(14): 11–19.

Smith, Ruth L. 1990. Order and Disorder: The Naturalization of Poverty. *Cultural Critique* 14: 209–29.

Strathern, Marilyn. 2004. *Commons and Borderlands: Working Papers on Interdisciplinarity, Accountability and the Flow of Knowledge*. Wantage, Oxon: Sean Kingston Publishing.

14

"Don't Use Your Data as a Pillow"

S. Eben Kirksey

A small feast had been prepared for my going away party: salty sago pudding, fish broth, fried papaya leaves, boiled yams, and chicken. It was a modest affair, organized by Denny Yomaki, a human rights worker, to mark the end of my fieldwork in May 2003. The event was scheduled to take place a few days before I returned to graduate school to begin writing up my findings. I expected the party to be a rite of passage marking a smooth transition into a new network of obligations and duties. What actually awaited me was a confrontation in Denny's living room that would question the basic value of my research. Here, at my own going away party, some of my basic methodological approaches and guiding principles were about to meet a head-on challenge.

I first came to West Papua some five years earlier, in 1998, to conduct research for my undergraduate honors thesis at New College of Florida. Then "West Papua" was officially known as "Irian Jaya." Initially I intended to study an El Niño drought that had hit the region. By the time I arrived, the rains had come. There was a marked lack of enthusiasm for talking about the drought. Indonesia's long-time ruler, Suharto, had just been deposed by a reform movement. The subject of the day was *merdeka* (freedom). Once the rallying cry of Indonesian nationalists in their struggle for independence from Dutch colonialism, *merdeka* was inspiring movements for independence from Indonesia in Aceh, in West Papua, and in East Timor. Initially I was perplexed. With a popular reform movement flexing its muscles throughout Indonesia after the ousting of Suharto, why bother to form new break-away governments?

After witnessing a series of Indonesian military massacres – where a student was shot in the head and dozens of other unarmed demonstrators were dumped into the sea to drown – I began to understand why many Papuans wanted to take the path of independence, not reform. A systematic campaign of genocide had been taking place (Brundige et al. 2003). The

Indonesian military had recently unveiled plans to increase its presence in West Papua to 50,000 troops; about one soldier for every 24 Papuans. By comparison, as the US occupation in Iraq hit a record high number of troops in November 2007, there was approximately one soldier for every 157 Iraqis.

As a graduate student at the University of Oxford, and then at the University of California, Santa Cruz, I made repeated trips to West Papua where I recorded distinctive indigenous stories. Some stories I heard will be familiar to anyone who follows daily news reports from other conflict zones – stories about torture, about the role of the US government in supporting a military occupation, and about aspirations for independence. Other stories surprised me. I learned about a campaign of terror triggered by "Dracula" and about how my ancestors, the Whites, stole the magic of modernity from indigenous Papuans. Unexpected discoveries forced me to rethink the terms of my research. Strange bedfellows – multi-national corporations and even covert Indonesian military operatives – have provided support to Papuan independence activists. Collaboration, rather than resistance, was the primary strategy of the indigenous political movement in West Papua.

Many Papuans sought me out as an ally, a potential collaborator. I found myself being drawn into the very movement that I had come to study. Human rights activists encouraged me to research campaigns of terror by Indonesian security forces. By studying the cultural dimensions of violence, I thought that I might help Papuans achieve freedom from terror within the current regime of Indonesian occupation. At my going away party my role was contested.

After Denny said a brief Christian prayer in formal Indonesian – giving thanks for our health and wishing me a safe journey – we heaped our plastic plates with food and sat around on the floor of his living room to eat. Once the plates were cleared away, we moved out to the front porch to chew betel nut – a green palm-tree seed that produces a mild, relaxing buzz. We begin swapping jokes in Logat Papua – the regional creole language. Propped up on my elbows and idly swatting at mosquitoes, I began chatting with Telys Waropen, a member of Komnas HAM, the National Human Rights Commission. Even though we had not met before, Waropen was invited to my party by Denny, the host. Waropen was a young firebrand in his late 20s, around my own age at the time, whose government post had been recently created in response to demands by Indonesia's reform movement.

Waropen originated from Wasior, a place where Indonesian police had recently conducted a sustained assault on alleged Papuan separatists aptly named "Operation Isolate and Annihilate" (*Operasi Penyisiran dan Penumpasan*). In the past weeks I had visited Wasior with Denny. We investigated rumors that Indonesian military agents were covertly support-ing a Papuan militia.

Our research in Wasior took place under conditions of intense surveil-lance. We only interviewed people who wanted to risk the chance of being seen with a foreign researcher in order to tell their stories. Denny and I used an elaborate protocol to protect the identity of our interviewees: we contacted them through back channels and set up meetings in the houses of neighbors in the dark of night.

Our ambitious research agenda had also initially included plans to inter-view renowned shamans in nearby mountains. Some of these shamans had been claiming responsibility for causing recent earthquakes in Indonesia's central island of Java and for downing an airplane carrying top Indonesian military brass. Since we were under surveillance, Denny and I did not risk contacting the shamans.

Weeks later at my going away party I learned that Telys Waropen had studied the Wasior shamans for his undergraduate thesis at a local univer-sity. As we were chewing betel with full bellies on Denny Yomaki's front porch, I began to see Waropen as an important source who might help fill in some gaps in my research. Here was my chance to learn about the shamans whom I had been unable to meet.

I asked Waropen for an interview, explaining in a well-rehearsed spiel that I would keep him anonymous, like the rest of my sources. Waropen recoiled. "What kind of research are you conducting," he asked, "where the identity of your sources doesn't matter? Wouldn't your data be stronger if you quoted credible sources?" By the time of my going away party at Denny's house, I had conducted more than 350 Indonesian-language inter-views with Papuan politicians, survivors of violence, political prisoners, guerrilla fighters, human rights activists, and indigenous leaders.[1] All of these interviews had been anonymous. As he questioned the value of my research a sinking feeling spread in my gut.

Informal advice from peers and mentors had led me to keep all of my sources anonymous in order to obtain an exemption from the institutional review board of my university. The guidelines state: "research involving surveyor interview procedures is exempt if in the researcher's private data (including field notes) as well as in any published material, responses are recorded anonymously and in such a manner that the human subjects cannot be identified, directly or through identifiers linked to the subjects."[2] Conducting fieldwork in West Papua had brought me to the conclusion that

---

[1]   Of these interviews, 144 were tape-recorded. A total of 405,000 words were transcribed from a selection of the tape-recorded interviews.

[2]   http://research.ucsc.edu/compliance/hsexempt.html.

keeping sources anonymous was not just a means to avoid bureaucratic rigmarole. Lives were and are at stake. But, by keeping sources anonymous was I erasing their identities altogether? Clearly some Papuans, like Waropen, want to be quoted – they want to be recognized as public intellectuals. This confrontation forced me to reconsider tangled personal, professional, legal, and ethical obligations.

Anonymous sources are viewed with a sense of suspicion and mystery by readers of newspapers and magazines. Journalists and editors usually use a rigorous set of guidelines to determine when to use an anonymous source (Boeyink 1990). These criteria guard against the fabrication of stories by unethical authors and the dispersal of misinformation by sources who gain the ear of reporters. Such citation strategies can also have an important juridico-legal function: this is how journalists and publishers protect themselves in libel lawsuits. Following standard ethnographic practices, I had approached my interviews with the idea that I might learn something even if my sources were anonymous, or even deliberately lying. There are some things that are well known – about lived experiences of terror or the disappeared – that cannot be spoken about in public or on the record.

When Waropen confronted me about the reliability of my "data," I tried to show him how insights from cultural criticism and post-structural theory might offer fresh perspectives on the conflict in West Papua. One route to *merdeka* (freedom), I suggested, might be understanding how rumors produce fear. He was already well aware that rumors help generate terror. But this insight was not helping him get traction in legal realms where a different standard of evidence prevails. He told me that he wanted to see members of the security forces prosecuted in Indonesian courts. Razed villages needed to be reconstructed. Waropen saw me as a potential ally, but one who needed some serious re-schooling.

I sat up as the conversation suddenly heated up. Initially I quibbled with Waropen: *Surely there are cases in human rights reporting where the identity of survivors and witnesses must be protected.* I also found myself trying to explain why a broad reading public would be interested in the shamans he had researched as an undergraduate. Then, after getting tired of arguing my case and justifying my research, I rested back on my elbows to listen. "Don't use your data as a pillow and go to sleep when you get back to America," Waropen insisted. "Don't just use this as a bridge to your own professional opportunities."

In part, Waropen was provoking me to become a reliable regional expert – someone who would know things with certainty and someone who would take questions of accountability seriously. Following Edward Said's critiques of Orientalist experts (1979), and Gayatri Spivak's characterization of liberal intellectuals who speak for subaltern subjects (1988), many cultural anthropologists are understandably wary about using their research to speak to power. Knowledge of Others can be used to further colonial, imperial, or professional agendas. Regional experts often ignore demands for accountability from the people they study. Opening up any issue of the *New York Times* illustrates that most people who are fashioned as regional experts by the media – government representatives, economists, and political scientists – appear untroubled by post-colonial critiques of knowledge production. The knowledges and concerns of people who occupy structurally marginalized positions continue to be underrepresented in the public press.

Waropen asked me to rethink what counted as "data" in cultural anthropology. He was prompting me to be a better, more authoritative, translator. Along related lines, Charles Hale has recently urged anthropologists to take positivist methodologies seriously in activist research: "To state it bluntly, anthropologists, geographers, and lawyers who have only cultural critique to offer will often disappoint the people with whom they are aligned" (Hale 2006). Waropen was challenging me to know about things that mattered and to know them well. This confrontation at my going away party prompted me to translate underrepresented forms of knowledge into legible narratives that might travel abroad.

Simply publishing my findings in a peer-reviewed journal, or otherwise using my data to advance my own professional opportunities, was clearly unacceptable to Waropen. Would writing about these issues in the popular press be enough? By the time I met Waropen, I had already published a number of newspaper articles about West Papua. For *The Guardian* of London I had written an experimental piece that explored how resistance to logging schemes and military troops was being inspired by a syncretic fusion of environmentalism and indigenous ritual practice (Kirksey 2002). Was this the right kind of "data" to be sharing with wider audiences? Waropen was prompting me to stick to the facts, more narrowly construed. He was also challenging me to take concrete action. This confrontation led me to think about how I might begin to do more than just write words – how I might begin to bring my knowledge about West Papua to the seats of global power.

While traveling to Wasior with Denny Yomaki, I researched rumors linking BP to recent violence. This company, formerly "British Petroleum," spent over £100 million to rebrand itself as "Beyond Petroleum." BP had just begun to exploit a natural gas field in West Papua that is expected to generate more than $198 billion (Vidal 2008). Reportedly, Indonesian military agents were provoking violence in an unconventional bid for a lucrative "protection" contract. Militia members, who claimed to be Papuan freedom fighters, had just killed a platoon of Indonesian police officers in Wasior. Rumors linked this militia to the Indonesian military. From afar, the identity of the different players was difficult to sort out: military provocateurs, police victims, and Papuan double-agents. Struggling to keep these people straight, I was skeptical. Why would one branch of the Indonesian security forces stage an attack on another branch? Why would Papuan "freedom fighters" collaborate with the Indonesian military? How is this related to BP?

In Wasior I managed to secure interviews with Papuan double-agents, the "freedom fighters" with alleged ties to the military. One of these men admitted, while my tape recorder was rolling, to murdering the Indonesian police officers. He also admitted to getting logistical support and intelligence from the Indonesian military. Through this source, and other interviews, I managed to substantiate the rumors linking the recent violence in Wasior to the BP project. This same man also told me that his life was in danger. He said that an active-duty military officer had tried to assassinate him because he knew too much. He looked to me for help in escaping his present situation – help which I was not able to provide.

Two weeks after Telys Waropen demanded that I do more than "use my data as a pillow," I found an opportunity to serve as an expert-in-action back in England, where I was a Marshall Scholar at Oxford. In late May 2003 John Rumbiak, a Papuan human rights defender, asked me to attend a meeting at the London headquarters of BP with Dr. Byron Grote, the Chief Financial Officer (CFO) of this petroleum giant. BP was training a "community-based security" force – a group of Papuan security guards who would minimize the need for collaboration with Indonesian security forces. Rumbiak had secured a meeting to talk about how BP's security policy was affecting the human rights climate in West Papua. Rumbiak asked me to join the meeting so that I could present my findings about militia violence in Wasior. With a gentler hand than Waropen, Rumbiak was fashioning me into a reliable witness – an expert on West Papua who would be prepared to make strong claims to knowledge.

Before the appointment at BP's headquarters I met up with Rumbiak, a thin man who is always quick to smile, in a coffee shop in central London. Not wanting to spring for a taxi, we got lost on the way to the meeting with BP. Walking around, we swapped stories about our recent travels, code-switching from Indonesian to English. After asking for directions from the guards at Saint James's Palace, the official residence of the Queen, we found the BP office. We were 20 minutes late.

Entering through the revolving glass doors of 1 Saint James's Square, a squat brick building, we were met by a smartly dressed young woman. She checked our names on a computer terminal, issued us visitors' badges, and instructed us to wait for our escort on some plush couches. When the escort arrived we were instructed to file one by one through a turnstile where we swiped our badges. Up in an elevator, down a hallway, and we found ourselves in a cramped room with CFO Byron Grote and John O'Reilly. O'Reilly was BP's Senior Vice President for Indonesia. Both Grote and O'Reilly had previously worked for BP in Colombia, where the company was embroiled in controversy when paramilitary death squads began assassinating environmental activists (Gillard 2002). Suddenly face to face with some of the most powerful men in Europe, I felt adrenaline rush through my veins.

Dr. Grote opened the meeting with a request that our conversations be off the record – that we treat the discussion as strictly confidential. Rumbiak immediately countered: "I'm sorry, that just is not possible. When I meet with you, the people of West Papua want to know what we talk about."[3] Rumbiak wasted no time. He immediately presented a clear message: the BP community-based security policy was inciting violence. The Indonesian state security forces made approximately 80 percent of their revenue from contracts to "protect" companies and BP's policy cut the military out of a lucrative deal. "Since this policy will establish a precedent that other companies in Indonesia might follow," Rumbiak said, "covert agents in the Indonesian military are determined to provoke violence until you relent and give them a security contract."

"Violence is bad for business," Dr. Grote responded. "Open societies are good and they create environments where business thrives. Working in West Papua is a huge challenge – one that we have to take. We are convinced that the community-based security policy will still work. If we cancel this project then another company that doesn't share our code of ethics will step in and develop this gas field." Grote's language was seductive, inviting. I found myself wondering if maybe this company could become a force to help sideline the Indonesian military in West Papua.

Rumbiak asked me to present my findings from Wasior. With my heart pounding, I tried to encapsulate a series of exceedingly complex events. I recounted my interview with the Papuan militia member who was afraid for his life: "He claims to have killed a group of Indonesian policemen with the assistance of Indonesian military agents. The Indonesian police later used this incident as a pretext for launching Operation Isolate and Annihilate. Both the police and the military want a protection contract from BP." The murder took place the very same day that John O'Reilly, the Vice

President who was sitting in the room with us, had been visiting the gas project site with British Ambassador Richard Gozney.

O'Reilly, a man with thick round glasses who was deceptively timid-looking, challenged my credibility: "Did the militia member who murdered the police officers explicitly say that the attack was planned to coincide with my visit?" "No," I admitted. The Indonesian military agents who were directing this militia had sent them letters with instructions to launch the attack the same week when O'Reilly was visiting. But these letters did not make explicit mention of the visiting dignitaries. During a fast-paced exchange with O'Reilly, I fumbled. I failed to make the complexity of the actors and the events legible.

John Rumbiak tried to intervene by providing more context: "The Indonesian police and the military are often in fierce competition over resources. Firefights among different branches of the security forces are not uncommon." My stories of double-agents and unlikely collaborators – Indonesian military operatives and Papuan guerrillas who work together – suddenly sounded implausible, maybe even paranoid. O'Reilly went further to completely discount the links that John Rumbiak had drawn between the violence of Operation Isolate and Annihilate and the BP gas project: "Wasior is 160 kilometers away from our project location. There are no roads or waterways linking the two sites. A mountain range and vast tracks of forest lie in between. We don't read what is happening in Wasior as a signal."

Drawing on another one of my interviews, I countered: "Wasior is a two-week walk from your site. Members of the same militia that murdered the police officers walked this distance in February 2001 to conduct reconnaissance near your base camp."

Dr. Grote was late for his next meeting. As we hastily concluded our conversation, Rumbiak made a specific request: "Use your influence with the Indonesian government to help make sure that the perpetrators of the violence in Wasior are prosecuted."

"We are not yet confident enough about the facts of this case to approach the Indonesian authorities," John O'Reilly responded.

Later, John Rumbiak urged me to go public with my findings from Wasior. In an e-mail he said that "we have to get this story published in a major paper." After our meeting at the BP headquarters we discovered that the corporation had, in secret, already reneged on its promises not to work with the Indonesian security forces. I cold-called and e-mailed a number of newspaper editors. After being turned down by five papers, I connected with an editor from *The Sunday Times*, one of Britain's largest newspapers with a circulation of 1.5 million.

Jack Grimston, then the Assistant Foreign Editor of the paper, called to ask if I would co-author an article with him. He traveled to Oxford by train. After poring over my maps, interview transcripts, and fieldnotes he placed a phone call to a senior editor in London. Grimston came back, saying that "the paper is still very interested in the story, but can not yet fully commit to publishing it. They want to print the name of the militia member who helped kill the police officers." Grimston took a train back to London while I mulled over the implications of going ahead with the story. Would the militia member be killed if we printed his name? Should he be held accountable for murder? I tried calling John Rumbiak, who was back in New York City, to ask for advice. No answer. I made my own decision and called Grimston. "We can't name the militia source," I told him. "His life might be in danger."

Over the next three days Grimston and I worked the phones, trying to confirm the details of BP's collaboration with security forces. The final article shared the back page with a story featuring a grinning picture of James Bond actor Pierce Brosnan. The militia member was only mentioned in passing:

> BRITAIN'S biggest company, BP, has angered human rights groups by becoming involved with Indonesia's brutal security forces in an attempt to protect a £28 billion gas production scheme. The company is using officers from the country's feared Mobile Police Brigade (Brimob) – which has been accused of numerous human rights abuses – to guard explosives. . . . Some critics believe the army may have already staged violent incidents as a pretext for intervention. One occurred in 2001, when five police officers were killed. . . . Barnabas Mawen, a pseudonym for one of the group which killed the policemen, told *The Sunday Times* that Indonesian military agents had supplied him with bullets, food, and money before the attack. BP said its security policy was designed to minimize the likelihood of military involvement.

Grimston and I reduced the complexity of the actors and the events that I had learned about during my fieldwork into a few legible paragraphs. By working with Papuan human rights activists and a British journalist, I had helped translate information gleaned from structurally marginalized sources into a genre of reportage that has currency in the halls of global power. In a sense, I had helped transform what Donna Haraway calls *situated knowledges* into *a view from nowhere*. Situated knowledges are faithful accounts of a real world that are simultaneously based in a no-nonsense commitment to realism and bound by radical historical contingency. This method of knowing is in contrast to a disembodied form of vision that claims to see everything from nowhere (Haraway 1999). In the article that appeared in *The Sunday Times*, "I" appeared to leave my own point of view behind and see the world from nowhere within it (cf. Nagel 1986: 67). "I" became *The Sunday Times*.

My translation work was, in part, compatible with Haraway's project: she has challenged us to "translate knowledges among very different – and power-differentiated – communities" (1999: 175). As with all attempts at translation, things were lost in the *Sunday Times* article: a detailed account of macabre human rights abuses in Wasior, the broader context of West Papua's independence movement, and competing Papuan views about the BP gas project. Yet, I found myself tussling with Haraway's ideas as my complex partialities and situated knowledges all but disappeared behind my byline in *The Sunday Times*. Passing, even if just for a moment, as an unmarked author with objective authority gave my work currency and credibility in social worlds where Papuans are largely excluded. An emergent coalition of Papuan groups – students, environmentalists, and human rights advocates – wanted to see the BP project stopped. My work was being drawn into this coalition. For some Papuans the publication of this short article represented a victory.

Telys Waropen, the human rights official who turned my going away party into a serious lesson about post-colonial knowledge politics, did not send a note of congratulations about my *Sunday Times* article. From a distance, I imagine how this story that just stuck to the narrowly construed "facts" might be useful in his struggle within the Indonesian government to get justice for the survivors of human rights abuses in Wasior. I also imagine the feelings of ambivalence that Waropen and others must have felt when this story appeared under my byline. Even as the disembodied subjectivity of the unseen "I" produced the effect of reliability and credibility, it hid painstaking research and advocacy by Papuan human rights workers. Ultimately, I was unable to respond to Telys Waropen's demand that I name my Papuan sources. In the hours before the story went to press, the *Sunday Times* editors cut the only sentence that quoted a Papuan source by name.

Even as my emergence as an expert-in-action was warmly greeted by Papuans who opposed the BP project, I drew criticism from some branches of the independence movement. Many Papuans saw BP as an ally in their struggle for freedom. The 2000 Papua Congress, an unprecedented event where hundreds of delegates united behind public demands for independence, had been funded, in part, through donations from BP.[4] The Papuan Presidium Council, the group that organized the Congress, received money from BP for their accommodation, transportation, and meeting venues (Richards 2002: 14–16).

---

[4] Brigham Golden, personal communication, New Orleans, November 20, 2002; Taha Al Hamid and Benny Giay, tape-recorded interview, Entrop, Jayapura, April 14, 2003.

Several months after my story ran in *The Sunday Times*, I found myself participating in a public conversation about BP with a member of the Papuan Presidium Council. The BBC radio World Service had scheduled an interview with me about BP's community-based security policy. In the hours just before the interview I learned that Viktor Kaisiepo, a Papuan independence activist who had lived much of his life in exile in the Netherlands, was going to be on the program as well. It was to be broadcast live.

As the radio show started, I quickly summarized the evidence that Indonesian military agents had provoked violence near the BP project site. I also recounted how BP had reneged on their promises to not work with Indonesian security forces. Kaisiepo did not directly engage with my claims about BP's community-based security policy, but stressed the importance of the project as a whole continuing: "Papuans as a people have the right to development." Met with this challenge, I found it difficult to represent the views of Papuan activists who opposed the BP gas project. Kaisiepo presented a direct challenge to foreign activists who want to see the BP project stopped.

Confrontations often mark moments of failure in cross-cultural mediations. Overt challenges test the allegiances of translators and culture brokers. I had come to know Viktor Kaisiepo years earlier, when I was just beginning my research on aspirations for freedom in West Papua. After the BBC radio program he sent me a friendly e-mail in the Papuan dialect of Indonesian. He addressed me as *Napi,* which means "you/friend" in the Biak language: "I'm glad to see that Napi is taking up the issue of BP and these military shenanigans. How can the international community force the Army to return to their barracks and stop all of this provocation?" Here Kaisiepo suggested how we might collaborate. While he clearly wanted the BP project to continue, he also wanted to stop the military violence. He was implicitly saying: "On this, at least, we can work together." Practical alliances, like confrontations, can produce an awareness of the relations of power that underlie the transfer of knowledge across cultural domains (Clifford 1997: 182).

Many people in West Papua sought me out as an ally. John Rumbiak and other close Papuan associates encouraged me to research the collaborations of the Papuan Presidium Council and other prominent independence leaders. I learned about the ties linking the Presidium to multi-national corporations and even Indonesian military agents. As I worked to understand these unexpected entanglements, I became allied with a particular faction of the movement.

The human rights activists who recruited me into their own projects of research and advocacy led me to meet with people whom I had not previously imagined as potential allies. In the face of being outflanked by big power, activists taught me the importance of incremental and partial victories. Securing a meeting with particular key officials, I came to learn, could be a significant achievement. I found myself donning a suit and tie to join Papuan activists during meetings with government representatives in Washington, London, and Jakarta. Meetings often involved specific "asks," or requests for action. Sometimes my meetings resulted in bringing a new ally into a fragile, contingent coalition that backed a particular initiative. As I tried to present compelling briefings to officials, I studied the architecture of power.

Serving as an advocate led me to think clearly and deliberately about why I write and who will read my words. I found myself putting in long hours to translate Indonesian-language human rights reports with the hope that my work might be read by a handful of key government officials. In other cases, I found myself writing up brief news items for electronic distribution to the small group of international advocates who are actively campaigning about West Papua.

Many other scholars have become advocates for the indigenous groups they study. Charles Hale, for example, has used rigorous forms of data collection, methods of causal analysis, and new computer-based cartographic programs to aid the political struggles of the weak. Positivists have long viewed politics as an influence to be purged from disinterested research. Hale has called for a rethinking of approaches to "activist" anthropology. He urges anthropologists to "deploy positivist social science methods and subject them to rigorous critique while acknowledging with acceptance the cognitive dissonance that results" (Hale 2006: 113).

Other approaches to the politics of knowledge avoid cognitive dissonance. Standpoint epistemologists see all knowledge projects as political – researchers are never free from the values and interests of particular social locations. Their subject positions shape the types of questions that they ask. Sandra Harding writes that it is "far too weak a strategy to maximize the objectivity of the results of research that empiricists desire" (1996: 241). She calls for a "strong objectivity" which requires that scholars "be integrated into democracy-advancing projects for scientific and epistemological reasons as well as moral and political ones" (2004: 136). Politically guided research projects, Harding argues, produce stronger claims to knowledge than those guided by the illusion of value-neutrality.

My own project wedded a rigorous empiricism with a commitment to listen to structurally marginalized narratives. During my research and writing I tried to keep my guiding questions open to renegotiation with Papuan intellectuals who sought me out as an ally. Overt challenges became opportunities for critical reflection even as they taxed my emotional and intellectual resources.

For Sandra Harding, standpoint theories are in direct opposition to the "God Trick" (Harding 2004: 128). Rather than critique the God Trick from the outside, it is possible to rescript it from within. We can be tricksters. We can play with the God Trick. While avoiding the temptation to try to see everything, we can see some things well and speak our knowledge with the voice of authority. Marking what we know as "activist knowledge" is a mistake. We can disappear at moments, blending into the architecture of knowledge/power, to emerge later with unexpected insights.

In creating an anthropology that is ready to travel off the shelf we should be prepared to face multi-directional demands for accountability – from informants who "talk back," from libel laws, and from a reading public who desire particular narrative forms. Being deceptive, presenting flimsy knowledge claims, will clearly not aid the political struggles of people who seek us as allies. Learning to follow the epistemological standards that operate in different domains, and mediating among these systems of knowing, can produce knowledge claims that stick.

As I finish this essay in November 2007 I look toward the final weeks of completing my Ph.D. dissertation, and beyond to revising the manuscript as a book. In this larger project I am juggling multiple genres and narrative forms: indigenous parable, figural realism, ethnography, oral history, and memoir. In trying to serve as a faithful translator, in trying to do justice to nuanced dreams of freedom in West Papua, I intend to do more than simply stick to the facts, narrowly construed. At the same time I work to know things that matter, and know these things well, I work to craft an ethnographic portrait of multiple coexistent realities in West Papua. Even as their dreams are dashed – by indifferent institutions of power, and by raw violence – Papuans imagine surprising futures. Chronicling such unexpected, hopeful visions might well generate emergent political possibilities.

Acknowledgments

Long conversations with Maria Puig de la Bellacasa, Jessica Falcone, James Clifford, Donna Haraway, Anna Tsing, and Maria Vesperi have helped me probe the limits of knowledge politics. Members of my writing group at UC Santa Cruz – Scout Calvert, Rebecca Schein, and John Marlovitz – proved to be thoughtful guides as I put pen to paper. Steinur Bell helped tighten the final draft.

References

Boeyink, David E. 1990. Anonymous Sources in News Stories: Justifying Exceptions and Limiting Abuses. *Journal of Mass Media Ethics* 5(4): 233–46.

Brundige, Elizabeth, Winter King, Priyneha Vahali, Stephen Vladeck, and Xiang Yuan. 2003. *Indonesian Human Rights Abuses in West Papua: Application of the Law of Genocide to the History of Indonesian Control.* International Human Rights Clinic, Yale Law School. www.law.yale.edu/outside/html/ Public_Affairs/426/westpapuahrights.pdf. Accessed August 28, 2008.

Clifford, James. 1997 *Routes: Travel and Translation in the Late Twentieth Century.* Cambridge, MA: Harvard University Press.

Gillard, Michael. 2002. Colombia Murder Claim Hits BP. *Sunday Times*, April 21.

Hale, Charles. 2006. Activist Research v. Cultural Critique: Indigenous Land Rights and the Contradictions of Politically Engaged Anthropology. *Cultural Anthropology* 21(1): 96–120.

Haraway, Donna. 1999. Situated Knowledge: The Science Question in Feminism and the Privilege of Partial Perspective. In *The Science Studies Reader.* M. Biagioli, ed., pp. 172–88. New York: Routledge.

Harding, Sandra. 1996. Rethinking Standpoint Epistemology: What is "Strong Objectivity"? In *Feminism and Science.* E. F. Keller and H. E. Longino, eds., pp. 235–48. New York: Oxford University Press.

Harding, Sandra. 2004. Rethinking Standpoint Epistemology: What is "Strong Objectivity"? In *The Feminist Standpoint Theory Reader: Intellectual and Political Controversies.* S. Harding, ed., pp. 127–40. New York: Routledge.

Kirksey, S. Eben. 2002. Spirited Fight. *Guardian*, May 29, Society: 9.

Nagel, Thomas. 1986. *The View from Nowhere.* Oxford: Oxford University Press.

Richards, Chris. 2002. Way beyond Petroleum. *New Internationalist* 344. Available on-line: www.newint.org/issue344/beyond.htm. Accessed August 28, 2008.

Said, Edward W. 1979. *Orientalism.* New York: Vintage Books.

Spivak, Gayatri Chakravorty. 1988. Can the Subaltern Speak? In *Marxism and the Interpretation of Culture.* C. Nelson and L. Grossberg, eds., pp. 271–313. Chicago: University of Illinois Press.

Taussig, Michael. 1984. Culture of Terror – Space of Death: Roger Casement's Putumayo Report and the Explanation of Torture. *Comparative Studies in Society and History* 26(3): 467–88, 492–7.

Vidal, John. 2008. Shattered Illusions. *Guardian*, March 19, Society: 8.

15

The Trope of the Pith Helmet: America's Anthropology, Anthropology's America

Micaela di Leonardo

I have long seen my role as that of a progressive political writer as well as a scholar. Given these concerns, the issue of the relative efficacy of my work looms large. In my youth, I had delusions of grandeur: I imagined, for example, that my first book, *The Varieties of Ethnic Experience*, would supplant Herbert Gans' *Urban Villagers* on college course syllabi and even in popular bookstores. I felt that I had a much better handle on the phenomenon of American white ethnicity than did Gans – especially in terms of its connection to race and racism – and wrote better than he did to boot. I thought that my historical political-economic and California regional contextualization and especially my feminist analysis of ethnic women's lives would capture the attention of scholars across several disciplines. Need I go on? I was a naive idiot.

Books do not become well known because of their virtues, although merit is usually a necessary if not sufficient feature. Books reach large audiences when they are well publicized (as *Varieties* was not), when their authors have influential patrons or friends who will write reviews and recommend the work (nope), and when their themes intersect in key ways with the zeitgeist, the spirit of the times. Alas, my leftist feminist analysis of the "white ethnic renaissance" was doomed on multiple zeitgeist grounds. I began research in the progressive 1970s, but published in the Reaganite mid-1980s. The flurry of public interest in hyphenated European-Americans was over, the glow of celebrity having shifted towards WASP wealth. "Leftist" anything, a draw from the late 1960s through the 1970s, became perceived as toxic, and, sad to say, the 1970s flurry of popular interest in feminist perspectives suffered the same fate. Finally, books with regional themes sell if the region described is also a key node of the literary and publishing industry. Nope again: post-hippie and pre-Silicon Valley Northern California was only of interest to itself. New York-based reviewers and press couldn't be bothered to investigate a book about a region where they hadn't grown up and didn't live.

Nevertheless, I was luckier than many. *Varieties* sold respectably if not wildly, was quite popular as a course adoption book in California, and gained staunch fans among progressives teaching all over the US. Despite lukewarm support from the publisher and the appallingly bad political context of its publication – which, after all, was much worse for the American minority poor, AIDS victims, and the Nicaraguans, among many others, than it was for me – my book stayed in print for thirteen years. I was even luckier with my two feminist anthologies, *Gender at the Crossroads of Knowledge: Feminist Anthropology in the Postmodern Era* (1991) and *The Gender/Sexuality Reader* (co-edited with Roger Lancaster, 1997), both of which, benefiting from the ongoing strength of feminist scholarship if not feminism in American public life, were academic best-sellers.

But then I spent a decade of my life working on one book, into which I poured accumulated knowledge and passion. Given the conservatizing times and my opposition, as I will explain, to key shifts in anthropological scholarship and especially to the Fourth Estate's very framing of our discipline, I couldn't expect it to be particularly influential. But I still had hopes – which were to be dashed by a completely unexpected, hilarious and yet disgusting shift in the zeitgeist. Let me explain.

Poor-Bashing and Halloween Costumes

Exotics at Home: Anthropologies, Others, American Modernity – which was published in 1998 – was born out of triangulated outrage, and a series of political and intellectual excitements. It is a study of the symbiosis between American anthropology and American popular political culture over the course of the twentieth century. I spend considerable time on the appearance of anthropology in the contemporary American public sphere, and since finishing the book, have maintained a watching brief on larger media developments. These developments not only further instantiate my original analysis of the uses of anthropology as trope in current American popular political discourse, but also help to explain, beyond the points I have laid out above, why and how – because I am not interested in guild defense here, but in politics – it is frequently so difficult to gain access to the contemporary public sphere for anthropological knowledge with progressive political implications. The trope of the pith helmet – the sets of discursive modes through which "anthropologizing" is publicly understood – affects us all, not just progressive anthropologists attempting to reach scholarly and popular audiences, but all American and global citizens attempting to apprehend Otherness as we live through the sped-up global trajectory of neoliberal capitalist growth.

The triangulated outrage, which gave birth to *Exotics*, is simply explained. First is the horror of living through the years of Reagan–Bush immiseration, as government support was withdrawn and private capital depredations encouraged, as the numbers of the poor and the extremely wealthy skyrocketed and the middle-income population dwindled, as American cities became spectacles of this increasingly concentrated, racially inflected inequality.[1] I experienced this immiseration as quotidian life on one block of a working-class neighborhood in New Haven, Connecticut that shifted, in the course of my five years' residence, from nearly all-white to nearly all-black as the drug economy and street prostitution became increasingly visible.

New Haven was and is for me field site as well as residence, and one of the most telling, and depressing, aspects of my ethnographic work in the 1980s and early 1990s was my white *and black* neighbors' unselfconscious use of underclass ideology in their attempts to make sense of the declining quality of life they were experiencing. As I and others have pointed out, this son-of-culture-of-poverty frame, popularly available throughout the 1980s and then made academically respectable through the 1987 publication of sociologist William J. Wilson's *The Truly Disadvantaged*, makes a series of empirically inaccurate claims about impoverished urban minority residents, and in so doing as well denies the operations of urban political economy. In addition, it neatly re-establishes anti-feminist notions of women's functions and legitimizes racist apprehensions – as long as they are directed towards only those nonwhites who are poor (di Leonardo 1998: chs. 2 and 6). Despite radical scholarship, despite gallant political organizing – against immigrant-bashing and so-called welfare reform, for example – and even in the midst of the political-economic lessons of the revived Clinton economy and the horror of the war years with George W. Bush, blame-the-victim underclass ideology, a key element of neoliberalism, is still pervasive across both academic and popular precincts of the contemporary public sphere.

But in anthropology, we actually saw very little underclass writing in the 1980s and 1990s. This was in part because of the relatively liberal cast of

[1]   This analysis is documented, with abundant citation, in di Leonardo 1988, chapters 2 (79–144) and 6 (pp. 314–67).

the field, but more due to shifting trends in the discipline. For many of us, the rise of postmodernism in the academy coincident with Reagan–Bush political-economic developments was the pouring of salt into open wounds. It was certainly the case that many radical scholars had fallen into economically reductionist arguments, and that discursive and cultural analyses can be extraordinarily useful. It was also the case that watching one's anthropological colleagues and graduate students become enamored of textual analysis, of chiasmus and aporia, and perturbed over power dynamics only insofar as they involved the textualization of a dyadically circumscribed ethnographic encounter, in the same years that the gap between rich and poor widened rapidly and homelessness grew exponentially, the federal government abandoned the cities, hate crimes rose horribly, and the United States reasserted its global imperial role, was an exceedingly annoying experience. Nor did it help to be informed that, in continuing to assert the necessity of analyzing gender- and race-inflected shifting capitalism, one was clinging to discarded modernist grand narratives (di Leonardo 1998: ch. 2). This phenomenon, then, was the second source of outrage that gave rise to my book. In *Exotics*, I offer careful critiques of postmodern anthropology and try to engage simultaneously in cultural and historical political-economic analyses. I try, in other words, to practice what I preach.

The third angle of outrage is familiar to many of us who work on the United States. It is that constellation of academic and popular constructions of anthropology that construes its subjects as exotics, primitives, Others, anyone "not-Us." This presupposition is not only profoundly anti-empirical, denying the long and rich history of self-study in both American and British anthropology; as I document in *Exotics*, it has led to the ridiculously repeated Fourth Estate *and anthropological* "discovery," since the 1940s, that anthropologists are "just now" turning their sights to the United States. It also defines Americanist anthropology, quite automatically, as declassé, lesser, not really anthropology, unlikely to lead to important theoretical and methodological insights (di Leonardo 1998: 25–78). And I allow my pique at this phenomenon free rein in *Exotics*.

But most importantly, this construction of anthropology effaces the contours of national and global power through the hiving off of cultural difference from historical political economy. I have identified (and here I am moving from outrages to political and intellectual excitements) in popular culture and literature, and even in use among anthropologists since the 1920s, a trope I label the anthropological gambit: the humorous assertion that "we" are *just like* the fill-in-the-blanks. Primitives "R" Us, Edith Wharton's novels, Gary Larson cartoons, the late Horace Miner's creation of the strange tribe the Nacirema ("American" backwards), and a host

of commercial advertising all make lavish use of this trope. I myself
enacted it in my first ethnography, when I complained humorously that my
Italian-American informants kept offering to look up the answers to my
questions: "To comfort myself, I imagined Trobriand Islanders answering
Malinowski's questions by referring to their *Fielding Guides*." My moment
of insight came when I realized that Americanist anthropologists working
with more stigmatized populations – racial rather than ethnic, impoverished
rather than working-class, sexual minorities – do not use the gambit: it is
no longer amusing when the population being compared to "primitives" or
"exotics" itself has been labeled primitive and exotic.

To identify and attack the gambit is not, then, to stand against cross-
cultural comparison, or to deny that citizens of advanced capitalist societies
perform rituals, attach themselves to totems, and so on. The "destructive
analysis of the familiar," as Edward Sapir put it, is one element of a liberatory cultural critique in use in the West at least since Montaigne's ironized
cannibals. It is rather to point out the ideological functions of ahistorical,
noncontextual "defamiliarization" – cross-cultural vignettes which place
Others at a temporal distance and thus efface the questions of history
and power on both poles of the contrast. Thus a seemingly benign, if
silly, phenomenon is revealed as both reflecting and enacting cultural
imperialism.

I identified as well a series of what I labeled anthropological "Halloween
costumes" into which, since the 1960s, the public has tended to squeeze all
anthropological knowledge. Each costume – Technicians of the Sacred, Last
Macho Raiders, Evil Imperialist Anthropologists, Barbarians at the Gates,
and Human Nature Experts – reflects minor strands in some past or present
anthropological writing. More important, each twists anthropological narratives in unintended, generally rightist, directions. The costumes, in other
words, act as Procrustean beds, amputating those pesky limbs of anthropological knowledge that flop outside their predetermined grids.

Technicians of the Sacred, for example, posits anthropologists as time
travelers who bring back to us visions of Noble Savages living non-
violently and cooperatively, practicing sexual equality, respecting the environment, and engaging in religious worship somehow more "spiritual" than
ours – and as time travelers who return from pilgrimage with comparative
ratings of quality ethnological commodities so that we can buy our salva-
tion as informed consumers. Last Macho Raiders imagines anthropologists
as a guild populated by cool Harrison Ford lookalikes, virile, positive
imperialists. Here the Other is terminally orientalized – a proven inferior
who must be forced to cooperate in studying his or her own present or past,
an exotic individual who, in the aggregate, can provide the *mise-en-scène*

for an infinite series of dramas of modern Western selfhood. The Evil Imperialist Anthropologist became a stock postmodern character in the 1980s, a readily available punching bag to stand in for whatever the writer disliked about the modern world. Marianna Torgovnick (1990), Trinh Minh-Ha (1989) and many others wrote about evil imperializing anthropologists without actually having read any post-World War II anthropological work. Of course there were many radical and native anthropologists from the 1920s forward as well. Barbarians at the Gates, on the other hand, is a rightist envisioning of anthropologists as foolish multiculturalists, misguided salespeople hawking inferior cultural materials to a gullible American public. The early 1980s American press free-for-all around Derek Freeman's attack on Margaret Mead's work in Samoa was redolent with this trope.

Finally, Human Nature Experts paints anthropologists as pure scientists – gatherers of facts alone (di Leonardo 1998: 25–78). This would seem an innocuous interpretation, if it were not for the fact that this frame has been most often used as a means of defining Others as "our" natural laboratory – and thus defining Others as inferior to ourselves without even the bother of overt deprecation. My overall argument, thus, was that we should do our best to avoid donning or having these costumes thrust upon us in the public sphere, as each is connected to retrogressive political projects.

There is much more in the book, as befits a decade-long project. For example, I chose a series of deliberately popular, successful ethnographies written by American anthropologists, published from the 1920s into the 1980s, and contextualized them in the politics and anthropological practice of their respective eras. I both offer textual analyses of these ethnographies and chase down popular and scholarly reviews of them as proxies for contemporaneous reception. In the process, I identify the trope of the Dusky Maiden in ethnography and follow its varying, still exotic appearances over the decades. And I give Margaret Mead's half-century career and presence in anthropology and the wider public sphere extensive and highly critical treatment, while also defending her against Derek Freeman's silly posthumous attack and the Reaganite sexist and racist media firestorm following his publication of *Margaret Mead and Samoa*.

I Did Not Have Sex with That Book

The University of Chicago Press marketed *Exotics at Home* as a trade book, and I received good reviews in the *Times Literary Supplement*, the *Village Voice*, and the *Boston Book Review*, as well as more scholarly responses in *American Anthropologist* and *New Politics*. I received an honorable mention for Best Senior Book from the American Ethnological Society, having had the poor judgment to publish *Exotics* in the same year as *Testing Women, Testing the Fetus* by the magnificent Rayna Rapp who was awarded the prize.

As well, scholars I attacked or whom I just annoyed got revenge in the pages of *Dissent* and *American Ethnologist*. Others, especially postmodernists, simply ignored the book, and for a short period I became the negative cynosure of the New Right, especially after pieces of mine bearing on Mead appeared in *The Nation* and the *American Anthropologist*. This was a very bitter pill to swallow: to be hounded as a Mead apologist when I had clearly said such nasty things about her – nasty enough to be jacked up by Mead-lovers at two different conferences. I comforted myself that it was yet another proof, as if proof were needed, that New Right acolytes are as abysmally stupid as we've all been saying all along, that they cannot read the very words in front of their eyes.

I did have great hopes of contributing to important scholarly conversations about gender, race, and class shifts in American history, politics, and culture. I have had modest success here in terms of the book becoming a mandatory text for progressive anthropology graduate programs such as the CUNY Graduate Center. And without expecting it, I did succeed in one arena: interdisciplinary American Studies, where *Exotics* has been heavily cited and assigned in courses throughout the United States and in Europe and even Japan. I do not, however, expect to reach a large popular audience with the book, because of its scholarly tone, because of its intransigent anti-postmodern stance, because of its radicalism in a conservative era – but most importantly, because the book offers a serious critique of precisely the public culture in which popular reviews would appear. I think that progressive anthropologists *can* reach large popular audiences, as I hope to do with my New Haven book, with skillfully written, accessible, historical ethnographic narratives that eschew biting the public cultural hand that feeds them.

There is, however, also a role for chance. I *was* in line to appear on Ray Suarez' National Public Radio book show – and then the Clinton–Lewinsky impeachment hearings began. After that, all bets were off, for me and for so many other authors, and indeed activists who wished to discuss burning political issues and were shunted off-track for months as the press went hog-wild over the story. I can say with some chagrin, then, that the ex-President's private member altered the course of my book, as well as of American history.

Let me just comment on some of the contents of the "anthropology as trope" media file I have amassed since finishing *Exotics*, and the implications of my analysis for all of us. Any collection of this sort is obviously partial, reveals the idiosyncrasies of the collector. I have done more standard LexisNexis searches on, for example, the media normalization of the New Right's attack on the concept of cultural relativism (di Leonardo 1998: ch. 6). But my obsessive reading and listening have caught *en passant* references that LexisNexis is not designed to winnow out. In my file from the late 1990s, a significant grouping, including several cartoons, engages in the anthropological gambit, happily nattering on about the "discovery" of "strange tribes" of elderly white Middle Americans, or noting that "Tribesman Practices Ritual Mammal-Meat Consumption," i.e. white businessman eats a hamburger.[2] Then there is a cluster of pieces arising from the merchandising elements in the Technicians of the Sacred construct: home design articles extolling "ethnographic" wood, and fashion pieces praising the "urban tribalism" of one designer – at one point, hilariously, referring in Mrs. Malaprop mode to "ethnocentric" garb – or even voicing fears that the fashion industry treats women of color as "exotics, tribal, ethnic, not just regular people" (Bucholz 1998).

A few pieces in the file are by or about anthropologists in the Human Nature Expert mode. In most cases – and this is a shift from the radical 1960s and 1970s that my book documents and analyzes – anthropologists who gain major press attention are either sociobiologists, or are engaged in work that, while it may be interesting and insightful, is of little threat to the powers that be.[3] My favorite Human Nature Expert example, however, comes from the Tom Joyner Morning Show, a syndicated black drive-time radio show about which I have since written three articles. On March 26, 1998, in the midst of discussion of Clinton's policies, Tavis Smiley – a Black Entertainment Television regular who was a guest that morning – commented: "And that's why I don't understand the uproar around his statement that we all come from Africa." Jay Anthony Brown, a comic and regular on the show, interjected: "It's an anthropological fact!"[4]

Then there are a number of relatively benign versions of the Pith Helmet – the anthropologist as the wacky adventurer. A *New York Times Magazine* piece, for example, begins, "For cultural anthropologists who monitor New York's tabloids, this season is already a textbook classic" (Tierney 1998).

---

[2] Roz Chast cartoon, "The Lost Tribe," *The New Yorker,* April 5, 1999; R. Bolling cartoon, "News of the Times," *Village Voice,* June 8, 1999.
[3] Good examples are Hafner 1999 and Shweder 1997.
[4] Tom Joyner Morning Show, WVAZ (Chicago), March 26, 1998.

Adventures in Friendly Fire

What I want to focus on and end with, though, is a rather sinister development – the sneering, negative citation of anthropology in order to define
the writer as a superior analyst of human social processes. Ten of my items
fit this category, and all of them appear in "respectable" middlebrow or
highbrow publications: two from the *New York Times*, two from the *New
Yorker*, two from *Harper's Magazine*, one from the *Village Voice*, one from
the *New York Observer*, one from the *Chicago Tribune Sunday Magazine*,
and the last from the *New York Review of Books*. Many of the writers are
well known, and of decidedly progressive politics: Mike Davis, Barbara
Ehrenreich, Tom Frank. Whatever is going on here?

Part of the process seems to involve the general middlebrow acquiescence
in the Barbarians at the Gates frame, the New Right attack on its own
falsely constructed, "anything goes" notion of cultural relativism that
I analyze in *Exotics* and in an article for *The Nation*. Here anthropology
is identified with and effectively substituted for a series of stigmatized
Others. A *New York Times* piece on Linda Tripp as part of a tradition of
"citizen denouncers," for example, first reports that "some historians . . . are
looking at denunciations not just as a political phenomenon but as an
anthropological one as well." "Anthropological" here means consideration
of phenomena across time and space, a process I thought was called
comparative studies and was commonly practiced across the humanities
and social sciences. At the end of the article, however, a historian "confesses
some discomfort with the anthropological approach," because he feels that
the United States cannot be compared in any way to totalitarian societies
(Waldman 1999). Similarly, a literary scholar who taught a Great Books
sequence at the University of Chicago notes that her students were "self-
selecting, choosing a course with an anthropological orientation," but that
she, "in what I hope was a usefully contrary spirit, [resisted] a kind of
cafeteria-style multiculturalism" (McLane 1999).

Then there are the reverberations from Derek Freeman's intellectually
bankrupt, but outrageously successful, Reagan-era attack on Margaret
Mead's Roaring Twenties interpretation of Samoan lives.[5] Adam Gopnik,
a *New Yorker* writer who seems to be negatively obsessed with our discipline, claims in one issue that "the Samoans, Margaret Mead's pick as the
gentle, sexually emancipated pastoral, are apparently as testy as a group of
Republican congressmen" (Gopnik 1999a). In another, he inveighs against

---

[5] Analyzed in *Exotics*, ch. 5: 263–313.

the use of the notion of "the culture of," as in post-Littleton "culture of violence." "To seek to anthropologize or philosophize it away," he writes, "to seek a 'deeper' or 'hidden' explanation – is to rob the event of its significance" (Gopnik 1999b).

This notion of "anthropologizing" as both an intellectually and morally inferior form of social interpretation is now widespread, but seems to draw not simply from Reagan-era Culture Wars epistemology. Tom Frank, in a piece titled "Brand You: Better Selling through Anthropology," indicts the new "ethnographic" movement in advertising that fits my Technicians of the Sacred costume: "It's Margaret Mead meets the Marlboro Man" (Frank 1999).[6] A *Village Voice* writer, praising a collection of photographs of drag kings, asserts that "they are not mere snapshots or *National Geographic* anthropological wonders" (Taormino 1999). And Barbara Ehrenreich, in a long investigative piece on low-wage women workers, sneers:

> Besides, I am not doing this for the anthropology. My aim is nothing so mistily subjective as to "experience poverty" or to find out how it "really feels" to be a long-term low-wage worker. I've had enough unchosen encounters with poverty and the world of low-wage work to know it's not a place you want to visit for touristic purposes (1999).

Ehrenreich, who holds a Ph.D. in biology – and who knows many cultural anthropologists, was even feted by feminist anthropologists at an American Anthropological Association Annual Meeting some years back, and therefore ought to know better than this characterization – took a strong pro-Sokal, "pro-science," anti-postmodern stance in the *Social Text* controversy of a few years ago. She seems to have decided that all cultural anthropologists are anti-empirical postmodernists who enter fieldwork in the spirit of Marie Antoinette playing shepherdess – that we all fit, in other words, a trivialized version of the costume I have labeled Good Subaltern, Evil Imperialist Anthropologist.[7] The *New York Times Magazine* ethicist, Randy Cohen, seems to share this notion. In a column responding to a reader asking if it was okay to visit a topless bar in an

---

[6] Frank does at one point absolve professional anthropology from his indictment. I think, however, that this is a Heisenberg effect: he had been given a copy of *Exotics* by my publicist, and cited it in the original draft of this article. He withdrew reference to it after I informed the *Harpers* fact-checker that I had never said that anthropologists hawk the Primitive, but rather that public culture does.

[7] The grand irony here, of course, is that it is precisely the postmodern anthropologists of the 1980s and 1990s who agonized at length in print about the ethics of "textualizing the Other." Ehrenreich just doesn't care.

"anthropological" spirit, Cohen wrote: "Nor am I persuaded that there's a meaningful distinction between 'anthropological' and 'condescending'" (Cohen 1999).

But radical historian Mike Davis, ironically, identifies all of anthropology with precisely the opposite construction available in popular culture – sociobiology. "The debate over the constitutive role of violence in human culture – killer apes, "Manson gangs" from Mexico, and all that," he writes, "belongs in the anthropology department. Historians are generally more struck by the changing scales and logics of violence over time" (1999).

Anthropologists are by no means the only intellectuals who can complain, in the Rodney Dangerfield line, that we don't get no respect. A late-1990s *New York Review* piece by Andrew Delbanco laments the public trivialization of literary studies in the wake of postmodern shifts. But then, again making the anthropology = postmodernism move, he asserts that the apotheosis of this shame is that "literature, in effect, became a branch of anthropology" (1999).

Our new role as the whipping boys and girls of middlebrow – and often highbrow – culture would not matter much if it were merely a question of damaged professional vanity. After all, many anthropologists already disseminate important knowledge in the public sphere through de-emphasizing their guild membership. What is genuinely important here are: (1) the ways in which these characterizations not only reflect but enact, often unconsciously, the revanchist race, class and gender politics of the post-Reagan era, and (2) the inability of radical, historicist cultural anthropologists to gain access not only to popular culture, but to representation inside the discipline – where recent debates have seemed to define all of us as either positivists – probably sociobiologists – or "pure" postmodernists. We all have a lot of work to do, inside and outside the academy. I hope that my analysis of what we're up against helps us to do it better.

References

Bucholz, Barbara. 1998. Upgrading Opulence. *Chicago Tribune Sunday Magazine.* October 18: 24.

Cohen, Randy. 1999. The Ethicist. *New York Times Magazine.* March 14: 22.

Davis, Mike. 1999. Repent! The End Is Near – And Much Worse This Time! *New York Observer.* January 18. Available at www.observer.com/node/40971. Accessed August 28, 2008.

Delbanco, Andrew. 1999. The Decline and Fall of Literature. *New York Review of Books.* November 4: 32–8.

di Leonardo, Micaela. 1984. The Varieties of Ethnic Experience: Kinship, Class, and Gender among California Italian-Americans. Ithaca, NY: Cornell University Press.

di Leonardo, Micaela, ed. 1991. *Gender at the Crossroads of Knowledge: Feminist Anthropology in the Postmodern Era*. Berkeley: University of California Press.

di Leonardo, Micaela. 1998. *Exotics at Home: Anthropologies, Others, American Modernity*. Chicago: University of Chicago Press.

Ehrenreich, Barbara. 1999. Nickel-and-Dimed: On (Not) Getting By in America. *Harpers Magazine*. January: 37–52.

Frank, Tom. 1999. Brand You: Better Selling through Anthropology. *Harpers Magazine*. July: 74–9.

Freeman, Derek. 1983. *Margaret Mead and Samoa: The Unmaking of an Anthropological Myth*. Cambridge, MA: Harvard University Press.

Gans, Herbert. 1982. *Urban Villagers: Group and Class in the Life of Italian-Americans*. New York: The Free Press.

Gopnik, Adam. 1999a. Animals Behaving Badly, *New Yorker*. July 19: 29–30.

Gopnik, Adam. 1999b. Culture Vultures. *New Yorker*. May 24: 27–8.

Hafner, Katie. 1999. Coming of Age in Palo Alto. Anthropologists Find a Niche Studying Consumers for Companies in Silicon Valley. *New York Times*. June 10: G1, G7.

Lancaster, Roger N. and Micaela di Leonardo. 1997. *The Gender/Sexuality Reader: Culture, History, Political Economy*. New York: Routledge.

McLane, Maureen. 1999. Who Says Great Minds Think Alike? *Chicago Tribune Sunday Magazine*. October 24: 12–20.

Minh-Ha, Trinh T. 1989. *Woman, Native, Other: Writing Postcoloniality and Feminism*. Bloomington: Indiana University Press.

Rapp, Rayna. 2000. *Testing Women, Testing the Fetus: The Social Impact of Amniocentesis in America*. New York: Routledge.

Shweder, Richard. 1997. It's Called Poor Health for a Reason. *New York Times*. March 9: E5.

Spindler, Amy M. 1997. Taking Stereotyping to a New Level in Fashion. *New York Times*. June 3: A21.

Taormino, Tristan. 1999. Of Butches, Kings, and Masculinity. *Village Voice*. October 5: 223.

Tierney, John. 1998. The Upside of Gossip. *New York Times Magazine*. January 25: 14.

Torgovnick, Marianna. 1990. *Gone Primitive: Savage Intellects, Modern Lives*. Chicago: University of Chicago Press.

Waldman, Amy. 1999. Before Tripp, A Long Line of Denouncers. *New York Times*. January 30: B9.

White, Constance C. R. 1997. Invoking Tribal Spirits as 90s Muses. *New York Times*. November 7: B13.

Wilson, William J. 1987. *The Truly Disadvantaged*. Chicago: University of Chicago Press.

16

The Book that Wrote Me[1]

Roger Sanjek

The Gray Panthers first entered the American national consciousness on a May weekend in 1972. Margaret E. Kuhn was a last minute stand-in at a press conference during the United Presbyterian General Assembly in Denver, and what seized the reporters were this elderly woman's persona and her words. The *New York Times* described a "slim 5-foot-3 militant [in] blue midi dress, whose slit revealed her stylish boots." The newspaper added, however, "Margaret Kuhn would not be flattered if someone told her she looked younger than her 67 years." Maggie, as everyone called her, left no room for doubt on this score. "I'm an old woman. I have gray hair, many wrinkles, and arthritis in both hands" (Blau 1972).

Such affirmation and realism about old age would be a continuing Gray Panther theme. Yet equally important, Maggie's message was not about senior citizen interest-group politics. She did raise issues concerning older people: increased Social Security benefits, resident rights in nursing homes, the inequity of mandatory retirement, "asinine" activities in "those damned golden age clubs." Yet, the *Times* continued, "her major concern is with issues that transcend age: war, peace, poverty, hunger, racial justice." And Maggie's feminist credentials were on her sleeve when she stated, "Ageism is just as pervasive in our society as sexism." She added that her group, numbering about one hundred, included some two dozen younger members, and she emphasized "the curious and wonderful" empathy between older and younger Panthers.

The Gray Panthers were first organized by Maggie in 1970, the year of her forced retirement at age 65 from the Presbyterian Church's national staff. Following her national publicity in Denver, this loose-knit group of retirees and students grew rapidly, with local groups, or "networks,"

---

[1] Portions of this essay are adapted from *Gray Panthers* (University of Pennsylvania Press 2009).

formed in New York City later in 1972, Berkeley, California in 1973, and points in between. By the first national convention in 1975 there were 28 networks. Six years later more than one hundred networks existed nationwide, with some thirty thousand financial supporters. Most active network members were over age 60, but about 10 percent were under 30. Members between 30 and 60 amounted to perhaps 25 percent, with great variation from one local group to another.

The Gray Panther movement was strongest in California, where I was a member of the Berkeley network in 1977–8. How I got there, and how my book, *Gray Panthers* (Sanjek 2009), was conceived, evolved, and completed has little to do with research proposals, standard fieldwork, or academic career hurdles. Still, it is the work of a social anthropologist who has attempted to employ an ethnographic sensibility and adhere to canons of validity he advocates (Sanjek 1990a). It is also, admittedly, the story of this activist movement as one Gray Panther lived and sees it – part ethnography, part history, part memoir.

What brought me to Berkeley was New York City's 1975 fiscal crisis. As an untenured assistant professor at Queens College, part of the public City University of New York, my job was in jeopardy. Luckily I was awarded a postdoctoral fellowship "in quantitative anthropology with public policy emphasis" at the University of California, Berkeley, where I could ride out the 1976–7 academic year on a leave of absence. My wife Lani Sanjek and I arrived in Berkeley in September 1976, intending to stay nine months. Lani had joined me in my dissertation fieldwork in Accra, Ghana, during 1969–71. After that she returned to Barnard College for courses in biology and chemistry, and then completed a second bachelor's degree in the nurse practitioner program at Lehman College, also part of the City University of New York. Once in Berkeley she became a volunteer at the Berkeley Women's Health Collective. On a visit to the Berkeley Free Clinic a staff member suggested she also consider the new Over 60 Clinic established by the Gray Panthers.

She did and was hooked, and soon I was too. Lani quickly became a full-time volunteer nurse practitioner at Over 60, and by December agreed to become director, and remained so for two years. She asked me to analyze the clinic's six hundred patient records (Sanjek 1977), a task suited to my novice computer skills – this was back in the day of feeding boxes of key-punched IBM cards into a card-reader attached to the campus mainframe. I was soon spending more time at the Clinic in South Berkeley than on campus. We were both now under the wing of our Gray Panther mentor, Lillian Rabinowitz, 66, a retired teacher and social worker, and a health care activist and visionary who had founded the Berkeley Gray Panthers.

In February 1977 I attended my first Gray Panther monthly meeting. I was struck immediately by the voluble energy of some two dozen gray-haired women and men talking about political issues and the activities of their "network." I quickly realized, first, that I had never been in a room with so many older people before, and, second, that whatever stereotypes of "senior citizens" I held had just flown out the window. I was 32, and for Lani and me the Gray Panthers transformed our notions of what our 60s, 70s, 80s, or 90s could be. For the next year and a half I was an active member of the Berkeley Gray Panthers as well as an Over 60 volunteer and secretary of its governing Gray Panther Clinic committee. In Berkeley we also met movement founder Maggie Kuhn. While there I applied for, but did not get, a position with the Alameda Health Consortium, an alliance of community clinics that Over 60 belonged to and I worked with on a large research project. In September 1978 I returned to Queens College where I have taught since.

During the next two years the need for "a book" preoccupied me. A prospectus for one based on my Ghana fieldwork had been rejected and I did not submit it elsewhere. Instead I focused on journal articles, which got me through the tenure hoop. I also began teaching a "Peoples of New York City" course to help formulate a new fieldwork project, which I eventually started in Elmhurst-Corona, Queens, in 1983 (a book from that came much later – Sanjek 1998).

Four months before leaving Berkeley I had read a paper about my Over 60 Clinic applied and advocacy roles to a CUNY Graduate Center anthropology colloquium while on a brief visit to New York. I dusted it off in 1980 to present to audiences at the University of Connecticut, the University of Massachusetts at Amherst, and the social medicine residency program at Montefiore Hospital in the Bronx (it was later published as Sanjek 1987). It was now dawning on me that the story of the Clinic and the Berkeley Gray Panthers could be the subject of a book. In Berkeley I never considered what I was doing to be fieldwork. I was a participant, not an observer, and I had taken no fieldnotes. But I did have reports, minutes, and other materials produced by me, as well as Clinic and Gray Panther documents, meeting agendas, and newsletters. I proposed writing a book utilizing these materials, plus my headnotes (see Sanjek 1990b), titled "Gray Panthers, Community Clinics, and Health Care Politics," and intended to devote a 1981–2 sabbatical year to it. Once it began, I decided first to visit the national Gray Panther office and archive in Philadelphia to gather material for an introductory chapter. There I found 29 boxes of materials, plus office files that traced the formation and growth of this political movement. The Berkeley story now took back seat, and during that year I wrote two chapters covering the life of Maggie Kuhn and the origin and first five years of the Gray Panthers.

Meanwhile I had joined the New York Gray Panthers in 1980, and was elected to the movement's National Steering Committee of 30 members in 1981. More of my energy was devoted to activism again, this time on housing issues in New York City (Sanjek 1982, 1984), but at the same time I kept at work on the book. In 1982 I revisited Berkeley to update the story there, and I began a chapter on the national movement from 1976 onward. In 1983 I resigned from the steering committee after a wrenching internal struggle between a "National" faction comprised of Philadelphia staff, organization officers, and Maggie, and a grassroots network faction that questioned "National's" decisions, particularly about the 1983 Social Security "compromise" and its purge of the knowledgeable and popular leader of the Panthers' national Health Task Force (these events are covered in my book). Dispirited, I was unable to return to the book for two years. In 1985 I completed a long chapter on Berkeley and Over 60. I circulated the three draft chapters to several national and Berkeley Panthers, who gave helpful responses. I also sent them to Maggie but she did not respond.

I hoped to complete the book in 1986 but that year my father died of prostate cancer and amidst mourning and family responsibilities (see Sanjek 1988) I made no further progress. By this time my Queens research project, as well as other professional activities as editor of the Cornell University Press Anthropology of Contemporary Issues Series since 1982, and Councilor of the American Ethnological Society during 1984–8, consumed my energies. In 1987 I was appointed director of a research center at Queens College, where I served for three years. Now unable to attend daytime meetings, I had to end my active membership in the New York Gray Panthers. I attended the network's twentieth anniversary celebration in 1992, and returned in 1996 to speak about my research on immigration and racial transition in Queens.

My Gray Panther chapters remained in a file drawer. In 1995 Maggie Kuhn died, but the movement persisted. My book on Queens, *The Future of Us All: Race and Neighborhood Politics in New York City*, was published in 1998. I then began thinking about returning to the Gray Panther manuscript, compelled by a sense of responsibility to the older friends and mentors I had known in Berkeley and New York, some now gone. With this in mind, Lani and I attended the 1999 Gray Panther national convention. There, thinking of myself as an observer rather than a participant, for the first time in my Gray Panther experience I took extensive fieldnotes. And with trepidation that my book might have been superseded, I also then read Maggie's autobiography, *No Stone Unturned: The Life and Times of*

Maggie Kuhn (Kuhn, Long, and Quinn 1991). Aside from personal details about Maggie, however, it contained relatively little about her career not found in previous writings, and surprisingly little about the Gray Panthers.

The aftermath of my Queens book and research project occupied me through 2002 (Sanjek 2004). When at last I turned to my Gray Panther manuscript I began by compressing and revising the three original chapters, which comprise about one-third of *Gray Panthers*. Next I read the files of newsletters I had continued to receive as a dues-paying member of the Berkeley, New York, and national Gray Panthers. I had by then decided to include the New York story in the book, and to cover the 1970s period before I joined as well as extend the account beyond 1987 to the present. As in Berkeley, I recorded no fieldnotes during my 1980–7 New York Gray Panther years but I did have files of documents to draw upon.

A 2003–4 John Simon Guggenheim Memorial Foundation fellowship allowed me to work on the book full-time. Shortly after the fellowship year began, my mother, then 86, had a stroke, which was followed by rehabilitation therapy and her move to an assisted living residence. A few months later I was hospitalized and spent a month in recovery. These experiences deepened my understanding of the late life and health care issues I was writing about. So did the last months and days of Lani's father, who died at 93 in 2006, and the hip fracture and recovery of her mother, 92, in 2007. Both of them aged in place at home with family members close at hand. Although nursing home reform was the cause that attracted the largest number of young Gray Panthers during the 1970s and 1980s (Sanjek 2009), I had not been active around or knowledgeable about long-term care alternatives. My experience while writing my book of visiting my mother during hospital stays and at her assisted living residence, however, made the saga of Gray Panther long-term care activism more meaningful to me.

In 2003 the New York Gray Panthers, with new leadership, resumed operations after a three-year hiatus. I attended a January 2004 meeting and later volunteered to become secretary and to restart the network newsletter. I came initially as an observer, and recorded fieldnotes. I was redrawn into activism, however, particularly around opposition to the war in Iraq, against which I have protested with the Granny Peace Brigade coalition at more than a dozen events, and in resisting President George W. Bush's crusade to privatize Social Security. As an active network member I felt recording fieldnotes about "us" seemed inappropriate, and in 2005 my notes trailed off. So in telling the New York story through 2007 I again relied on meeting minutes and newsletters (which I produced) and other documents. I did, however, take fieldnotes at the Gray Panther national convention in Seattle in 2004, and also during a visit to Berkeley and attendance at a Gray Panther National Board meeting in 2007.

The passages of my book that proved most difficult to write were those in which I am a participant. I could not responsibly leave out my involvement in helping stabilize the Over 60 Clinic after Proposition 13 in 1978, participation in Gray Panther local–national conflicts during 1982–3, years as convener of a New York City umbrella group of nine networks during 1982–7, housing activism in the early 1980s, or public speaking on Social Security in 2005 and testimony on accessible and visitable housing before the New York City Council in 2007. But this is a tiny part of a larger movement, now spanning nearly four decades, which involved thousands of others, including many who inspired and conspired with me. I found I had to write out in full detail the sections in which I figured, and then edit them down, or completely edit them out. In several instances the writing process released and then tamed pent-up emotions, particularly about intra-organizational disputes. Once these events were captured on paper several seemed less significant than they did at the time, and a few even unnecessary in the full sweep of the narrative.

What remains, and certainly whatever "ethnographic truths" my book contains, is "thus inherently *partial* – committed and incomplete," as James Clifford puts it (1986: 7). In writing *Gray Panthers* I have realized more than ever that ethnography is always autobiographical to some degree – that, to quote Johannes Fabian (1983: 87–8), "anthropological discourse formulates knowledge that is rooted in an author's autobiography." But I also understand, as Judith Okely observes, that "if we insert the ethnographer's self as positioned subject into the text, we are obliged to confront the moral and political responsibility of our action" (1992: 24), and that, in the words of Clifford Geertz, "the responsibility for ethnography, or the credit, can be placed at no other door" than that of its author (1988: 140). These thoughts have continuously occupied me in writing this book, not only regarding what to write but also what to leave out.

Let me now round out the story of what I learned from my three lives as an active Gray Panther (during 1977–8, 1980–7, and since 2004), and from my even longer view as anthropologist and historian. The older people who became Gray Panthers in the 1970s realized that "At no point in one's life does a person stop being himself [or herself] and suddenly turn into an 'old person.'" Yet they also understood that in the society around them "the public image of most older people is far more negative than the view that [those] 65 and older hold of themselves" (Harris 1975: 52–3, 129). Negative characterizations and treatment of the old became more pervasive with the United States' transition from nineteenth-century pre-industrial republic to twentieth-century corporate state (Achenbaum 1978; Fischer 1978; Haber 1983). In 1968 Robert Butler coined the term "ageism" to describe them.

> Ageism is the systematic stereotyping of and discrimination against people because they are old. . . . Old people are categorized as senile, rigid in thought and manner, old-fashioned in morality and skills. . . . Ageism allows the younger generation to see older people as different from themselves; thus they subtly cease to identify with their elders as human beings. . . . Ageism is manifested in . . . outright disdain and dislike, or simply subtle avoidance of contact; [in] discriminatory practices in housing, employment and services of all kinds; [in] epithets, cartoons and jokes. (Butler 1975: 12; see also Shield and Aronson 2003: 103–10, 131)

Maggie Kuhn and the Gray Panthers offered something different. As she put it,

> Aging begins with the moment of birth, and it ends only when life itself has ended. Life is a continuum; only we – in our stupidity and blindness – have chopped it up into little pieces and kept all those little pieces separate. . . . Old age is nothing to be ashamed about. Rather, it is a triumph over great odds, something to be proud of. To be old and gray is beautiful. . . . [D]on't deny your history. . . . Review what you've done and be strengthened by it. . . . Old age should be esteemed as a flowering not a fading of life. . . . We're the elders of the tribe and the elders are charged with the tribe's survival and well being!

Maggie's message resonated with many of those in their 60s or early 70s whom she targeted as Gray Panther recruits – former union organizers, peace activists, leftwing political party supporters, women's rights advocates, retired social workers – and who first became politically active in the 1930s. They were also attracted by the Panthers' active protesting of the war in Vietnam, which distinguished this movement from self-identified "senior citizen" organizations.

The anti-war stance was also the initial link to young recruits, and peace and opposition to US foreign intervention remained central Gray Panther causes. The young Gray Panthers of the 1970s and 1980s had been molded by the decade of the 1960s. In addition to the Vietnam War, which did not end until 1975, they had lived through African American civil rights struggles and the assassinations of President John F. Kennedy, Malcolm X, Martin Luther King, Jr., and Senator Robert Kennedy. They had participated in or been exposed to "[t]he student movements of the 1960s [which] represented a backlash on the part of middle-class youth against the . . . failure of America to live up to its moral claims" (Evans and Boyte 1992 [1986]: 101).

It was the union of these two generations that made the Gray Panthers the unique organization it was. For both generations the political was already personal, and each brought their experiences and values with them. Both the young, not yet encumbered with the demands of careers, and the old, now freed from theirs, had time to devote to activism. The Panther intergenerational milieu was new to each cohort, as were the friendships rooted in shared political commitments and activities that crossed three, four, even five decades.

For young Queens Gray Panther and medical anthropologist Susan Meswick, her membership gave her "a different sense of aging – something to look forward to. Not retirement [but] an enlightenment, a renaissance – to use those years to do the things you really wanted to do." She admired the older women who "had seen the role of women change in their lifetimes, and wanted to expose other women to that." Meswick, in her early 30s, became close to Central Queens Gray Panther convener Evelyn Neleson, who was in her early 70s. "I was her daughter in some ways. I could talk to her about things her daughter didn't, and she talked to me about things she didn't with her daughter." At steering committee meetings, "There was always a social component – discussions, a very comfortable situation. . . . I thrived on it too, the mutual respect and learning." My own Gray Panther experiences resonate with those of Meswick.

The Gray Panthers bequeath us an activist ideology and tactics still relevant and usable, a generation of young Panther "alumni" now approaching our own elderhood, and a social justice agenda not yet fulfilled. Whether or not today's Gray Panthers survive or flourish, we will need something like them – for their perspective on the human life cycle, their intergenerationalism, and their readiness, as Maggie Kuhn urged, to "get out there and do something about injustice."

References

Achenbaum, W. Andrew. 1978. *Old Age in the New Land: The American Experience since 1790*. Baltimore: Johns Hopkins University Press.
Blau, Eleanor. 1972. Gray Panthers Out to Liberate Aged. *New York Times*, 21 May: 68.
Butler, Robert. 1975. *Why Survive? Being Old in America*. New York: Harper & Row.

180   *Roger Sanjek*

Clifford, James. 1986. Introduction: Partial Truths. In *Writing Culture: The Poetics and Politics of Ethnography*. James Clifford and George Marcus, eds., pp. 1–26. Berkeley: University of California Press.

Evans, Sara and Harry Boyte. 1992 [1986]. *Free Spaces: The Sources of Democratic Change in America*. Chicago: University of Chicago Press.

Fabian, Johannes. 1983. *Time and the Other: How Anthropology Makes Its Object*. New York: Columbia University Press.

Fischer, David Hackett. 1978. *Growing Old in America*. New York: Oxford University Press.

Geertz, Clifford. 1988. *Works and Lives: The Anthropologist as Author*. Stanford: Stanford University Press.

Haber, Carole. 1983. *Beyond Sixty-Five: The Dilemma of Old Age in America's Past*. New York: Cambridge University Press.

Harris, Louis and Associates. 1975. *The Myth and Reality of Aging in America*. Washington, D.C.: National Council on the Aging.

Kuhn, Maggie, with Christina Long and Laura Quinn. 1991. *No Stone Unturned: The Life and Times of Maggie Kuhn*. New York: Ballantine.

Okely, Judith. 1992. Anthropology and Autobiography: Participatory Experience and Embodied Knowledge. In *Anthropology and Autobiography*. Judith Okely and Helen Callaway, eds., pp. 1–28. London: Routledge.

Sanjek, Roger. 1977. *A Profile of Over 60 Health Services Users: A Report and Recommendations*. Berkeley, CA: Over 60 Health Clinic Geriatric Health Services Program.

Sanjek, Roger. 1982. *Federal Housing Programs and Their Impact on Homelessness*. New York: Coalition for the Homeless. Reprinted in Jon Erickson and Charles Wilhelm, eds. *Housing the Homeless*, pp. 315–21. New Brunswick, NJ: Rutgers University Center for Urban Policy Research.

Sanjek, Roger. 1984. *Crowded Out: Homelessness and the Elderly Poor in New York City*. New York: Coalition for the Homeless and Gray Panthers of New York City. Reprinted in *Homeless Older Americans: Hearing Before the Subcommittee on Housing and Consumer Interests of the Select Committee on Aging, House of Representatives, 98th Congress*, Comm. Pub. No. 98–461, pp. 119–84. Washington, D.C.: Government Printing Office.

Sanjek, Roger. 1987. Anthropological Work at a Gray Panther Health Clinic: Academic, Applied, and Advocacy Goals. In *Cities of the United States: Studies in Urban Anthropology*. Leith Mullings, ed., pp. 148–75. New York: Columbia University Press.

Sanjek, Roger. 1988. Preface. In *American Popular Music and Its Business: The First Four Hundred Years* (3 vols.). Russell Sanjek, vol I., pp. v–vii. New York: Oxford University Press.

Sanjek, Roger. 1990a. On Ethnographic Validity. In *Fieldnotes: The Makings of Anthropology*. Roger Sanjek, ed., pp. 385–418. Ithaca, NY: Cornell University Press.

Sanjek, Roger. 1990b. A Vocabulary for Fieldnotes. In *Fieldnotes: The Makings of Anthropology*. Roger Sanjek, ed., pp. 92–121. Ithaca, NY: Cornell University Press.

Sanjek, Roger. 1998. *The Future of Us All: Race and Neighborhood Politics in New York City*. Ithaca, NY: Cornell University Press.

Sanjek, Roger. 2004. Going Public: Responsibilities and Strategies in the Aftermath of Ethnography. *Human Organization* 63(4): 444–56.

Sanjek, Roger. 2009. *Gray Panthers*. Philadelphia: University of Pennsylvania Press.

Shield, Renée Rose and Stanley M. Aronson. 2003. *Aging in Today's World: Conversations between an Anthropologist and a Physician*. New York: Berghahn.

17

Fighting Words

Paul Farmer

Anthropologists are members of a tribe that spends most of its time talking and writing about other tribes. Over the last few generations, the understanding of fieldwork has changed, and so has our sense of what our books and papers are supposed to do. No longer content to "document the last vestiges of a vanishing way of life," to paraphrase the elegiac tone that runs through so many familiar monographs, we also hope to piece together a larger story that will include the "people with history" and the "people without history" (in Eric Wolf's [1997] pungent formulation), show the connections among our worlds and tribes, and perhaps, through literary representation, help to win a greater degree of respect and autonomy for the usually disempowered people with whom we spend years of our lives. But our projects – and projections – always need to be re-evaluated in terms of outcomes. What does our writing do? How do we come to writing, and what happens when we have been lucky enough to capture the attention of some part of the public? Here I will tell a little bit about my own work, but also point out its limitations.

I had the good fortune to be in Haiti when it was time to prepare the proposal for my Ph.D. dissertation. I assembled a grandiose document about what I wanted to do in my thesis, which was to look at several different afflictions and ailments, including (in keeping with the times), an interesting and little-studied "culture-bound disorder" (Farmer 1988a). Of course, it is not possible to do that – one cannot really write a Ph.D. thesis on several different things at once while completing medical studies, which I was also doing. So in the end I narrowed my focus to two: tuberculosis, an old disease, and AIDS, a new disease.

I had worked hard to get a couple of articles out when I was a graduate student, one in *American Ethnologist* (1988a), and another in *Dialectical Anthropology* (1988b), both of which, I suppose, had and have a very restricted readership. I was proud of the acceptances, of course; one of the articles was based on two years of ethnographic research. But we should be, let's say, sociologically realistic about the impact that one has in writing for a specialized journal: readership is limited, though libraries keep one's article on the shelf for the potential ideal reader.

Then Stan Holwitz, a wonderful editor from University of California Press and a friend of my mentor, asked if I would like to publish a book with them. I had just finished medical school, and of course no one had ever said anything like that to me before. I replied, "Yes, absolutely!" I spent a good deal of my non-clinical time over the next year shortening my thesis so that it could be published as a book.

AIDS and Accusation appeared in 1992. The book was "critically successful" (which means that someone beyond one's mother and thesis advisors liked it a lot) and UC Press kindly kept it in print. A few years later, this publisher asked me to write a preface for a new edition of the book (2006), which I wrote in Rwanda in August of 2005. This was a very gratifying experience because it allowed me to reflect on exactly the issues that the editors of *Anthropology off the Shelf* have asked us to consider: Why do you write? For whom do you write?

The answer to the second question was easy. Of course, I had written this book for my peers. I did not write it for the people whom I had the great privilege of serving as a physician. Even when *AIDS and Accusation* was later translated into French, I knew that it would never be read by anyone who was likely to end up as one of my patients in rural Haiti. They do not speak French any more than they speak English, and many of them do not read or write at all. This gap between our two audiences, our two foci of authorial responsibility, creates a feeling of unease in many of us – even among those anthropologists and ethnographers who do their work in a place where their "informants" (as we like to say in anthropology) are able to and do read their books.[1] Not only are my "informants" unlikely to read my writings, but in all of the 25 years that I have worked in Haiti, no one has ever asked me to write about their suffering – not ever, not once. I've written and conducted research for other reasons.

I would like to think that I've grown into those reasons. Twenty years ago, when I was a graduate student, I might have said that I was doing this in

---

[1] See, for example, the controversy sparked by Nancy Scheper-Hughes's (1979) book *Saints, Scholars and Schizophrenics: Mental Illness in Rural Ireland*. Of course, many anthropologists' work is read eventually by those whose societies are depicted; fierce debates may ensue over contested issues, from kinship to patterns of violence. Scheper-Hughes herself discusses this in her 2001 essay "Ire in Ireland," and one recent example is found in Borofsky's overview of the Yanomami debates (2005).

order to serve the destitute, or to speak truth to power. Nowadays, I would ratchet down my expectations of what it is that ethnographic inquiry does and says. I would say that I think with my hands, that writing books allows me to think, to process problems and solutions. I have met people who are able to think without preparation, without writing things down. I am not able to do that, however. I have to work things out by writing. Perhaps books allow a reader to process problems and solutions too.

Since I am a physician as well as an anthropologist, I also write for a medical audience. Those are my other peers, my medical peers. But I cannot honestly claim after twenty years of such writing that this medical work is going to be read by or to directly influence those who determine the fates of many people we serve as physicians. For it is, in the places I've worked, politicians and generals who control the salient dimensions of our patients' worlds, and they are probably immune to the results of technical discussion in medical journals.

Another example may bring home the bifurcation of our audiences and the limits to our effectiveness. Twelve years ago, our group[2] wrote a book called *Women, Poverty, and AIDS*. The primary contributors were medical anthropologists, and the Society for Medical Anthropology of the American Anthropological Association awarded the volume its Eileen Basker Prize. Getting this recognition was nice, but the things that we predicted twelve years ago about poverty, gender inequality, and AIDS have all come to pass. One could say that the confirmation by experience shows that our book was significant, but all of us would have preferred to be proven wrong. Sadly, I don't think that any of us who participated in the book believe that we did much to alter the trajectory of this epidemic through our writing. And yet none regret having invested a great deal of time in working on this and other projects, because it allowed us to clarify our own positions and to understand what it was that we were doing.

I've sounded this note twice now: the benefit of writing works of medical anthropology is primarily to the writers. This may sound selfish. How do others benefit from my prolonged out-of-doors education? Wouldn't I be better advised to spend more hours with my patients and leave the writing to journalists? I would argue that the benefits of writing are the benefits of thinking, but with an added, communal dimension. Before testing them through the struggle to make them obey the rules of logic, grammar,

---

[2]   The Institute for Health and Social Justice, the research and academic arm of Partners In Health (www.pih.org).

organization, and demonstration, my ideas, like anyone else's, are apt to be patchworks of anecdote bullied around by the pressures and interests of the moment. Writing brings clarity, some degree of generalizability, and a wider context of understanding. It is sometimes through writing that I discover what the real stakes are. This activity, seemingly far removed from "action" (a Che Guevara fantasy is common among medical anthropologists, and the word "action" often summons it up), is indispensable to figuring out what actions are needed and where they should begin.

Among the books I've written, *The Uses of Haiti* is closest to me. The book was not written for my peers in medicine or anthropology, but rather for a broader audience, with the intention of affecting US policy towards Haiti. The audience in the end was not large, though gratifyingly diverse, and I learned that it had been very naive on my part to assume that historical and moral arguments would influence one iota the brutal course of my country's behavior toward its impoverished neighbor. Originally published in 1994, *The Uses of Haiti* is still in print, and now boasts more introductions and prefaces and postfaces than any book really needs. Though swollen to the size of the Gutenberg Bible or thereabouts, and quite futile as an effort to change United States policies towards Haiti, it did, I hope, help to inform an American public that was awakening to the troublesome issues of global trade policy, immigration, foreign aid, and political meddling that are at the top of any Haitian's list of concerns. Moreover, in the aftermath of publishing the book I did something else: if you can imagine it, I decided that I would embark on an activist tour.

It was the summer of 100 talks – literally. I ended up going to places such as Fort Leavenworth, Kansas, places in the middle of the country that I did not know very well. I stayed at church ladies' houses, slept on sofas, and gave AM radio interviews.

I recall one interview with a South Florida radio station. I grew up in Florida, so I gave myself a certain latitude there. People were calling in, saying, "Who does Dr. Farmer think he is? We can't have Haitians coming to our shores – you know, *boat people*." And I said, "Why not? I'm a boat person." This confused the listening audience significantly. I didn't mention which boats, but it is true that my forebears had come here on boats. My joke didn't register.

And so I have had these two very different writing experiences: writing for a university press – for my peers – and writing more broadly for the American citizenry. Two very different experiences, two different audiences, and yet I cannot claim to have gone very far even on a scale of argumentative effectiveness. For the intellectual or writer who gets up every morning hoping to change the world through words and ideas, the slogan "Never Again" serves as a grim reminder of the limited power of reason, principle, or storytelling. In Haiti, I see the same problems that my predecessors saw a hundred years ago, aggravated daily, and renewed by the same crimes and different perpetrators. In 1994, Rwanda was the scene of a genocide with 800,000 or more people killed in just 100 days. This is one of the most abundantly documented episodes of mass violence on record, with photographs, real-time reporting, and even scholarly work published in newspapers, books, and on the Internet. It happened only 50 years after the "never again" of the death camps of the Holocaust; 20 years after the "never again" of the Khmer Rouge in Cambodia; ten years after the "*nunca más*" of mass disappearings and torture in Argentina; concurrent with the "never again" of ethnic cleansing in Bosnia and Herzegovina; and nine years before genocide started again, this time in Darfur.

The recurrence of such events should make us pause. The destruction of the European Jews during the Second World War, which was to have set a milestone of horror never again to be reached, gave rise to the slogan "never again" but leaves the scope of its applicability undefined. All right, perhaps such things will "never again" happen at that scale in certain European countries, but they continue to occur elsewhere with a frequency that makes the slogan "never again" hollow, hypocritical, or Eurocentric. Some of us have worked on presentations for the American Anthropological Association on the topic of mass violence and its prevention. But I do not think that any of us can say with any conviction that getting information and documentation "out there," in the spirit of the Enlightenment ideal, is adequate to prevent mass violence. It would be disingenuous for writers and historians to say otherwise.

A few years ago I met a woman in the airport in Kigali, Rwanda. I had just purchased an enormous book called *Rwanda: Death, Despair and Defiance* (African Rights 1995). I was sitting right there reading it, and as it turned out the woman who wrote it, Rakiva Omaar, was sitting next to me.

We started talking, and she signed my book. She was running a human rights group, and had written and published that book within months of the genocide. Imagine that. Imagine having that sort of documentation – hundreds of pages of documentation.[3] Omaar, who was not Rwandan

---

[3]   The original edition, published in 1994, was about 750 pages; the revised edition, published a year later, is 1200 pages.

herself (she was actually from Somaliland), had been there almost by accident. She was so traumatized by what she saw in the first half of 1994 that she could not leave, and to this day has never left. She still works on this topic. I asked her, "You got this written in September of 1994?"

"Yes," she said.

I kept looking at this copyright date, September 1994, over and over, aghast at the failure of the notion of "never again." How could this happen if people *knew* that it was happening?

But people knew about the Rwandan genocide; it was very well documented. And it happened anyway.[4]

In a 2004 op-ed essay on Darfur in the *New York Times*, "Will We Say 'Never Again' Yet Again?" Nicholas Kristof urged that informed people should call a spade a spade and do so loudly. He advocated using the term "genocide" as opposed to "ethnic cleansing," and tried to press the American government to use this trigger term publicly. The assumption was that "nothing is so effective in curbing ethnic cleansing as calling attention to it." But I am afraid that this claim was optimistic. Since Kristof's article appeared, the US government has indeed called the killings in the Sudan a genocide – the first time in history that my country has done so while the violence was ongoing – and taken the further step of imposing sanctions, but the violence continues unabated. Clearly, writing about and documenting an event such as this one are not always enough to "curb" mass violence.

I realize that I am giving a glum view of writing books about some of the kind of things that anthropologists write about: mass violence, or the oppression of poor or subaltern peoples. I think it is important not to fool ourselves about what it is that our books do. Some books break out of an academic setting, like Howard Zinn's *A People's History of the United States* (2003). But generally, if we're lucky, our books are read by 5-, 10-, 15,000 people or maybe a few more – but the sales don't lie. This is the sociology of the knowledge we produce: on the whole, it does not reach a very broad audience.

Do we really need to claim that we are altering the impact of noxious social forces with our writing? I think it is better to simply acknowledge that we don't, and then have our own reasons for doing what it is that we do. Reasons such as being able to clearly explain what has happened, if we are looking backwards in time, or what *is* happening, as Rakiva Omaar

---

[4] I've discussed this at some length in *The Tanner Lectures* (2006b): "Never again? Reflections on human values and human rights."

did in Rwanda in 1994. I think it is enough to be able to document carefully and clearly what is happening. That is my idea of speaking truth to power with books. Of course I wish that we were able to alter the fates of impoverished, oppressed, subaltern peoples with our writing. But I am not sure that we can.

I think there is a saving grace for writers if we choose to link our work to activism. And we should not be embarrassed as anthropologists or sociologists or historians – as people who have been trained in scholarship – or apologize for our activism, or for being part of a movement. Looking back at the classic and successful movements – the movement for civil rights, the movement for women's rights, and the abolition movement in England and the US – one can mark their strategy: they wrote books. They wrote reports on slavery, the nineteenth-century precursors of human rights dossiers. They wrote them in settings in which the vast majority of the populace did not have the right to vote, and so they wrote for governments. But most importantly, they linked their writing to activism: for example, the English abolitionists moved around the United Kingdom, parts of Europe, and even the United States on horseback to gather 500,000 signatures on their petitions to Parliament. I think this is a very inspiring example for those of us who are interested in activism and in changing the way things are.

There are also examples for our times. A few years ago, Howard Zinn introduced me to the book *Green Parrots: A War Surgeon's Diary* (2004). It was written by an Italian named Gino Strada, a surgeon-writer who moved from front line to front line over fifteen years, all the while noting in his journal what he saw in the places at war where he worked: Afghanistan, Peru, Rwanda, Iraq, and Bosnia, among others. This entry, from Kurdistan, is dated April 5:

> Heider arrives in the Hospital. He comes from a mountain village in the Sidikhan valley, a three hour drive from Choman . . . He was herding a flock of goats up on the mountain slopes. He saw the mine at the last moment, one second before stepping on it. We operate immediately, but for that leg there is nothing left to do. The day after surgery we show him the mine "catalogue" that we have put together, like criminal identification photos in a police station. He recognizes a VS-50, one of the many small mines manufactured in Italy. "But I did not see that black plug in the middle," he says. It is the rubber plate, which detonates the mine when stepped on. He has been lucky. Probably that mine was upside down, so a good deal of the explosion was unleashed toward the ground, and the boy has "only" lost a foot. (2004: 13–14)

This book, originally published about a decade ago, closes with a description of the organization Emergency, which Strada helped found. Emergency provides medical and surgical assistance to civilian (and sometimes military) war victims. Strada notes that "for years Emergency has been committed to persuading Italy to abandon the use of anti-personnel mines. On October 27, 1997, the Italian government approved a law which bans manufacture or sale of these devices" (Strada 2004: 144).

This triumph – the triumph of banning the production of landmines in a sophisticated European country – was not accomplished by his book. It was done by activism, by organizing the population to send letters and cards to their elected officials in Italy. Gino Strada and the laypeople of Italy, like the abolitionists of an earlier era, exemplify the power of integrating the production of knowledge with broad-based, unified activism. If we want to contribute to improving the fates of impoverished, oppressed, subaltern peoples, as I know many of us do, we are going to have to broaden our notion of how books work, and what we can do with them.

Acknowledgments

I am grateful to my friend and life-long editor, Haun Saussy, who has helped me "think with my hands" through writing, and to friends at the University of California Press, especially Stan Holwitz and Naomi Schneider, who have kept my books in print and introduced them to a broader audience than I anticipated upon publishing my first book with them.

References

African Rights. 1995 [1994]. *Rwanda: Death, Despair and Defiance*. London: African Rights.

Borofsky, Robert. 2005. *Yanomami: The Fierce Controversy and What We Can Learn From It*. Berkeley: University of California Press.

Farmer, Paul E. 1988a. Bad Blood, Spoiled Milk: Body Fluids as Moral Barometers in Rural Haiti. *American Ethnologist* 15(1): 62–83.

Farmer, Paul E. 1988b. Blood, Sweat, and Baseballs: Haiti in the West Atlantic System. *Dialectical Anthropology* 13(1): 83–99.

Farmer, Paul E. 2003 [1994]. *The Uses of Haiti*. Monroe, ME: Common Courage Press.

Farmer, Paul E. 2006a [1992]. *AIDS and Accusation: Haiti and the Geography of Blame*. Berkeley: University of California Press.

Farmer, Paul E. 2006b. "Never again? Reflections on human values and human rights." In G. B. Peterson, ed. *The Tanner Lectures on Human Values, Vol. 26*, pp. 137–88. Salt Lake City: University of Utah Press.

Farmer, Paul, Margaret Connors and Janie Simmons, eds. 1996. *Women, Poverty and AIDS: Sex, Drugs and Structural Violence*. Monroe, ME: Common Courage Press.

Kristof, Nicholas. 2004. "Will We Say 'Never Again' Yet Again?" *New York Times*, March 27.

Kristof, Nicholas. 2008. "A Genocide Foretold." *New York Times*, February 28.

Scheper-Hughes, Nancy. 1979. *Saints, Scholars and Schizophrenics: Mental Illness in Rural Ireland*. Berkeley: University of California Press.

Scheper-Hughes, Nancy. 2000. Ire in Ireland. *Ethnography* 1(1): 117–40.

Strada, Gino. 2004. *Green Parrots: A War Surgeon's Diary*. Milan: Edizioni Charta.

Wolf, Eric. 1997. *Europe and the People without History*. Berkeley: University of California Press.

Zinn, Howard. 2003. *A People's History of the United States: 1492–Present*. New York: HarperCollins.

18

Taking Chances

Maria D. Vesperi

Partway through junior high my class was assigned to write essays for the annual Daughters of the American Revolution American History Essay Contest. An envoy from the DAR turned up to explain the spirit behind the competition, and at first all eyes turned to this novel presence. She spoke about patriotism and history for a while, and perhaps she went on to provide some rules about formatting our entries. I'm not sure, because my attention wobbled and dropped out a wide, oak-framed window during that part. I found gazing outdoors the most reliably engaging subject in our curriculum, and I generally liked to study ahead.

Most everyone saw the history assignment as a "research" project, which meant a trip to the public library and diligent paraphrasing from the dog-eared offerings on hand in the Juvenile Section. Mildly intrigued by the prospect of roaming further, I daydreamed about an afternoon set loose in the stacks. I had already breached the forbidden Adult Section for a biography of Andrew Jackson, provoking a swift rebuff from library staff. That news raised a flash in my mother's green eyes and prompted a rare but always effective telephone call.

Henceforth I was granted free if grudging access to all collections. The librarian was reduced to shaking her head in a way that foretold a debauched future in the company of adult fiction.

At best, I figured, one among us might gratify teachers and parents with an essay contest win, place or show. At worst, the DAR. assignment was a chance to meet friends while loitering in the library with its mysterious old smells – smells that lent temporal depth to the books on the shelves and the frozen face of the sentinel grandfather clock, its hands and pendulum stilled halfway through the phases of some long-ago moon. Either way, we were made to understand, the writing competition meant mandatory, non-negotiable homework.

My mother found humor in the essay contest, signaled by the mischief around her mouth when I requested back-story on the DAR. Both my parents excelled at explaining the *why* behind the *what*, particularly when it offered an object lesson about unfair treatment based on language, looks or religion. Had I asked my dad, I'm pretty sure he would have said that the DAR took pride in reminding us they were here well before the Irish, Italians and Jews. My mom explained simply that DAR members traced their ancestry to the early English settlers. Then I caught that look again. Only later could I see the irony that had made her smile: rows of desks occupied by the spawn of more recent immigrants, heads bent over patriotic tributes as they swam upstream toward a club they could never join.

My folks could have used this moment to relate how Eleanor Roosevelt quit the DAR back in 1939, after Marian Anderson was barred from its concert hall. They knew me too well, though. Armed with that news I might have dawdled fatally over the assignment, a move they would be hard-pressed either to contradict or to explain to my teacher. Worse, I might have written the kind of "story" that had taught my mother to check my homework carefully – *very* carefully – before I turned it in.

It was the Space Age and my bedroom boasted a transistor radio and a 1960 *World Book* in a long shelf of red volumes. The set stretched to subsequent annual yearbooks, where the NASA program was prominently featured. I was genuinely inspired by space travel and I figured astronauts were safe patriotic subjects, contrasted as they were at every turn with those space-racing Soviets who rocketed hapless dogs and monkeys to near-certain death from Behind the Iron Curtain. I had John Glenn in mind when I found myself writing from the viewpoint of an astronaut in his capsule, gazing at Earth and contemplating re-entry.

It was fun to craft thoughts about science and space, using facts to create a mood that I hoped evoked history in the making. I copied my essay neatly, following the mysterious but rigid entry rules which by then had been hammered home by our teacher. Quite familiar with the mindless, lock-step reports we were trained to produce in school, I took for granted that my entry would be disqualified. I smiled a secret smile as I turned it in, and I cared not at all.

I was daydreaming again when the slender, neatly coiffed descendant of Our Founding Fathers reappeared. We were told that the local chapter had found its winner, and that person was a member of our class! My interest was piqued and I glanced speculatively toward the most likely suspects: three high-achieving girls. Somehow I didn't think a boy would win. It had crossed my mind that the *daughters* of Paul Revere might have chips on their shoulders – born too late for the glory of forcing a Redcoat retreat and unfit regardless because they were female. It had been my experience that such groups, like the Girl Scouts and Camp Fire Girls, might have something to prove in the "we-can-do-anything" department.

Then time began to slow in the dissociated way that can accompany shocking news. I heard my name and I saw myself from a slight distance as I stood to accept my prize, a small box that contained a bronze medal suspended on grosgrain ribbon. Schoolwork was generally so rote and unchallenging in my late-industrial mill town that I sometimes felt guilty about collecting good grades. This time, though, I felt empowered. I took a chance with my writing, and I won.

My approach to the craft of writing began to take shape and direction that day. A long-held suspicion was dramatically confirmed: coloring inside the lines was not just boring – it wasn't enough. I began to appreciate how vital it was to immerse oneself in a situation, either by reading intensely or, where possible, through direct experience. Then it was time to construct a detail-rich platform and take an imaginative leap. I began to see that serious writing was active – athletic even – and that immersion, intensity and leaping were only the preparatory stages to writing itself.

Over time I began to notice also that some students and colleagues get stuck at this point, more or less in midair. They might be gifted and intrepid fieldworkers, meticulous readers, spectacular thinkers. When it comes to the craft of writing, though, they seem afraid even to pick up their tools. They approach it with the dread I reserve for exploring the guts of stuttering major appliances – Do not remove protective cover! Tampering with circuits voids warranty! – or film-inspired nightmares about grabbing the controls of a plane when the trained professional goes unconscious. Scary stuff. Painful endings.

I would rather take that chance, though. Giving up is hazardous in a different way. My *beau idéal* is the main character of Richard Russo's *Straight Man*, the beleaguered chair of an English department at a backwater college. At midlife he is reduced to regretful glances at the centerpiece of his book collection, his own slender, early novel that once held the portent of a fine literary career. Instead, he finds himself in a windowless office, trying half-heartedly and failing to dodge a relentless barrage of scutwork.

Where did that second novel go? He thinks he knows: "The academic memo, the voice message, the e-mail (which I don't receive) taken together are the cotton plugs that drown out the siren's song. At first resentful, we scholar-sailors come to be grateful for them" (Russo 1997: 175).

For many would-be anthropologist-writers, students and colleagues alike, self-confident beginnings give way to punishing self talk, procrastination, endless Internet "research." As they soldier on toward burnout, the work of writing is never described as playful, never fun. The papers and books they eventually produce are dutifully factual and well hedged with citations. I can see that the subjects who inhabit these pages are respectfully, carefully, even lovingly described. But they don't, in the words of Stephen King, "walk and talk."

As an undergrad anthropology student I learned that functionalist theory, while tidy, is predictably static in its application. A must-avoid. No one mentioned that writing styles have similar predictive value; like theories, they create known effects. That I had to learn for myself through trial and error, and from articles such as Tom Wolfe's "Seizing the Power," a short course on what a handful of carefully honed techniques can do. Dissecting the "new" journalism that thickly described the events of the 1960s, Wolfe claims it as writing that called out, "Hey! Come here! This is the way people are living now . . . You won't be bored! Take a look!" (1973: 28).

Wolfe pinpoints precisely how Jimmy Breslin, Joan Didion, Gay Talese and others "seize the power" to draw readers to non-fiction through their use of dialogue, scene-by-scene construction, third-person point of view and the rich detail he summarizes as "symbols of status life." He explains that fiction writers abandoned realism in favor of "novels of ideas," passing up countless opportunities to tell the important stories that were unfolding in the nation's cities. Along the way, he notes smugly, "In abandoning social realism novelists also abandoned certain vital matters of technique" (1973: 29–31).

I think third-person perspective is best left to novelists; anthropologists are well rid of the omnipotent conceit that they can look through others' eyes and represent what they see, think or feel.[1] Wolfe's larger observation about abstract, minimalist novels remains relevant, though. "Ideas" are important, but not at the expense of holding the vibrant, fractious, awe-inspiring world in view. Since anthropologists volunteer – and dare – to mediate and translate "the way people are living now," it seems foolish not to keep the tools of the writer's trade sharp and close at hand.

Dialogue, for example, has gained new respect in ethnographic writing; it has been lifted to the level of an "approach" in some quarters with help from terms such as dialogic and polyphonic. While these literary concepts

---

[1] Kathleen Stewart's *Ordinary Affects* (2007, Duke University Press), uses third-person perspective to refocus attention on stories drawn primarily from her own life experience.

and the debates that surround them might seem a step back in the direction of jargon, I believe they have helped to refocus attention on the walking, talking human actors in ethnographic tableaus. Minimally, ethnographers are reminded that it's not enough anymore to lift blocks of transcription from one's interviews and plunk them down in the middle of a narrative.

That said, getting dialogue right remains truly difficult. Both Wolfe and James Clifford point to Charles Dickens as a master of this technique; Clifford positions it against Flaubert's "'free, indirect style,' a style that suppresses direct quotation in favor of a controlling discourse" (1988 [1983]: 47). Clifford points to *The Nuer* as an exemplar of masterful but controlling non-fiction, a theme picked up by Renato Rosaldo (1986), Clifford Geertz (1988) and many others.

Seeking stronger command of dialogue, I find it useful to examine how Dickens's characters talk to *each other* rather than to the reader, as ethnographic subjects are often made to do. Isolating quotes as bits of data has the effect of turning dialogue into monologue, desituating and decontextualizing people when fully situated subjects are in fact the writer's goal. Those in search of more recent examples should not be above a close look at contemporary novelists, including Stephen King. Forget the plots; Dickens's rambling serials weren't that well organized, either. Concentrate on how much is revealed through conversation.

Scene-by-scene construction – entering the field site, looking around, transporting the reader from one place or event to the next – is a hallmark of vivid ethnographic work and contemporary non-fiction as well. And Wolfe's "descriptions of status life" are the anthropologist's bread-and-butter catalogue of morals, manners and material culture: "the recording of everyday gestures, habits, manners, customs, styles of furniture, clothing, decoration, styles of traveling, eating, keeping house, modes of behaving toward children, servants, superiors, inferiors, peers, plus the various looks, glances, poses, styles of walking" (Wolfe 1973: 31, 32).

Wolfe's discussion prefaces an anthology that richly illustrates these four techniques, and many authors represented in *The New Journalism* continued to perfect them. Joan Didion's 1979 tour of gubernatorial real estate, "Many Mansions," serves well as a short but stunning example of how powerfully scene-by-scene construction and status life can be combined. Walking readers from room to room in the residence commissioned by Ronald Reagan during his term as California's governor, she points to concrete walls that "resemble" adobe and a vinyl counter that "resembles" slate. The kitchen suggests a house "built for a family of snackers," although Didion notes that the place was never occupied by Reagan or by his successor, Jerry Brown (1979: 67–9). The very emptiness of the structure conveys a texture of its own.

Then Didion takes readers on a parallel tour of the old governor's mansion, now vacant but still crowded with material symbols of a fine-grained, if idealized, upper-middle-class American world. There is a pastry marble in the kitchen, a gilt mirror frame that incorporates a bust of Shakespeare in the library. She finds bathrooms large enough "for chairs on which to sit and read a story to a child in the bathtub" (1979: 71–2).

Didion's descriptions of objects and spaces say much about the lives for which they were intended. She leaves readers with the question: "Which culture do you want?" without ever stating that marble is superior to plastic or that Ronald Reagan "resembles" a governor, but might indeed be something else.

In anthropology as in journalism, descriptions of status life are among the most powerfully subjective elements at a writer's command. Katie Trumpener and James M. Nyce explore how anthropological perspectives and archaeological techniques guide the use of this device in their analysis of Edith Wharton's 1929 novel, *The Age of Innocence*. Wharton, they explain, achieves "an ethnography of a distinctive set of customs and a way of life which no longer exists save in sentiment and memory" (1988: 162). Of course, Wharton wrote her books when most novelists were intently focused on the details of daily life, long before the rejection of collecting and cataloguing that Wolfe describes.

The better writers are at what they do, the more effortless and transparent their work appears. This can lead readers to assume that there is no mystery, that the "sites of production" are themselves transparent. I think this is why some social scientists are so quick to analyze popular media without doing fieldwork – without setting foot in a newsroom or production studio. If the writing is so accessible, it seems, there can't be much behind it.

There is danger in this assumption, and it is never accurate. Anthropologists know from experience that issues of judgment and balance plague any descriptive project. Decisions about what to emphasize, what to leave out, confound ethnographers from their first student field trips to their most mature works. There are questions of relativism, heterotopic representation, distortions of time. One way or another, though, collections from the field will be made to assume ethnographic form. The process should be active and intentional, guided not by a version of automatic writing but by the same level of strategic decision making that informs fieldwork itself.

Some ethnographers write novels or poetry as well, and a few are really good at it. That form of chance-taking never tempted me seriously – I find "writing about culture" to be challenging enough. I approach it from two directions that inform each other as I move along, as one might plot and plant a garden or design and build a piece of furniture. Substance resides in content, but craft means understanding the interplay between substance and form. In the case of writing, craft requires confidence in handling words, making them fit and support each other so that concepts at the core of a project can begin to emerge. For me, this is hard but satisfying work.

I have written a few long pieces about nursing-home life: first as a student, then as a journalist and, most recently, as an academic (Vesperi 1995, 2003). In each case I was motivated to work toward a phenomenological awareness inspired by the work of Eugene Minkowski (1970) and Alfred Schutz (1971), positioning myself as closely as possible to how things look, sound, smell, taste and feel in daily institutional life. Nursing-home stories need a point of view, but most visitors don't tarry long enough to develop one and most residents are too frail or too fearful to speak of their condition. Most, but not all:

> A bank of windows next to T.D.'s bed faces obliquely on the yellow brick wall of an adjoining wing of the nursing home. These windows are large and the building is low, so he also commands a patch of grass and a smudge of sky. In this part of the country, the intensity of light against buildings and trees reveals a lot about the weather and the changing seasons.
>
> "Do you know how long you have been here, in *this* place?" I asked him, curious about the sense of time afforded by his fixed view of winter, spring, summer, and fall.
>
> "I have no idea," T.D. said, pinning me with a keen look. "I'm afraid to ask. I don't know if they would tell me. I haven't asked in quite a while, probably two or three months. If they don't watch me, I'm gonna die here. And I don't wanna die. I'm afraid of death. And I can do a lot of things. My brain isn't that bad." (2003: 89)

"The only thesis I ever had to read with a drink in my hand" was a grad school mentor's comment on my master's work, a study of symbols and self-image in two nursing homes. I took that for the compliment it was, and later he encouraged me to revise it as an article for the *New York Times Magazine*. The *NYT* editor ultimately turned it down, but "The Reluctant Consumer" saw two academic publications (Vesperi 1987 [1980]). I also submitted it as a writing sample when the *St. Petersburg Times* was trying to decide if a college prof with no journalism training could help write an investigative series about low-income urban elders, the subject of my dissertation research. I got the chance, then a job, and used articles from the series to help turn my dissertation into a book, *City of Green Benches: Growing Old in a New Downtown* (1998 [1985]).

I stayed at the *St. Petersburg Times* for a dozen years and along the way I learned to think about style, voice and audience as if my livelihood depended on it, which of course it did. Losing the pedantic edges of my writing style was easy; drafts of stories were shared around and there was no place to hide from the cut-and-paste squad. Editors and colleagues just kept grabbing my props and crutches until to my own surprise I no longer seemed to need them. I learned to stop hedging statements with qualifiers and harrumphs; "somewhat" vanished quickly along with most parenthetical phrases. I came to see them as forms of dissembling and equivocation that protected me, the writer, but did little to help readers focus sharply on the subject at hand.

Organization was much trickier. Shorter sentences and paragraphs looked vulnerable, naked, and burying one's point at the end of an article is a defensive academic reflex that dies hard. When I was stubborn about it, an editor's well-placed ridicule sometimes worked wonders. Readers won't stay with you that long, I was told. Copy editors cut from the end, so don't blame them if your final draft is a buildup to nowhere.

"Voice" was something I brought along from my DAR essay days but it was hard to modulate in the newsroom setting. I tried, but I couldn't write consistently in the neutral tone required for many news stories. I wrote features; I was given a column. Eventually I moved to the editorial department, where I could combine reporting and analysis. I went out in the field for long investigative pieces that ran in the Sunday op-ed section and I continued to report on issues as a columnist. So-called "signature" columns are routinely accompanied by stamp-sized photos, encouraging readers to link a face with the writer's "voice." I guess mine was a mismatch because more then one reader blurted out at first meeting: "Wow, I thought you were taller!"

As an editorial writer I learned to imagine the audience for each day's topic. Economy of style is important because space is tight; some editorials are as short as 300 words. For a piece to be effective overall, each phrase must resonate with readers. The broader the audience for persuasive writing, the harder it is to select the right style.

Occasionally an editorial has "a readership of one" – a land developer, for instance, or the governor. The topic may be complex, but the writing task is usually less daunting. In such cases the terms are already engaged; there's a fight underway between A and B and the well-informed writer knows just what to shout from the sidelines to get their attention. In a similar way, it is relatively easy to draw the attention of academic peers by joining an ongoing battle over data or theory. Much harder, I think, to attract general readers with anthropological writing that calls out loud enough to be heard.

Deborah Tannen explains that coherent, involved conversation relies in part on repetition, which builds familiarity and lets others join in (2007: 61). Academic conversations, usually carried out in print, rely heavily on the familiarity scholars build through repetitive jargon. I must note with all irony in mind that citations are a form of academic repetition too. General readers find these markers unfamiliar and exclusive, even if the topic is important to them – or about them.

The most intriguing aspect of journalism for me has been the challenge of using anthropological perspectives and theories to tell stories without relying on jargon. Doing this well requires clarifying my own grasp of the models involved to the point where they become part of my thinking. I count as a failure in this regard the story that yielded a heavily accented call from a Latvian man in his 80s; he claimed he could see right through it to the Marxist foundation below. Calls like that prompted me to critique my drafts with a more skeptical imaginary reader in mind, a smart person with no time or patience for convoluted discourse.

At a journalism seminar I heard someone talk about "rendering" a narrative, as in cooking something down to the essence. For me, the space constraints of writing columns and editorials revealed the benefits of rendering ideas to roux, so that they could be used creatively to support a story without overwhelming it.

In his classic study of spacing behavior, Edward T. Hall notes that the eyes must work more to see a visage up close than at a distance. At intimate distance the face is just an ear, perhaps, or a mouth, and at arm's length "the gaze must wander around the face" to apprehend it fully. Only from a social distance of seven to 12 feet can one person "take in the whole face" of another without shifting the eyes (1969: 117–22). In the same way, writers who hold their work too close risk exhaustion and uncertainty about the shape and character of their own creations.

Sharing drafts with the widest available group of readers allows writers to step back and take full measure of the texts they produce. I have participated regularly in an informal writers' group and I sit in on professional workshops whenever I can. I read books about writing as if they were theoretical texts or ethnographies in my areas of interest – as if they could help me to glimpse the shape and colors of my future work. And in a very tangible way, they can.

A senior thesis is required for graduation from New College of Florida, where I teach. Most anthropology students base their theses on fieldwork, sometimes conducted under challenging conditions, perhaps in a second language. Some students present their findings at professional conferences; some texts they produce could qualify as MA theses elsewhere. Writing up is a bear, though. It doesn't help that campus culture glorifies the suffering of thesis students, pale and glassy-eyed despite the sun and the organic garden and all the places to bike or swim.

I try to keep anxiety from becoming global by advising students to compartmentalize their writing tasks ruthlessly, as people who write for a living do. I suggest that they dedicate a generous block of time to the keyboard each day and defend it against all distractions. When time is up, I say, walk away until tomorrow. Don't feel guilty about doing something else; all that does is foster resentment toward the writing.

I tell my students other things as well, such as not to address the reader as you, us, or we. These are sustaining pronouns in many kinds of writing, but they are inherently hegemonic and they can create volatile relationships with readers. *Bright Lights, Big City* by Jay McInerney provides a good illustration. This short, unpleasant novel is addressed entirely to the reader as "you," as in: "If you were Japanese, this would be the time to commit "*seppuku*" or "You go off to buy a drink, keeping both eyes peeled for lonely women." Identity transpositions such as this can easily backfire. The one time I assigned the book, students hated it. This lively group of male and female, gay and straight young adults said they felt an unwilling complicity in the main character's unsavory behavior because the narrator kept addressing them as "you." It was mercifully toward the end, but the passage that really set them against the book was this one: "*Pantene Shampoo. Pantene Conditioner.* Doubtless this should not make you think of *panties*, but it does" (1984: 25, 49, 140, italics in original).

"We" and "us" are also presumptive inclusions, and they invite resistance as well. "Maybe *you* do but *I* don't," I heard an African American student mutter when another girl went on about how "in American society, we. . . . "

At other times, "we" is a prelude to self-indictment or a generalized call to action: "As anthropologists, we do/don't/should. . . ." I hear that often and my first thought is almost always, "Maybe *you* do. . . ."

I hope that anthropologists never trade away the primacy and privilege of writing extended, eyewitness accounts of community life. I say this because I am concerned that so many of my peers are transfixed by the raw immediacy of the Internet. I used to regard television as the babysitter of my generation's middle age, tasked with keeping potentially troublesome characters socially sedated and off the street. Now that job has fallen to the Web. As a group, anthropologists have yet to appreciate the dangers it poses to what they do best – spending time with people in their daily lives and trying hard to write about it.

Journalists do know what's at stake, and for some it is already too late. Harassed by the glut of information and the pressure of 24-hour news cycles, they are clocking less time on the streets and more time managing information. Those who spend much of their workday tethered to computers in harshly lit newsrooms understand how thin their descriptions have become. The more frantically absorbed they are in the task of retrieving information collected by others, the less time remains for the first-hand encounter, the fresh take, the news in the true sense of "new." Journalists were once ridiculed and excoriated for being too eager, too much on the scene, making pests of themselves in a bird-dog effort to get the scoop. These days they are often criticized for being too remote, too intellectually and viscerally and bureaucratically removed from current events. I listen to the stories they tell about their writing today and remember that I am fortunate.

This poetic commentary on his master work, *The Pleasure of Fishes*, has been attributed to the thirteenth-century painter Chou Tung-ch'ing:

> Not being fish, how do we know their happiness?
> We can only take an idea and make it into a painting.
> To probe the subtleties of the ordinary,
> We must describe the indescribable.

The inspiration for this quote can be linked to a well-documented exchange between Taoist philosopher Chuang Tzu and Hui Tzu, a logician. As for the commentary, though, I'm not sure this is what the artist said. I found it attributed this way with a reproduction of the painting and it moved me, so I wrote it down. I share it here because it speaks to the challenge of anthropology and the craft of writing as I understand them.

I do know that Vincent Crapanzano wrote this: "It was Tuhami who first taught me to distinguish between the reality of personal history and the truth of autobiography" (1980: 5). The real and the true, two sides of the coin that anthropologists turn endlessly in their hands. Then they turn to the keyboard, and they write.

References

Clifford, James. 1988 [1983]. On Ethnographic Authority. From *The Predicament of Culture: Twentieth-Century Ethnography, Literature, and Art*, pp. 21–54. Cambridge, MA: Harvard University Press.

Crapanzano, Vincent. 1980. *Tuhami: Portrait of a Moroccan*. Chicago: University of Chicago Press.

Didion, Joan. 1979. Many Mansions. From *The White Album*, pp. 67–73. New York: Pocket Books.

Geertz, Clifford. 1988. *Works and Lives: The Anthropologist as Author*. Stanford, CA: Stanford University Press.

Hall, Edward T. 1969. *The Hidden Dimension*. Garden City, NY: Anchor Books.

McInerney, Jay. 1984. *Bright Lights, Big City*. New York: Vintage Contemporaries.

Minkowski, Eugene. 1970. *Lived Time: Phenomenological and Psychopathological Studies*. Chicago: Northwestern University Press.

Rosaldo, Renato. 1986. From the Door of His Tent: The Fieldworker and the Inquisitor. In *Writing Culture: The Poetics and Politics of Ethnography*. James Clifford and George E. Marcus, eds., pp. 77–97. Berkeley: University of California Press.

Russo, Richard. 1997. *Straight Man*. New York: Vintage.

Schutz, Alfred. 1971. *Collected Papers 1: The Problem of Social Reality*. The Hague: Martinus Nijhoff.

Tannen, Deborah. 2007. *Talking Voices: Repetition, Dialogue and Imagery in Conversational Discourse, 2nd edn*. Cambridge: Cambridge University Press.

Trumpener, Katie and James M. Nyce. 1988. The Recovered Fragments: Archeological and Anthropological Perspectives in Edith Wharton's *The Age of Innocence*. In *Literary Anthropology: A New Interdisciplinary Approach to People, Signs and Literature*. Fernando Poyatos, ed., pp. 161–9. Amsterdam: Benjamins.

Vesperi, Maria D. 1980. The Reluctant Consumer: Nursing Home Residents in the Post-Bergman Era. *Practicing Anthropology* 3, 1. Reprinted in Jay Sokolovsky, ed. 1987. *Growing Old in Different Societies*, pp. 225–37. Littleton, MA: Copley.

Vesperi, Maria D. 1995. Nursing Home Research Comes of Age: Toward an Ethnological Perspective on Long Term Care. In *The Culture of Long Term Care: Nursing Home Ethnography*. J. Neil Henderson and Maria D. Vesperi, eds., pp. 7–22. New York: Bergin & Garvey.

Vesperi, Maria D. 1998 [1985]. *City of Green Benches: Growing Old in a New Downtown*. Ithaca, NY: Cornell University Press.

Vesperi, Maria D. 2003. A Use of Irony in Contemporary Ethnographic Narrative. In *Gray Areas: Ethnographic Encounters with Nursing Home Culture*. Philip J. Stafford, ed., pp. 69–102. Santa Fe, NM: School of American Research Press.

Wolfe, Tom. 1973. Seizing the Power. In Tom Wolfe and E. W. Johnson, eds. *The New Journalism*. New York: Harper & Row.

Index

Aboriginal Americans *see* Native
  Americans
absurdity, literature of 20
academy, the 36, 42, 43–5; black
  writing 86–7; current dilemmas of
  academic writing 128–32;
  stereotypes of 142; writing for 5,
  39, 61, 80, 111, 112–13, 114,
  182–3, 184, 185, 199; and writing
  process 3, 21–34, 35, 36–7, 71, 74
  (*see also* citation(s))
acting white 80, 84–6, 87–8
activism 8–11, 44, 107; black
  writing 5, 80, 87–91; efficacy of
  books 15–20; feminist
  anthropology 5, 22–30, 32–3; Gray
  Panthers 172–81; medical
  anthropology 185, 188–9;
  poverty 5, 67–70, 134–45;
  progressive politics 160–2, 170;
  racism 58, 93–100; regional
  expertise 149–58; and violence 11,
  35–45
advocacy anthropology xv; *see also*
  activism
Afghanistan 188
Africa 26, 35–6, 40; culture 53, 87
African Americans: culture 53, 57;
  women and work 29; *see also*
  black ...
Agamben, Giorgio 39
ageism 172, 178

AIDS 36, 65–78, 183, 184
alignment strategy 135
Allison, Dorothy 106, 109
American Anthropological Association
  (AAA) 71n, 186; meetings 2–3, 25,
  37, 101, 104, 128, 129, 169; Society
  for Medical Anthropology 184
American Anthropologist 165, 166
American Dream 46, 51, 99
American Ethnological Society 166
American Ethnologist 77, 140, 166,
  182
American Studies 166
Anderson, Benedict 82
Angell, Roger 6
anonymity 148–9
Anthony, Susan B. 89
anthropologist(s): accountability 10,
  149–50, 158; passion and
  emotion xiv, 2–3, 7, 11, 35–45,
  110, 112, 113, 115, 177; as regional
  expert 149–58; responsibility 1, 10,
  37, 110, 123, 149, 177; support
  from 36–7, 44; use of concepts of
  race and culture 56–8; voice xiv,
  198; voyeurism 67; as writer
  1–11; writing for oneself 71, 184–5
anthropology xiii–xv; history 4–5, 9,
  52–3, 54, 56–8; popular political
  culture and 161–70; *see also*
  methodology; theory
Anthropology News 129, 130

aporia 163
applied anthropology 68; *see also* activism
Argentina 186
assimilation 53
Atlantic Monthly 74
audience 3–6, 142–4; anthropology as literature 109, 111–15; black writing 80, 90; journalism 198–9; Marxist-feminist anthropology 23, 29–30, 31, 32, 33; medical anthropology 182–3, 185, 187–8; progressive anthropology 160–1, 166; view of anthropology 164–5; work on homelessness 139–42; work on single mothers 136–9; work on violence 35–45; writing on poverty 70–3; *see also* academy, the; general reader; media; students
authenticity 55
authority, attitudes to 46–54, 57–8
autobiography, ethnography as 177
autonomy 182

Babb, Florence 126
Baker, Lee D. 4–5, 8, 9, 46–59
Baldwin, James 19, 124n
Balinese cockfight 107
Ball, Sharon 6, 11, 101–5
Bao Ninh 44
bard, role of 35–45
Barnes, Andrew 1–2, 4, 60–2
BBC radio 104, 156
Beam, Alex 76n
Beard, Charles 17–18
Behar, Ruth 3, 5, 7, 106–16; *An Island Called Home* 2, 106–9; *The Presence of the Past in a Spanish Village* 112–13; *Translated Woman* 113–14, 121, 129; *The Vulnerable Observer* 109–11, 114, 124, 129
Belize 121–8

Benedict, Ruth 107, 108
Berger, John 113
Bigelow, Bill 19
black anthropology, influence of Zora Neale Hurston 6, 119–33
black family structure 82
black feminism 125
black history 87
black people: cultural and racial politics 8, 46–59; and knowledge 17, 19
Black Power movement 53
black women: poverty 65–78; writing by 5, 7, 8, 79–92 (*see also* Butler, Octavia E., Hurston, Zora Neale)
Blakey, Michael 126
Boas, Franz xiv, 52, 55
Bolles, Lynn 126
Borofsky, Robert 37, 183n
Bosnia 186, 188
Boston Book Review 165
Bourdieu, Pierre 39
Boyte, Harry 179
BP 150–8
Breslin, Jimmy 194
Brettell, Caroline B. 122–3
Briggs, Charles 55
Brodkin, Karen 4, 5, 21–34; *Caring by the Hour* 5, 28–30; *How Jews Became White Folks and What That Says about Race in America* 8, 31–2; *Making Democracy Matter* 32–3; *Sisters and Wives* 27
Broussard, Carol 46, 50
Brown, Jay Anthony 167
Brown, Jerry 196
Bucholz, Barbara 167
Burma 37
Bush, George H. W. 18
Bush, George W. 98, 162, 163, 176
Butler, Octavia E. 6, 11, 101–5; *Fledgling* 105; *Lilith's Brood*; *Kindred* 104; *Parable of the Sower* 102;
Butler, Robert 178

Cambodia, Khmer Rouge 186
campus culture 54
Canada, homelessness 139–42
capitalism 94, 162, 163, 164
Cardinal, Marie 4
Caribbean Studies Association 128
Carson, Rachel 18
chaos theory 42
chiasmus 163
Chicago Tribune Sunday Magazine 168
China 23, 24
Chou Tung-ch'ing 201
Christian, Cora 128
Chronicle of Higher Education 99
Chuang Tzu 201
Cisneros, Sandra 113
citation(s) 4, 21–2, 61, 194, 199
City Newspaper 88
Civil Rights movement 23, 24, 29, 53, 178, 188
class xv, 9, 18, 23, 26, 29, 31, 32, 50, 52, 73, 94, 95, 97, 162, 166, 170, 196
Clifford, James 6, 55, 121, 129, 177, 195
Clinton, Hillary Rodham 89
Clinton administration 162, 166, 167
Cobbs, Montague 126
Cohen, Randy 169–70
Cole, Johnnetta B. 126
collaboration, human rights in West Papua 147–58
collective activism 28–30
colonialism xiv, 4, 146
Columbus, Christopher 19, 82
comparative method 26
Conan, Neal 101
Congress of Racial Equality 24
consciousness raising and changing 9, 11, 15–20, 22–5
contextualization 2, 141, 143, 160–1
corporate culture 54
counternarrative(s) 5, 79–92

Crapanzano, Vincent 121, 129, 201
creativity 37, 38, 108
critical poverty theory 73, 76
critical race theory 32
critical studies of whiteness 32
cross-cultural comparison 143
Cuba 23, 24, 25, 106, 108
Cullen, Countee 19
cultural criticism 149
cultural imperialism 164
cultural relativism xv, 167, 168
culture xiii–xiv, 54–6, 108; displacement of black women 79–92; and race 46–59
culture wars 57, 169
CUNY Graduate Center 166, 174
cynicism, young people 47–8

Darfur 186, 187
Das, Veena 44
Dash, Leon 73–4
data 18–19, 194; anonymity and reliability 148–50; translating and interpreting 22, 126, 128–32, 140–2, 149–58
Daughters of the American Revolution 191–3
Davis, Mike 168, 170
deaf culture 55
Delbanco, Andrew 170
DeLillo, Don 71
Democratic Party 98
deviance 55
di Leonardo, Micaela 4, 74, 160–71; *Exotics at Home* 9–10, 161–7, 168; *The Varieties of Ethnic Experience* 160–1
Dialectical Anthropology 182
Diamond, Norma 26
Dickens, Charles 16, 18, 195
Didion, Joan 194, 195–6
differences *see* diversity
Discourse & Society 137
displacement 79–92, 108

Dissent 166
diversity xv, 86, 139–40, 141
Domínguez, Virginia 110
Douglas, Mary xiv
Douglass, Frederick 89
Drake, St. Clair 125, 126
dramaturgy 126
drug addiction 65–78
D'Souza, Dinesh 76
Duke University, Policy Research
    Center 28–30

East Timor 146
education, childhood experience of
    writing 7, 8, 80–6, 87–8, 191–3
Ehrenreich, Barbara 73, 168, 169
Elbow, Peter 8
Emergency (organization) 189
emotion *see under* anthropologist(s)
empiricism 157
Engels, Friedrich 25
Englander, Nathan 115
environmentalism 150, 155
equality/inequality xv; gender 4, 25,
    26, 27, 29, 89, 184; race 89, 96, 97,
    98
Erickson, Frederick 140
essentialism 55
ethics xv, 2, 8
ethnic cleansing 186, 187
ethnicity 9, 160–1; *see also* race
ethnocentrism xiv, xv
Europe, race 98
Evans, Sara 179
Evans-Pritchard, E. E. 129, 195

Fabian, Johannes 177
facts *see* data
Farmer, Paul 1, 8, 9, 37, 58, 71,
    182–90; *AIDS and Accusation* 183;
    The Uses of Haiti 185
fashion, racial and cultural politics
    46–54, 57–8
Faulkingham, Ralph 130, 131

feminism 172; Marxist-feminist
    consciousness 23–33
feminist anthropology 25–33, 113,
    114, 125–6, 160–1, 169
Feminist Studies 128
Fernandez, James 112
fiction writing 6, 7, 21, 101, 194, 195,
    196, 200
fieldwork 41, 107, 124, 182, 200; *see
    also* research
Fischer, Dawn Elissa 126
Flaubert, Gustave 195
Fletcher, Alice 52
folklore 124
Fordham, Signithia 5, 7, 8, 79–92;
    Blacked Out 85–7
Foreman, Sylvia H. 130
Foster, Kevin 126
Foucault, Michel 37, 40, 134
framing 2, 5, 21, 30–1, 32, 141, 142
France 98
Frank, Robert 76n
Frank, Tom 168, 169
freedom, West Papua, 146–59, *see also
    merdeka*
Freeman, Derek 165, 168
functionalism 194

gang violence 46, 47, 48
Gans, Herbert 160
Geertz, Clifford xiv, 6, 107, 108, 129,
    177, 195
gender xiv, 9, 31, 50, 120–4, 135,
    163, 166, 170; equality,
    inequality 4, 25, 26, 27, 29, 89,
    184; life history method 122–4; in
    writing 79–92
general reader 5, 9–10, 23, 31, 80,
    166, 185, 199; anthropology as
    literature 2, 106, 108–9, 111–15;
    observations about writing 4, 60–2
genocide 146, 186–8
Ghana 48–9
Gilliam, Angela 126

Gilman, Sander 69, 73
Glenn, Evelyn Nakano 28
global imperialism 163
Goffman, Erving 134, 135
Gopnik, Adam 168–9
Gordon, Deborah A. 114, 121, 129
Gough, Kathleen, reaction to speech at
  Brandeis University 23–4
Gozney, Richard 153
Gramscian ideology 22, 94
grand narratives 163
Granny Peace Brigade coalition 176
Gray Panthers 10, 172–81
Green, Felix 24
Green, Vera 126
Gregory, Steven 31
Grimston, Jack 153–4
Grote, Byron 151–3
Guardian 150
Gwaltney, John 107, 126

Hafner, Katie 167n
Haiti 182, 183, 185
Hale, Charles 150, 157
Hall, Edward T. 199
Hall, Stuart 136
Haraway, Donna 154–5
Harding, Sandra 157, 158
Harper's Magazine 168, 169n
Harris, Louis 177
Harrison, Faye V. 126
Haughton, James 97n
Healey, Eloise Klein 31
health care 29
Heller, Joseph 20
Herkouf xiv
Herrnstein, Richard 76
Hersey, John 20
Herzegovina 186
hierarchies xiv, 45, 93, 103
Hiroshima 20
history 55; *see also under*
  anthropology
HIV/AIDS 36, 65–78, 183, 184

Holocaust 32, 186
Holwitz, Stan 183
homelessness 65, 67–8, 70, 75; 163;
  Canada 139–42
Howell, Algie 50
Hughes, Langston 126
Hui Tzu 201
human rights, West Papua 146–59
Hurston, Zora Neale xiv, 11, 48, 80,
  107, 108; as example 6, 119–33;
  Mules and Men 119, 120; *Their
  Eyes Were Watching God* 120–2
Hyatt, Sue 127

Ibn Battuta xiv
identity 42, 55, 80–1, 87, 108; clash
  of identities 51; national 31
ideology 96–7; Gramscian 22, 94
imperialism 26
Imus, Don 49, 89–90
indigenous ritual practice 150
individualism: cult of 73;
  possessive 143
Indonesia, human rights 146–59
injustice *see* justice
institutionalized racism 58, 93–100
intellectual communities 5, 22,
  23–33
interests 17–18, 94
Internet 194, 201
interpretive anthropology 125, 128
Iraq war 147, 176, 188
Israeli politics 32
Italy, ban on landmines 189

Jackson, Antoinette 126
Jackson, George 126
Jackson, Jesse 98
jargon 4, 22, 31, 40, 96, 195, 199
Jencks, Christopher 67n
Jet Magazine 47
Jews 8, 31–2, 106, 186
*Journal of Community and Applied
  Social Psychology* 138

journalism 5, 21, 74, 101, 149, 194, 195–201
judgment 18–19, 196
justice, injustice 22, 87, 124n; Gray Panthers 10, 179; law and 16–17

Kafka, Franz 20
Kaisiepo, Viktor 156
Kapferer, Bruce 37
Kennedy, John F. 178
Kennedy, Robert 178
King, Martin Luther, Jr. 178
King, Ryan S. 66
King, Stephen 194, 195
Kingfisher, Catherine 4, 9, 134–45; *Women in the American Welfare Trap* 134–9
kinship 27
Kirksey, S. Eben 8, 10, 146–59
Kleinman, Arthur 44
knowledge 8, 144; and activism 189; different kinds 19–20; popular conceptions of anthropology 164–5; theories 40–1; transformation of 10, 154–8; *see also* data
Kristof, Nicholas 187
Kuhn, Margaret E. 172, 174, 175–6, 178, 179
Kurdistan 188

Labor Studies Journal 30
Lamphere, Louise 26, 27, 126
landmines 19–20, 188–9
language *see* writing style
Latina self-sacrifice 109–10
law, and justice 16–17
Le Pen, Jean-Marie 98
Leach, Edmund xiv
Leacock, Eleanor "Happy" 97n
Lee, Dorothy xiii
Left 27
leftist anthropology 160–1
Lemann, Nicholas 74
Lévi-Strauss, Claude xiv, 107

Lewinsky, Monica 77, 166
LexisNexis searches 167
life history method 122–4, 129, 130
literature, relationship to anthropology xiv, 5–7, 106–16, 126–8, 131–2
literature of absurdity 20
long-term care *see* nursing homes
low-paid workers 135–9
lynching 93, 94

Malik, Kenan xv
Malinowski, Bronislaw 164
Marcus, G. 6, 121, 129
Marcuse, Herbert 23
marketing 2, 61–2, 76–7, 106, 108–9, 160, 165
Martin, JoAnn 37
Marx, Karl 18
Marxist-feminist consciousness, development of 23–30
Mathis, Greg 47
matriarchy 27
Mauer, Marc 66
McClaurin, Irma 1, 6, 119–33; *Women of Belize* 121, 122–4, 126–7
McCourt, Frank 62
McGrath, Charles 77
McInerney, Jay 200
McLane, Maureen 168
Mead, Margaret xiv, 25, 80, 83, 165, 166, 168
media: and anthropology 161, 163, 165, 166–70, 196; black writing 5, 85–6, 87–91
medical anthropology 182–90
Melville, Herman 16–17
merdeka 146, 149; *see also* freedom
Meswick, Susan 179
methodology 136–7; challenges to 146–59
Minh-Ha Trinh, T. 121, 165
Minkowski, Eugene 197

miscegenation laws 52
misogyny 103
Monge, Luigi 120n
Montaigne, Michel de 164
Mooney, James 56, 57
Morgan, Robin 25
Morgenthau, Hans J. 94
motherhood 134–9
Moynihan, Patrick 82
Mozambique 35
Ms magazine 29
Mullings, Leith 52
multiculturalism 165
multi-national corporations, human
    rights in West Papua 147–58
Murray, Charles 76
Mwaria, Cheryl xiii–xvi, 126
Myerhough, Barbara 107

NAACP 24, 57
narrative 2, 6, 61, 75–6, 81, 122–4;
    see also storytelling
Nation, The 166, 168
National Association for the
    Advancement of Colored People 24,
    57
National Association of the Deaf 55
National Geographic magazine 83,
    169
national identity 31
national interest 17
National Public Radio (NPR) 6, 61,
    101, 102, 103, 104, 166
Native Americans 52, 56–7, 108;
    homelessness 139–42
native anthropology 125–6, 165
native voice 7, 81, 83, 85, 91
nativism 103
Neleson, Evelyn 179
nerdiness 88n
New College of Florida 200
New Haven, Conn 162, 166
New Journalism, The 195
New Orleans 67n

New Politics 165
New Right 166, 167, 168
New York Observer 168, 170
New York Post 16, 112
New York Review of Books 61, 168,
    170
New York Times 61, 67n, 76n, 89,
    150, 168, 172, 187
New York Times Book Review 77
New York Times Magazine 167,
    169–70, 197
New Yorker 167n, 168–9
New Zealand, targeting
    audiences 137–9
Newman, Louise 89
Nordstrom, Carolyn 3, 7, 11, 35–45
novels *see* fiction writing
NPR *see* National Public Radio
Nugent, Benjamin 88n
nursing homes 172, 176, 197
Nyce, James M. 196

Obama, Barack 55, 89
Ogbu, John 87
Okely, Judith 177
old age 172–81
Omaar, Rakiva 186–8
orality 82
O'Reilly, John 152–3
Other 73, 86, 90, 134, 139, 140, 150,
    163, 164, 165, 168

Palacio, Ludwig V. 126
"paper babies" 79–80, 83–5, 90–1
Papua Congress (2000) 155
Papuan Presidium Council 155–6
pariah groups 134–45
Paris Review 71
Partners in Health, Institute for Health
    and Social Justice 184n
patriarchy 25, 27
Paynter, Robert 131
peer audiences *see* academy, the
personhood 134–45

Peru 188
peyote use and abuse 56–7
phenomenology 197
Piven, Frances Fox 135
poetry 108, 126–7, 196
policy change 9, 15, 68, 136–42, 185
politics: anthropology and xiii, xv; human rights in West Papua 10, 146–59; progressive anthropology and popular political culture 160–71; and race 97–8
positivism 150, 157, 170
post-colonial critique 149–50, 155
postmodernism 84, 163, 165, 166, 169, 170
post-structuralist theory 137, 149
poverty 5, 65–78, 134–45, 161–2, 184
Powell, Colin 103
power 47, 70, 103, 163; human rights in Indonesia 146–59; speaking truth to 1, 9, 15–20, 22, 23, 67, 70, 93–100, 150, 188 (*see also* activism)
Pratt, Mary 74
progressive anthropology 160–71
public decency laws 46, 50, 58
public policy *see* policy change
public sphere: anthropological knowledge 161–2, 170; black women's writing 87–91; institutionalized racism 58, 93–100
publicity *see* marketing
publishing 2, 9, 44, 86–7, 106, 108–9, 161; racism 93, 94, 98–9; rejections and errors 89–90, 98–9
Pulitzer Prize, process of winning 60, 62

Rabinowitz, Lillian 173
race xiv, 95–8, 160, 163, 166, 170; and cultural politics 46–58; feminist anthropology 8, 29, 31–2; in writing 79–92

racism 2, 4, 8, 9, 19, 47, 50, 51, 52–4, 58, 103, 104, 141, 142, 160, 162, 165; institutionalized 58, 93–100
radical anthropology 165, 170
Ramphele, Mamphela 44
rape 36, 38, 42–3
Rapp, Rayna 26, 166
Reagan era 160, 163, 165, 168, 169, 195–6
reality 201
reflexivity 6, 36, 121, 125, 128, 129
religious freedom 56–7
Remy, Dorothy 28
Republican Party 97–8
research 7, 22, 41–2, 70–1, 191, 193, 194, 200–1; "going native" 84; "strong objectivity" 157–8; *see also* data; fieldwork; methodology
respect, disrespect 143, 182; urban young black people 46, 47, 49, 50
reviews 2, 61, 99, 160, 161, 165–6
Reynolds, Pamela 44
Robbins, Tony 37
Robinson, Dianne 50
Rone, Tracy 126
Rosado, Sibyl Dione 126
Rosaldo, Michelle 25–6, 126
Rosaldo, Renato xiv, xv, 43, 195
Roy, Albert 50
Royal, Ségolène 98
ruling elites, and institutionalized racism 94, 97–8
Rumbiak, John 151–3, 154, 156
Russo, Richard 193
Rwanda, genocide 186–8

Safa, Helen 126
Said, Edward 149
Sandford, Victoria 37
Sanjek, Lani 173, 174, 175, 176
Sanjek, Roger 31; Gray Panthers 10, 172–81
Santería 111
Sapir, Edward 164

Sarkozy, Nicolas 98
Scanlan, Chip 8
Scheper-Hughes, Nancy 69, 183n
Schofield, Virginia 77
schooling *see* education
Schutz, Alfred 197
science fiction writing 6, 101–5
sexism 2, 8, 25, 27, 28, 165
sexuality 9, 95
shamans 148, 149
Shweder, Richard 167n
Simmons, David 126
Simmons, Kimberley Eison 126
Simon, Scott 104
single mothers 134–9
Singleton, Anne 108
Singleton, Theresa 126
Skidmore, Monique 37
slavery 82, 87, 91; abolition
    movement 188
Slocum, Karla 126
Smiley, Tavis 167
Smith, Ruth L. 134
Smith, Sarah A. 132n
Snow, Edgar 24
social commentary 101
social control 68
social engineering 143
Social Housing in Action (SHIA) 139,
    140, 141, 142
social movements 23–5, 33; *see also*
    Civil Rights movement
social problems 67–70, 141
social programs 68
social scientists 9, 55, 58
Social Security 172, 176, 177
social systems and structures 141, 142;
    inequality 52, 58
Social Text 169
socialism 23–5
Society for the Anthropology of North
    America (SANA) 71n
Society of American Indians 56, 57
sociobiology 170

sociology 55
Spain 112–13
Sparrow-Clarke, Paul 140
Spears, Arthur K. 7; *Race and
    Ideology* 9, 93–100
Spivak, Gayatri 149–50
Sri Lanka 35–6, 40, 41
St. Petersburg Times 5, 197–8
Stack, Carol 28
standpoint theories 157–8
Stanhope, Ruth 108
state xiv, 17–18; institutionalized
    racism 93–100
status 196
Steele, Claude 80
Steele, Danielle 112
stereotypes 70; of academics 142;
    black women's writing 80, 91;
    homeless 139, 140, 141, 142; of old
    age 174, 177–8; racist 95–6
Stewart, Kathleen 194n
storytelling 10, 21, 22–3, 31, 32, 61,
    62, 74, 113, 115, 134; about
    racism 93–100
Strada, Gino 19–20, 188–9
Strathern, Marilyn 144
Strathmann, Cynthia 30
structural inequality 52, 58, 67–70,
    72, 75, 142, 150; by gender 27, 31;
    by gender and class 135; by race 54,
    93, 141; by race and gender 29, 90
structuralist theory 137
Strunk, William, Jr 6
student movements (1960s) 178–9
Student Nonviolent Coordinating
    Committee Freedom Summer 24
students: advice to 37–8, 200; lack of
    instruction in writing 128–32;
    reception 30; writing for 4–5, 9, 23,
    31, 52, 95–9, 136, 166
Students for a Democratic Society 25
style *see* writing style
subversion 48–9, 90
Sudan 18

Sunday Times 153–5
Susser, Ezra 65n
Sutton, Connie 126
Swift, Jonathan 20

Talese, Gay 194
Tannen, Deborah 199
Taormino, Tristan 169
textual analysis 163
theory 2, 22, 74–5, 76, 96, 136–7;
  relationship to application 35–45
thick description 107
Thomas, Deborah 126
Thomas, Elizabeth Marshall xiv
Tierney, John 167
Time magazine 23–4
Times Literary Supplement 165
Toor, Rachel 99
Torgovnick, Marianna 165
Tripp, Linda 168
Trumbo, Dalton 20
Trumpener, Katie 196
truth 201; and power *see under* power
Tsing, Anna 131
Tuck, Lily 71
Turnbull, Colin xiv
Turner, Victor xiv
Twain, Mark 20

underclass 74, 162
unions, and women's work 28–30
United Nations Conference on Racism 103
University of Florida, writing 129–30, 131–2
University of Michigan 24–6, 30, 113
urban young people 46–54, 57–8

Valentine, Charles 76
values, clash of 51
Vanidades 112
Vesperi, Maria D. 5, 7, 191–202; *City of Green Benches: Growing Old in a New Downtown* 198

Vietnam War 24, 178
Village Voice 165, 167n, 168, 169
violence 11, 19–20, 35–45, 146–59, 170, 186–9
voice xiv, 198; native 7, 81, 83, 85, 91
Vonnegut, Kurt 17, 20

Waldman, Amy 168
Walker, Alice 16
war 11, 19–20, 35–45, 188–9
Waropen, Telys 147–50, 155
Washington Post 50, 85
Waterston, Alisse 10; *Love, Sorrow and Rage* 5, 65–78
Weik, Terry 126
welfare providers 135–9
West Papua 146–59
Wharton, Edith 196
White, E. B. 6
white ethnicity 160–1
white supremacy 52; institutionalized racism 93–100
Williams, Brett 76
Wilson, William J. 162
Winddance-Twine, France 126
Wolf, Eric 27, 182
Wolfe, Tom 194, 195
women: social position 120–8; and work 27–30
women's rights 89, 188
Women's Studies 22, 30
work 135; self-help through 46, 51, 73; women and 27–30
World War II 20, 186
Wright, Richard 19
writer's block 8, 104–5
writing 3, 193–4; anthropologist as writer 1–11; benefits to writer 71, 184–5; challenges and confrontations 72–5; childhood experiences 7, 8, 80–7, 191–3; difficulties of participant observation 177; efficacy and power of 8–9, 15–20, 67–70, 86–7,

109–11, 123, 143–4, 160, 182, 184, 186–8; general reader's observations on 4, 60–2; honesty 40, 108, 111; progression of 3, 111–15; reading about 199; reasons for 1–2, 20, 21–2, 54, 58, 69–70, 71, 114–15, 182, 183–5, 187–8; reception 2, 8–10, 19, 77, 85–6, 109–11, 122–4, 165–7, 183 (Zora Neale Hurston 6, 119–33) (*see also* audience, reviews); strategies and techniques 2, 21–2, 75–6, 128–32, 134–5, 140–2, 143, 194–7 (*see also* contextualization, framing, storytelling, writing style); vision of alternatives offered by 22, 32–3
writing style 4, 6, 21–34, 61, 74, 75–6, 128–32, 140–1, 194–7, 198,

200; black people 5, 7, 8, 79–92; role of bard 7, 35–45; *see also* jargon
WVAZ radio 167n

X, Malcolm 19, 178
xenophobia 103

Yomaki, Denny 146–8, 150
young people: membership of Gray Panthers 172–3, 174, 178–9; race and culture 46–54, 57–8

zeitgeist (spirit of the times) 160, 161
Zinn, Howard 9, 15–20, 188; *A People's History of the United States* 19, 187
Zitkala-Ša 56–7